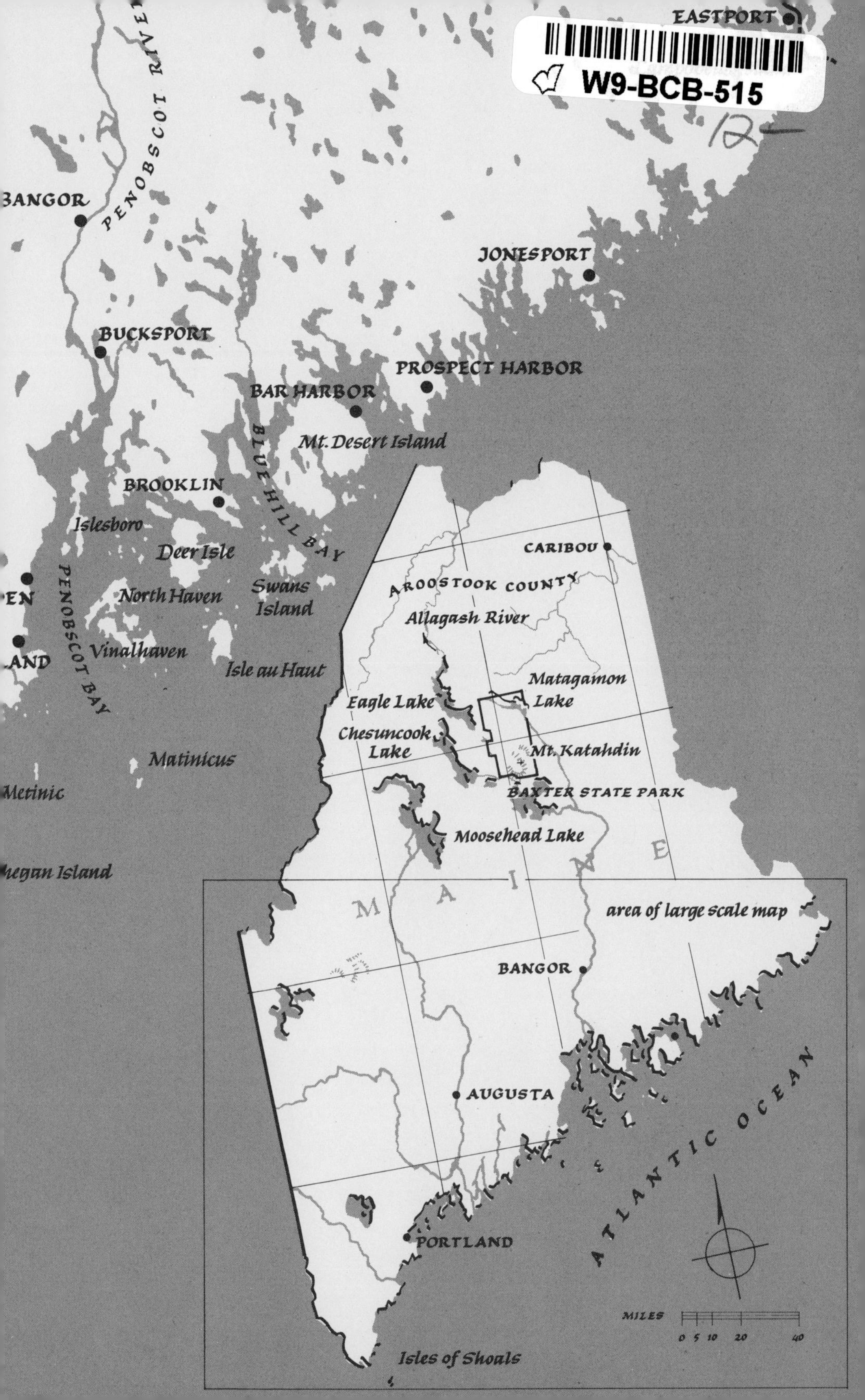
EASTPORT
PENOBSCOT RIVER
BANGOR
JONESPORT
BUCKSPORT
PROSPECT HARBOR
BAR HARBOR
Mt. Desert Island
BROOKLIN
BLUE HILL BAY
Islesboro
Deer Isle
North Haven
Swans Island
PENOBSCOT BAY
Vinalhaven
Isle au Haut
Matinicus
Metinic
hegan Island
CARIBOU
AROOSTOOK COUNTY
Allagash River
Matagamon Lake
Eagle Lake
Chesuncook Lake
Mt. Katahdin
BAXTER STATE PARK
Moosehead Lake
MAINE
area of large scale map
BANGOR
AUGUSTA
ATLANTIC OCEAN
PORTLAND
MILES
0 5 10 20 40
Isles of Shoals

RIVERS of FORTUNE

By Bill Caldwell

by Bill Caldwell

ENJOYING MAINE	(1977)
MAINE MAGIC	(1979)
ISLANDS OF MAINE	(1981)
RIVERS OF FORTUNE	(1983)

First edition July, 1983. Printed in the United States of America by Gannett Graphics, Augusta, Maine 04330.

Published by Guy Gannett Publishing Co., Portland, Maine 04101, July, 1983.

Library of Congress Catalog Card # 83-081302

ISBN # 0-930096-45-2

RIVERS of FORTUNE

Where Maine tides and money flowed

By Bill Caldwell

Guy Gannett Publishing Co.

Portland, Maine

For John and Susan
who have brought so much joy
to our river.

Contents

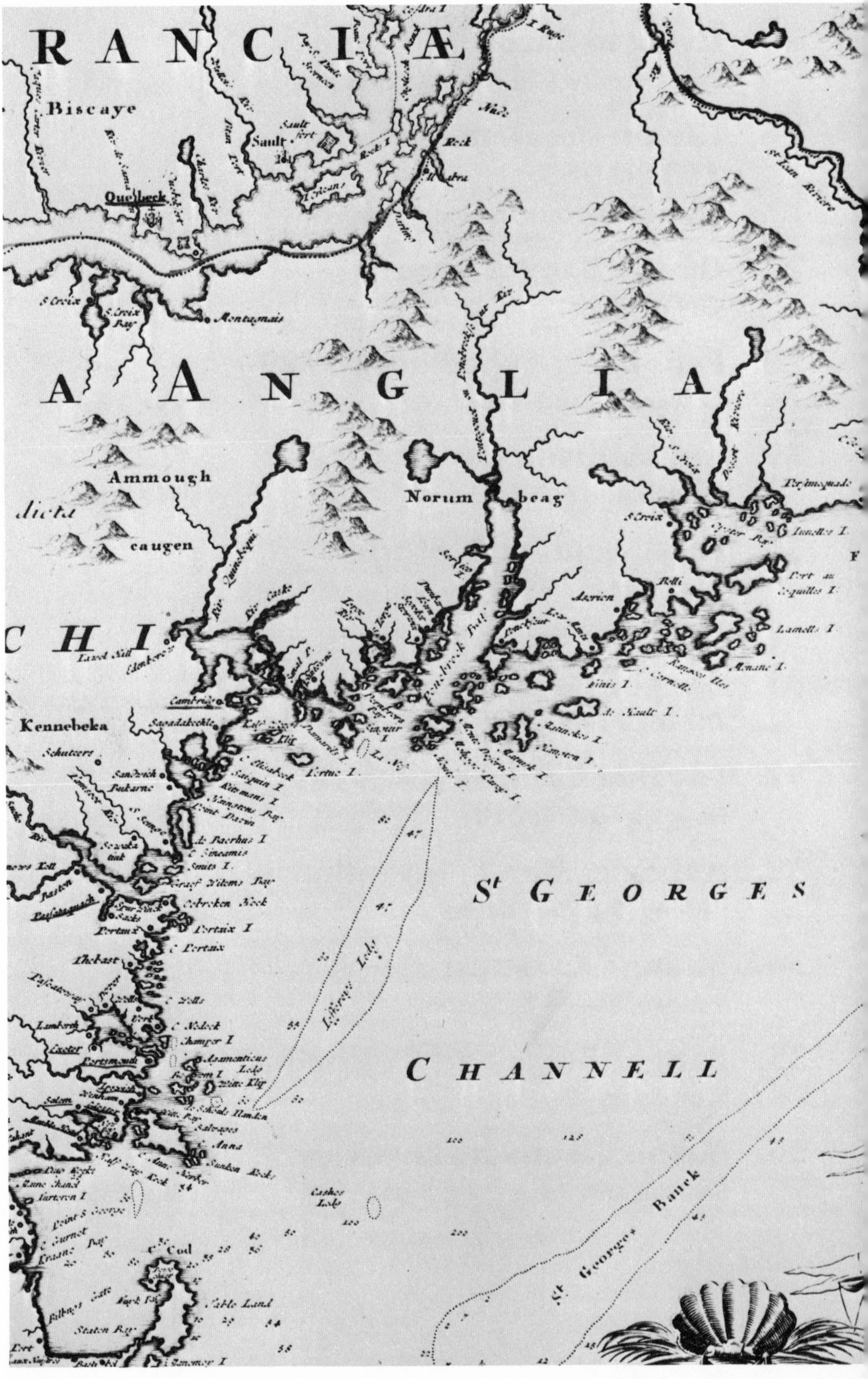

RANCIÆ
Biscaye
Sault
Quebeck
Montagnais
ANGLIA
Ammough
dicta
caugen
Norum
beag
CHI
Kennebeka
Cambridge
St GEORGES
CHANNELL
St Georges Banck
C. Cod
Staten Bay
Portsmouth
Exeter
Sunken Rocks
Cashes Ledg

1.

Tides of Men and Money:
Rivers of Maine

The coast is forever in the spotlight. But the rivers have been pushed almost off stage.

The coast of Maine is so fabled, so long, so beautiful and so written about that the rivers of Maine are largely overlooked.

Yet Maine is blessed with 5,000 rivers and streams. The 20 longest rivers in Maine stretch together over 1800 miles, the equivalent of more than half the breadth of the United States.

The longest is the St. John, barely known except to canoeists (who think it is Paradise) and lumbermen with long memories who remember the Madawaska Driving Co. once employed 1,500 men to drive 127 million feet of lumber down the St. John River in a single springtime. The St. John is 331 miles long on its southwest branch.

Next longest is the Penobscot, 240 miles on one branch, 237 on the other; then the Androscoggin, 174 miles long; then the Kennebec 170 miles, then the Saco 121 miles.

These last four are navigable from the ocean mouth to far upstream. A man could sail upstream and find shelter from the ocean, be close to forest and lumber, to farmland, and still have the river highway at his door. When he needed to buy, trading ships could come easily to where he lived; when he had something to sell, he could get it to market. With a river to ride on, nothing offered better transport until 19th century trains and 20th century highways. But trains and highways could take a man or his goods only to where the North American continent ended. Rivers and oceans could take a man or his goods to every place on earth.

Thus the navigable rivers of Maine became the arteries of Maine. The lumber, the ice, the ships, the men and the cargoes which started from these rivers could travel to every port in the whole world. The brute strength of the rivers' flow was harnessed by dams, converted to power, and ran the sawmills and textile plants.

On these great arteries, the fortunes flowed.

On the Penobscot River, we'll see how lumberjacks and rivermen, shanty Irish and Indians, made the Bangor millionaires and lumber barons. On the Saco River, we'll see how thousands of farm girls made fortunes for the owners of textile mills. On the Damariscotta River, we'll see how Maine bricks built seacoast cities and how early Indians feasted on oysters thousands of years ago.

The Kennebec is where the fortunes have flowed longest and richest.

The first ocean-going vessel built by white men in North America was built near the mouth of the Kennebec in 1607. She was the 30-ton pinnace Virginia, built by the first colony attempted in America, at Popham, Maine. Their vessel later carried supplies to the colony established at Jamestown, Virginia.

The first murder involving a newsy name was committed in 1634 on the Kennebec, at a fur-trading station near Fort Western in Augusta. John Alden of the Plymouth Company and "Speak for yourself, John" fame was arrested on a murder charge. It was big news when the upright Alden, the Pilgrim credited with being the first man from the Mayflower to set foot on Plymouth Rock, had to appear in court to answer a murder charge. After long deliberations, the court found him guilty of "excusable homicide." (There will be more detail later on the Alden scandal.)

Not long after Alden was charged with murder on the Kennebec, William Phips was born near its banks at Woolwich, on February 2, 1650. He was scarcely noticed in the family at first, for he was one among 26 children, of whom 21 were sons. But this Kennebec boy grew up to become a treasure-hunter and took almost $1.5 million of silver, gold, pearls and jewels out of a Spanish wreck in the Bahamas. For this, King James II made young Phips the first knight born in America and gave him $75,000 as his share of the treasure. As Sir William he led the British in an invasion of 40 ships and 4,000 men upon French Nova Scotia in 1690. It failed. Then there was no money to pay the troops in sterling.

To prevent mutiny, the troops were given scrip or dollar bills. Such is the origin of paper money. Phips, the Kennebec Kid, became governor of Massachusetts in 1692 for 30 months. Then he was called to London to answer charges of violence, and died in England in February, 1695.

Another early rags-to-riches and power story from the Kennebec features William King. Barefoot poor at 13, young King left his father's home at Scarborough and drove two oxen as his stake in the world. He wound up in Bath, prospered as a shipowner. When in 1820 Maine won its independence from Massachusetts, King was elected the first governor of Maine. After re-election he resigned to negotiate the U.S. purchase of Florida from Spain.

Politics and the Kennebec mixed well. For starters, the state capital was at the head tide of the Kennebec in 1827. Six years later Melville W. Fuller was born in Augusta. His name doesn't ring many bells today, but he was Chief Justice of the United States for 22 years (1888-1910) and wrote 800 decisions. Growing up in Augusta at the same time as Fuller was James G. Blaine who chalked up another kind of political record; he was a founder of the Republican Party, speaker of the U.S. House of Representatives, secretary of state under three presidents, and in 1884 was GOP candidate for president, narrowly beaten by Grover Cleveland.

Downriver at Bath, the Kennebec produced Arthur Sewall, the biggest ship owner of sailing vessels in America. He ran for vice-president on the Democratic ticket in 1896 — the losing ticket with William Jennings Bryan at the top of it.

But it was money even more than politics which flowed and flowed along the Kennebec; lots of big money in the shape of lots of big ships. More ships have been built on the Kennebec than on any body of water the same size in America.

We'll look at the flow, the ebb and sometimes the scandals of the fortunes of the Hydes, the Sewalls, the Morses. We'll see how Charles W. Morse, whose name now graces Bath high school, made millions in robber-baron fashion, shook Wall Street, was sentenced to 15 years in a federal penitentiary, wangled a presidential pardon from President Taft through a faked illness and then so milked the U. S. government in ship-building deals in World War I that he settled by paying back over $11 million.

We'll see how the mighty Bath Iron Works fell with such a crash that it was sold at auction on the court house steps to a New York junk dealer named Theodore Friedburg in the 1920s.

Sailing ships from Bath raced to the forty-niners in San Francisco in the great California gold rush; carried wheat around the Horn to Europe; square-rigged Downeasters from Bath traded in

China, carried ice to Calcutta. In World War II, 12,000 people in the Bath Iron Works launched more destroyers than the entire empire of Japan.

Bath, for many years the greatest ship building town in America, began as an offshoot to her big sister Georgetown. Bath was nicknamed "Twenty Cow Parish."

We'll see the Kennebec when 384 ships came and went through its mouth in a single day, see it when a man in a rowboat rowed passengers the 16 miles to Boothbay for 50 cents; and when thousands of men and hundreds of horses cut a million tons of ice and sold the crop they never had to plant for millions of dollars year after year.

The Kennebec men of the 1600s who settled the river banks may have been a special breed. A journal of Levi P. Lemont carries this strange report:

> "The men of Bath in the 17th century were reckoned half a head taller than the men of any other community in the country. There were no small men among them and very few medium sized ones. They might well have been called a race of giants in size and strength. There were few men that weighed less than 180 pounds and from five feet and six inches to about six feet and two inches in height. The heaviest men among them were Capt. Levi Peterson, he weighed nearly 500 pounds, and Isaiah and Crooker Jr., weighed 360 pounds."

Such were some of the men and fortunes which flowed along the Kennebec.

Bath on the Kennebec about 1840, from an old lithograph. (Maine Maritime Museum)

BIW on the Kennebec River

Carlton Bridge over the Kennebec, 1927, just before it opened for traffic.

2.

Carlton Bridge: 1927

First over the Kennebec

America was booming and Americans were celebrating good times in October 1927. So was Bath. Bath citizens were gearing up for the big day when the first train would cross the Kennebec by bridge instead of ferry boat.

Shortly before 8:15 a.m. October 24, 1927, locomotive engine No. 378, from Rockland eased onto the Woolwich end of the Carlton Bridge, and crossed the Kennebec River, pulling carloads of 700 dignitaries and officials from Rockland. More than 2,500 spectators cheered as the first train across the new bridge pulled into Bath station. The Bath brass band outblew the Rockland band aboard the train in the rowdy sounds of welcome.

Fifteen minutes later at 8:30 a.m. train No. 55 pulled out from Bath, heading east to Rockland, the first eastbound train to cross the Kennebec by bridge. Not a seat could be had for love nor money. Even the car platforms and steps were filled with waving, shouting passengers on the first run east.

The morning was crowded with trains, jammed with first-day passengers. At 11 a.m. a giant engine, No. 501, one of the largest on the Maine Central Railroad, pulled the first eastbound freight across the bridge, 14 cars heavily loaded with cement from Pennsylvania, to be used in building the new cement plant at Thomaston, a $4,000,000 investment by Lawrence-Portland Cement Co.

In late 1982 Martin-Marietta closed that now enormous cement plant, which was bought in 1983 by the Maine firm called Cianbro. This raised the question of closing the railroad link, from Bath to Rockland, which depended for revenue on carrying cement. In turn this raised the question of whether the Maine Central Railroad would remain responsible for raising and lowering the Carlton drawbridge when ships passed under it. For 55 years there had been a Maine Central man on duty in the bridge house 24 hours a day, 365 days a year, at a cost of almost $100,000 a year. But the number of bridge raises had dropped from the thousands to 500 a year, so each raising cost the railroad $200. How the old circus train would appreciate the bridge! When the Barnum & Bailey circus came to Maine in the summer of 1890 and wanted to cross the Kennebec, the ferry had to make 33 trips to carry 66 circus cars and engines across the river to Woolwich.

The $3 million bridge (and $3 million in 1927 is the equivalent roughly of $30 million in 1983) was an enormous feather in Bath's cloth cap and heartily approved by Bath voters. In Bath the referendum question of issuing state bonds to pay for the bridge was won with 2,800 "yes" votes and only 103 "no" votes. With commendable neighborly jealousy nearby Richmond and Bowdoin voted against the bridge. It was called the Carlton Bridge because Frank W. Carlton was the state senator from Woolwich who in 1925 introduced legislation to fund the bridge. On opening day Carlton was of course conspicously present to take the kudos.

The bridge was originally the idea not of Carlton but of Luther Maddocks of Boothbay Harbor. Maddocks launched his brainchild a full five years before Carlton got his bill before the legislature. In 1920 Maddocks had toured the local counties trying to drum up support. He had little success until he found a quorum gathered in the Lincoln County Courthouse one day just before court opened. There Maddocks whipped out the bylaws for the group sponsoring the bridge idea. There and then, Judge Cyrus R. Tupper was elected president, Arthur Littlefield of Rockland secretary and William D. Patterson of Wiscasset treasurer. Maddocks was named manager and given the job of raising funds. After 60 days and nights of buttonholing, Maddocks had raised $1,700, including $100 from the Portland Chamber of Commerce. They used $500 to hire engineers to "learn the nature of the riverbed." And in the bitter cold of November the engineer put down 13 holes through 60 feet of water and 40 feet of mud. Carlton then was given the job of getting a bill through the state legislature. There was so much wrangling over whether the bridge should be privately or publicly owned, whether it should be a toll bridge or a free bridge, that Carlton dug into the slim treasury and paid another engineer $25 a day to set up a model, along with charts and blueprints, in the corridor of the State House in Augusta, so lawmakers could see what they would be voting on.

On the day the Carlton Bridge opened in 1927, the Maine Central ran a big, pompous and boastful advertisement. In part the ad said the $3-million, 3000-foot bridge was:

> "A splendid example of the mutual benefits from cooperation between a public servant, typified by the Maine Central Railroad, and the public as a whole, represented by the State Government of Maine. Maine Central urges readers of the Bath Daily Times to remember every time one crosses the bridge — on rubber or on rails — that 55 percent of the cost of erection and maintenance of this splendid structure is borne by the Maine Central Railroad."

The Carlton Bridge is a heftily handsome, massively ugly, green engineering feat. When built, it was an engineering marvel; one pier was sunk 118.7 feet, deepest in the world; and the structure was built to withstand tons of immense pressure from ice buildup and tide flow. The metal in it weighs more than 9,000 tons. The bridge is 3,090 feet long, of which some 2,000 feet are over water and 1000 feet are approaches. There are seven spans. The largest weighs 980 tons and is 275 feet long.

One day when I was impatiently waiting in a long line of cars because the central span was up to let through a boat, I decided an interview with the man who raises the span would make newspaper column. So next day I climbed a steel ladder to the penthouse office above the bridge and met Bill McBurnie, junior partner in the foursome of Mank, Grant, Ryder and McBurnie, the team which manned the span around the clock in eight-hour shifts. They were all railroad men. For this is still a railroad bridge, though only one train a day uses the single track railway on the lower level, hidden from both view and knowledge of most.

McBurnie's office on the bridge had a splendid view. Windows on all four sides commanded the river north and south, the BIW shipyards, and the whole City of Bath below. It was furnished with an old oak desk, a rickety wooden swivel arm chair, a radio, a coal-burning Franklin stove and four large panels of gauges, and push buttons. There was one commercial telephone and one railroad "bug line" to call up and down the tracks between Portland

Building the Carlton Bridge, Bath, 1926.

and Rockland. Above this room was the workshop, reached by a ladder of iron stairs. This housed 55 two-volt batteries producing the 110 volts needed to activate the railroad smashboards and rail locks. The smashboards are exactly that; a train must smash through them if it should mistakenly go through the stop signals.

McBurnie and his coworkers on the other shifts had not much business from passing ships. Shipping under the bridge, like railroading on the bridge, saw busier times long ago. McBurnie's old logbooks show that in 1931, the bridge went up 1,300 times. By the 1980s it was going up only 500 times. The bridge had twin turbines which convert power from Central Maine Power to the 440 volts required to operate the two 150-horsepower motors which raise and lower the bridge. At full lift, the center span of the bridge can be lifted 135 feet. In the engine room, the 1928 gasoline motor, there when the bridge opened in 1927, was still working more than 55 years later, as a standby in case of power failure.

The signal to "Open the bridge, please!" is three blasts from a ship's whistle. Three reply blasts or three flashing yellow lights mean the operator is ready to raise. If a train is coming or if for some other reason the operator cannot raise the bridge, he replies with five blasts or five red light flashes.

"Usually," McBurnie said, "we clear a ship through in about five minutes. If she is baulky and awkward it might take 15 minutes. And then you should see the traffic pile up on the highways!"

In the spring of 1983, these two vital questions had not been answered; Will Maine Central keep trains running over the Kennebec? If not, then who will raise and lower the bridge?

Cars lined up to board the Woolwich ferry in 1920s, before the Carlton Bridge was open. (Maine Maritime Museum)

3.

BIW Sold at Auction: 1927

But its roots began in 1792

The view from the new Carlton bridge was not all good in 1927. The same issue of the Bath paper which ballyhooed the opening of the bridge reported with yearning, "Shipyard may reopen soon."

Bath Iron Works had gone broke two years before. The final blow had been ignominious, cheap and dreary.

On a raw windy day, Sept. 24, 1925, the Iron Works had been sold at auction on the courthouse steps, knocked down to a junk dealer from New York city named Theodore Friedburg. There had been only three bidders; William S. (Pete) Newell, the Bath man who had worked at BIW for 25 years until it went bankrupt, and who later was to bring BIW to new heights; William E. Reid of Portland; and Ralph O. Dale, a Bath lawyer bidding on behalf of Friedburg.

A shivering crowd of 100 spectators watched Newell open the bidding at $90,000. Before long Reid dropped out. The duel was between Newell and Friedburg's agent, Dale. Dale would raise Newell by a miserly $100 after every bid by Newell. The bidding reached $185,000. Then Newell, in his last move, raised by $8000. Friedburg's agent raised by $100 again. But Newell was out of funds. Friedburg got the Bath Iron Works for $193,100 and paid another $25,000 for all supplies and stock on hand. Friedburg sold off BIW's machinery, and what he couldn't sell he junked for scrap. The shipyard closed.

In the proud yard where thousands had built warships in World War I, there was only one job — a watchman. But the phoenix was to rise from the ashes.

The roots of BIW go back to 1792, three years after George Washington had been elected the first president. That was the year Jonathan Hyde, a sickly and restless 30 year-old from Lebanon,

Connecticut, arrived in Bath after a long horseback ride to seek a new life of health and wealth. He found both. The Hyde family started BIW and made it into one of the best known and personally profitable shipyards in the nation.

When the first Hyde arrived, Bath was a quiet village. A mark of distinction was its lady doctor, Mrs. Samuel Lombard, whose practice stretched from Merrymeeting Bay to Phipsburg (now spelled as Phippsburg.) James Sullivan was Bath's one lawyer. He had begun practicing in 1760. Later Sullivan became governor of Massachusetts. There was a small tavern on High Street, run by Joseph Lambert, which had opened in 1774. At Dresden — an hour away on horseback — stood the only important building in the area, the handsome Pownalborough Courthouse, built in 1761 and still there. There was a schoolhouse on High Street, not far from the Lombard tavern. Joseph Sewall, later a lawyer and collector of taxes, built it and a Mr. Hobby was the teacher. Forty pounds a year was the school budget, raised to $400 a year in 1796. The U.S. mail was brought to Bath from Portland by Richard Kimball, who made the journey on foot once a fortnight. Luke Lombard took the mail to Boston on horseback once every two weeks, the trip lasting three days. (When Bath sent 10 soldiers to Boston, they walked the distance in six days.) The population of Bath was about 1,000 souls on the day 30-year-old Jonathan Hyde rode into town from Connecticut in 1792.

When this Jonathan Hyde was 87 years old he recalled those first days. He wrote in 1847:

> "All below Bath on the river, the seaboard, the islands were covered with trees; Seguin Island (now bare) was like a dark forest standing in the ocean; Wood Island, Stage and Pond were tree-covered then, though barren by 1847. Bath did not appear very much like a village; a few stores and a few houses scattered along a country road, which is now High Street; it was chiefly pasture where the city stands now."

After working for 15 years in stores and boatyards for others, Jonathan Hyde opened a general store of his own in 1807. Three years later, he sent word for his half-brother, Zina Hyde, to come up from Connecticut and join him. Together, they expanded the store into a ship chandlery and started a ferry service across the river. Bit by bit they moved into shipping and insurance. Then Zina split off, started his own store and prospered greatly. Zina went on to serve in the legislature.

Jonathan stayed close to home, and was elected selectman of Bath a half a dozen times and became president of the Lincoln Bank, which was started in 1813. The half-brothers and their families survived the plague of smallpox which hit Bath hard.

Zina, the big money-maker of the family, took his wife voyaging to the Mediterranean in 1841. While there, a son was born to them in Florence, and they christened him Thomas W. Hyde. This baby grew up to become the brilliant Civil War soldier who won the Congressional Medal of Honor and achieved the rank of general at 24. When he came home from the war Gen. Thomas Hyde opened his Bath Iron Works.

The story of Thomas and his son John Hyde and their impact on lives along the Kennebec, Maine, the United States and the seven seas will be told later. But first, the setting. What was life like in Bath during the early part of the 1800s?

I've taken a few items from a staccato little volume by Levi P. Lemont titled "1400 Historical Dates and Events in the Town and City of Bath and Georgetown from 1604 to 1874," published in Bath by the author in 1874. This rare book was lent to me by William F. Mussenden, who retired as vice-president of BIW in 1982. Lemont, the compiler of this Bath record, had long roots here, and facts about Lemonts pop up throughout his 104-page book. We first hear about the long-lived Lemonts under the date of 1722:

> "John Lemont settled near where the railroad now crosses the New Meadows river, and built a garrison. He was born 1704, died 1766. His children lived to a great age; one daughter lived 100 years, another 99 years, a son 96 years, another 86, and one 76 years. He built vessels at this place as early as 1745."

Bath had no sidewalks, but about 20 rough roads laced the town. Five ferries were running across the Kennebec, "all propelled by hand," until the first steam ferry in 1837, run by Peleg and Henry Tallman. Fires were a constant danger. In 1722, the Elkins house was burned by Indians. The schoolhouse burned down in 1800; Donnell's blacksmith shop went up in flames in 1805; in 1813 John Parshley's hotel burned, killing two children. David Pettingill was scalded to death while making salt at the New Meadows river.

Right after Dr. John Stockbridge's home on High Street burned in 1817, Bath organized its first fire company, "each member furnishing himself with two leather buckets and a knapsack." After putting up with some lemons in the way of engines, Bath purchased a "first class machine, a suction hose engine" costing $1000 in 1838.

Between the Revolution and 1825, more than a dozen taverns and hotels were opened, a sign of more and more travelers coming to the courthouse at Pownalborough and the shipyards. Among them were the Bath Hotel, opened by John Ring in 1806, and the Commercial House. The Bath Bank opened in 1810, with Gen. (later first governor of Maine) William King as president. This was quickly followed by the rival Lincoln Bank in 1813, with Jonathan Hyde as president. Then came the Commercial Bank. By 1836 Joseph Sewall was president of yet another, the Sagadahoc State Bank. From 1865 to 1868, a veritable rash of banks broke out, until Bath had a dozen different banks. In 1868 the only Bath bank with an unpretentious name opened its doors: The Peoples Twenty Five Cent Savings Bank.

Shipping was Bath's lifeblood from the start. Most vessels were small, usually under 300 tons. Tonnage recorded at Bath, which had become a port of entry in 1780, was 5,407 in 1794; jumped to 10,666 in 1804; and doubled again to 20,258 tons in 1815.

These Bath boats traveled far and often. In 1800 William King sent his 281-ton ship Reunion to England and back three times in three years. But King's knowledge of the U.S. coast was vague. When he launched his brig Androscoggin in 1802, he ordered Capt. Nehemiah Harding to sail for New Orleans. The Captain asked King where New Orleans was, and was told: "somewhere on the Gulf of Mexico." Capt. Harding luckily found an old Spanish chart; by that he found his way to New Orleans. This was the first vessel to sail from Maine to New Orleans.

The most exciting event in Bath in 1818 was the arrival of the first steamboat, the little steamer Tom Thumb, no more than 30 feet long, owned by a Mr. Dodd. She came steaming up the Kennebec, an open boat, all machinery in clear sight, with side wheels pushing her along. She created a sensation. And so excited Seward Porter that he immediately fitted out his flat river scow with a steam engine and christened her grandiosely, Kennebec. But her engine was so small, she couldn't make headway against the current. So the ambitious Porter went to New York in 1823 and bought the fine steamboat Patent. He stopped in Boston; then made the Boston to Portland leg in seventeen and a half hours. Thanks to Porter, Bath passengers could now ride on his steamer Patent to Boston, fare $7. By 1832, the Patent was carrying passengers from Bath to Portland for $1. This put Bath business really on the map.

Bath people endured very hard times, financially and climatically, in the early 1800s. Shipbuilding almost stopped because of the embargoes and blockades of the War of 1812. Then in 1816 came the winter that lasted all year long. Snow fell on June 8. The ground was frozen so hard that farmers could plant no corn. Farmers sold their land and migrated west, mostly to Ohio. There was no money in circulation. Gen. William King, Bath's leading citizen came to the rescue.

> "King had a cargo of corn come in and he would not sell over two bushels to any one person, and he trusted it out all through the country. By his extra perseverance, Wm. King got the Betterment Act through, which much relieved farmers. Corn was selling at $2.50 a bushel."

From 1820 to 1823, reports Lemont:

> "All kinds of produce were very low and no money to buy with; everything barter and a very little labor to be found, and low wages. Mechanics wages from 75 cents to $1.00 a day; laborers 50 cents; a good dressmaker or milliner 25 cents a day, and work from sunrise to sunset and glad to get it. Kitchen girls got 25 to 50 cents a week, and work all the time at kitchen work, sewing, knitting, or otherwise till nine or ten at night.
>
> "Here are the prices of some provisions; salmon three cents a pound; flour $4.50 a barrel; corn 50 cents a bushel; apples 10 to 25 cents a bushel; butter 10 to 25 cents a pound; Mutton 5 cents a pound or less; same for chickens and turkeys."

Sail-ferry carrying horse drawn wagon and ox drawn cart over the Kennebec.

These hard years were barely over when in 1836 the whole United States suffered a crop failure. The price of flour rose from $4.50 to $14 a barrel. Banks across the nation stopped specie payment or closed entirely.

As shipping was their prime business, Bath businessmen used the mail more than most. They paid postmaster Thomas Eaton 12½ cents on letters to Boston, 18¾ cents on letters to New York and 25 cents on letters to New Orleans or anywhere in the U.S., 500 miles or more distant.

This was the Bath world where Thomas W. Hyde, the boy born in Florence, made his mark on American shipbuilding that has lasted over the centuries.

General Thomas Worcester Hyde, president and founder of Bath Iron Works, 1884-1899.

4.

Thomas Hyde: The Founder

1884 — BIW begins

Zina and Eleanor Hyde brought their infant son, Tom, home to Bath by sailing ship from Italy, where he had been born, January 15, 1841. He grew up in the luxury of Elmhurst, the new 160-acre estate, which Zina Hyde built in 1842 from the profits of his Bath business.

Tom Hyde graduated from Bath High School in 1856 and went on to study at nearby Bowdoin College.

But he had an itch to study more technology than Bowdoin then offered, so in the fall of 1860 he went west to enroll in a class of three seniors at the University of Chicago. While in Illinois, 19-year-old Hyde met Abraham Lincoln, then a candidate for president. Hyde was present at a friend's house there when Lincoln first met Hannibal Hamlin, the Maine man who became Lincoln's vice president.

Young Hyde often went to Lincoln's law office in Springfield to help answer the mail for the president-elect. He was shocked by mail from Southerners who hated Lincoln for his anti-slavery stand and sent him dead rattlesnakes and Negro doll babies.

The night the Lincolns left Springfield to go to Washington and the White House, young Hyde was invited to a farewell party at Lincoln's home. Years later, Hyde wrote that Lincoln had invited him to travel to Washington with him and that, "Mrs. Lincoln was almost in a state of nervous prostration at the many stories rife of the dangers of the journey to Washington."

The student decided to stay in Chicago to complete his degree at the university. But in the spring of 1861, when President Lincoln called for 75,000 volunteers to put down the rebellion of the southern states, Hyde joined the Chicago Zouaves as a private and learned how to drill. But no call to battle came his way. So he took his university degree and returned to Maine to complete his studies at Bowdoin.

On the Bowdoin campus, Hyde taught fellow-students the intricate Zouave military drills. When the Union Army was soundly defeated at Bull Run, Hyde and his friends resigned from the Brunswick Zouave unit and in a patriotic fervor took the next train to Augusta to form Company D of the 7th Maine Regiment. Hyde was named captain, largely because of his experience in close-order drill. He and his company camped out in white tents on the long lawn between the State House and the Kennebec. Years later in his book, "Following the Greek Cross," Hyde recalled that night, writing:

> "Soon after supper it began to rain hard and . . . so I mustered the company and marched them off through the rain to the nearest hotel and put them up at my expense. I then invited the lieutenants to sleep in camp with me so we could inure ourselves to campaigning . . . but with the novelty and excitement, we sat up and told stories till it was time to go grand rounds . . . Before morning the rains ceased, but not the mosquitoes . . . and when the company sauntered leisurely down to breakfast, they saw their officers looking as if they'd spent all night watching with the sick."

Orders arrived for the 7th Maine Regiment to go to the war. But the colonel and lieutenant colonel — experienced soldiers — had not arrived in Augusta. So the job of heading the 7th Maine fell onto the shoulders of 20-year-old Hyde, who had been appointed major.

He marched a thousand Maine men to their encampment at Baltimore. (He'd risen from private to major in four months!) His camp was surrounded by grog shops, to which he quickly lost his unruly mob of 1,000 Maine soldiers. Hyde reported as ordered to General Dix. He immediately requisitioned handcuffs on an urgent basis, and by night had his most unruly soldiers handcuffed to the bandstand. Within a few days his colonel arrived to take charge.

From then on, he saw action. He was at the seige of Yorktown, fought in the second Battle of Bull Run, led a bayonet charge at

Williamsburg, fought at the battles of White Oak Swamp, Gannett's Hill, Golden's Farm, Savage's Station, Gettysburg and helped capture Gen. Stonewall Jackson's headquarters. He had three horses shot under him at Antietam, and wrote his mother;

> "My horse was shot through the mouth and hip; he, rearing, fell and I under him; and I saw between his legs the colors of the enemy near enough to read the names emblazoned on them."

Hyde was a tough, sometimes even brutal officer. When he found a Union soldier who wouldn't stand up and fight, Hyde, like an early version of World War II's General Patton, took out his sabre and ran it through the coward's leg. "That seemed to bring him to a sense of duty," said Hyde, barely 23 years old.

By the time he'd reached the age of 24, Hyde had won the Congressional Medal of Honor and was a brigadier general. After the surrender of Lee in 1865, this battle-tried, bemedaled veteran returned to Bath. Soon he married a hometown girl named Annie Hayden.

The ex-brigadier had plenty going for him in Bath. His uncle Jonathan had been prominent in local business and state politics; he himself had a college degree, a hero's war record and a loving eye for a local girl, and a very warm-hearted, if sometimes brutal, way with working men.

Looking for a way to make a livelihood in Bath, young Hyde leased the old Moses foundry on Water Street. He christened it the Bath Iron Foundry, and with seven men on the payroll began making railings, castings and pipes. He proved to be good at his job. By 1871 he had designed and patented the famous Hyde windlass, which soon became standard equipment on ships for raising anchors. With these profits, he bought the foundry he had been leasing and expanded and modernized its equipment. By 1879, he had 25 men on his payroll, making brass and iron castings and fittings for the shipping trade.

On October 15, 1884, former General Hyde (he kept using the military title all his life) walked into the registrar of deeds at the courthouse and filed the papers incorporating Bath Iron Works Ltd. Hyde, now 44, and his wife were the sole owners. Entire ownership of the hugely profitable BIW stayed exclusively in the Hyde family until 1918, except for a wild, brief period when his son John got mixed up in a high-flying game with Charles Schwab of Bethlehem Steel, a story which will be covered later.

Just four years after Hyde incorporated BIW, the nearby Goss Marine Iron Works on the banks of the Kennebec went broke. This gave Hyde a headache and an opportunity. The headache came from the fact that he was the principal creditor. Goss had been making boilers and engines for the wooden ships being built on the Bath waterfront in enormous numbers. Hyde had done the foundry work for Goss. The opportunity came from the fact that Hyde was able to pick up the bankrupt Goss Marine Iron Works cheaply and tuck it into BIW.

Hyde grabbed the opportunity. He turned Goss Marine into the southern (or downriver) division of BIW. Thereby he got valuable land and valuable business. But Hyde hoped for more. He saw the chance to use Goss as a stepping stone into building steel-hulled ships.

Hyde's neighbor, friend and rival, Arthur Sewall, was on the verge of turning his merchant fleet from wood to ships of steel. From this time on, Hydes would forever be planning and plotting how to keep even with or a step ahead of the Sewalls.

The one advantage Hyde had over Sewall was in personality. Sewall, even when being the politician, running for the vice-presidency with Bryan on the Democratic ticket, even when speechifying that he was the true friend of the working man, was a cold fish. Hyde, on the other hand, could walk through the streets of Bath, call three out of four working men by their first names, stop, shake hands, talk easily with every one of them. Sewall could never do that.

Hyde used this gift when he persuaded U.S. government inspectors to visit his combined BIW and Goss plants the year after he had acquired Goss. With the steel-ship business in mind, he gave them a complete tour and enthusiastic sales talk. "Here are the skilled workers and all the equipment for building steel-hulled government ships, Navy ships," he told the government men. That was in June 1889.

Arthur Sewall watched this ploy, and topped it. Sewall got President Benjamin Harrison himself plus members of his cabinet to visit the Sewall Yard and the Bath waterfront in August of 1889. It poured rain all day. The president spent his time sheltering inside the pilot-house of the ferryboat talking to the skipper. General Hyde, however, wangled his way aboard with the presidential party. He cornered the secretary of the Navy, Benjamin F. Tracy, and bent his ear talking steel-hulled Navy ships and BIW's ability to build them.

The resultant good news came in February 1890, less than two years after Hyde had acquired Goss, only a few months after the president's visit, and Hyde's hour with the secretary of the Navy.

BIW and Hyde had won government contracts to build two 190-foot steel gunboats. All Bath celebrated. The local paper reported:

> "There was more handshaking indulged in on street corners of Bath during the 30 minutes after the news flashed through the city than at any similar period in Bath history. Half a bushel of cannon firecrackers were fired off, creating a Fourth of July on a February day. Fish horns sounded along the waterfront. Every boat let go with a blast."

On a wintry day in December 1891, BIW launched its first Navy vessel, the steel-hulled gunboat Machias. Five months later, the second gunboat Castine went down the ways into the Kennebec. To the delight of the Navy and BIW both ships did well on sea trials; both exceeded the speeds specified in the contract. Thus began more than 92 years of steel-hulled ships and Navy contracts at BIW.

Even before the hulls on Machias and Castine were thoroughly salted, Hyde was signing his next Navy contract. And a weird one it was. It was to build a monstrous-looking ship, an experiment for use in ramming rather than shooting the enemy. The design was the wild idea of an admiral. No other shipyard in the nation wanted any part of it.

The ship had an enormous ramming rod built into her bow, a freak weapon which weighed 15 tons.

This unlikely vessel, christened Katahdin, was launched February 4, 1893, and won no friends for BIW. In sea trials she failed to make the 17 knots specified in the contract. For a desperate few months it seemed as though Hyde and BIW might be stuck with a ram ship and lose all the money it had cost to build her. Because Katahdin did not meet specifications, the Congress balked at approving the dollars to pay for building it.

But General Hyde called in all the I.O.U.s owed him by friends in Washington. They came to his rescue. The upshot was a special act introduced and passed by Congress, which permitted the Navy to accept Katahdin and pay in full for her. Hyde was happy to see the last of her.

But the ram ship got only as far as Newport News. There she

spent the rest of her life rusting and rotting, and never ramming at all, ever, anywhere.

Then another disaster hit Hyde. Fire in February 1894 all but destroyed BIW, and almost lost the Iron Works to Maine forever. As flames spread through the shipyard, blinding snow and ice handicapped Bath firefighters, but the cruelest blow was that the water pressure failed. Only the blinding storm, which piled four feet of snow in the city, stopped the fire from spreading throughout all the south end of Bath. At BIW, the plant was nothing but ashes and twisted metal: 800 men were thrown out of work. And Gen. Tom Hyde was mad as a bull.

He was mad because right was on his side. He and others had been urging the city fathers for over a year to increase water pressure in fire hydrants by tapping the Androscoggin. Their pleas had been turned down. Now because of lack of water pressure, the yard which Hyde had started with seven helpers, which had grown to employ 800, was burned to the ground. The infuriated Hyde told a local reporter for the Bath Times:

> "You may say the Iron Works will never rebuild here in Bath. We feel very hard against a city that used us so badly."

Rival cities leaped at the chance to get the Bath Iron Works to move out of Maine. New London offered to lease Hyde 1200 feet of prime waterfront for $1 a year, and to rebate taxes for 10 years. Three railroads serving New London offered to make special track connections. Local businessmen there offered to build a $700,000 drydock if BIW and Hyde would come to New London. But the general, still only 53 years old, cooled off. He decided to rebuild in Bath. He went out and bought the newest equipment available. He and BIW were soon back in business.

His first launching after the fire was the luxury yacht Eleanor, built for William A. Slater of Slater Mills in Slaterville, R.I. She was 230 feet long, carried three huge masts and 11,000 square feet of sail when all were raised. To raise them required a crew of 30 men. Some of those 30 men tended to the whims of Slater and his guests. His yacht had six luxurious guest staterooms. After she was launched Slater and his guests set off on a two-year cruise to Norway, Egypt, India, Japan and China. Later, in World War I, the Eleanor joined the U.S. Navy as a gunboat, and was renamed Harvard, because Harvard men manned her. After that war, she wound up as a passenger vessel in Greek hands, sailing between Greece and Italy as late as 1948, when she was 54 years old and the Hydes had long since left BIW.

The Eleanor led directly to a still bigger, more spectacular luxury yacht. Col. Oliver Payne, a rich and sybaritic bachelor from New York City, had chartered the Eleanor for a Mediterranean cruise and was bewitched by her luxury and beauty. But Payne was also canny. When he found that the BIW-built yacht had logged 80,000 miles without costing a dollar for repairs, he ordered Hyde to build the yacht Aphrodite for him. This super pleasure craft would be 302 feet long, require a crew of 56 and carry not 11,000 square feet but 17,000 square feet of sail flying from her three masts. To guard against getting fat while being waited upon by a crew of 56, Payne ordered a bicycle track built for riding around the decks. Inside, the entertainment salons were housed within a 160-foot-long deck house, faced with mahogany inside and out.

Gen. Hyde retired at age 58, in September 1899. He died two months later. The boy general at age 24 had become a millionaire shipbuilder. The foundry he began with seven workers had become famous the world around. The Army general turned Navy shipbuilder had supervised 28 ships under construction at BIW. The presidencies of BIW and Hyde Windlass were inherited by his sons, John S. Hyde, 32, and Edward W. Hyde, 30.

Wood engraving made in 1891 for first BIW catalog

John S. Hyde, president of Bath Iron Works 1899-1917.

5.

John S. Hyde: The go-getter 1899-1917

Big Money for the Family

The founder of BIW was not long dead before his sons won a contract which made the general spin in his grave with pride: the one and only contract BIW has ever had to build a battleship.

She was the Georgia, 438 feet long, 76 feet wide and 15,000 tons, designed to fire 12- and 8-inch guns and to make a top speed of 20 knots. Her contract price was a $3.5 million, a gigantic sum in 1899. Getting this award was the pride of Maine. The Georgia took five years to build. And when she was launched into the Kennebec in October 1904, 20,000 spectators mobbed Bath to cheer the new battleship down the ways.

But landing one of the biggest of shipbuilding contracts in the U.S. turned the heads of the young Hyde brothers, who were still under 35 and new at the controls of BIW. They got themselves, BIW and Hyde Windlass into a financial mess.

Two years before the Georgia was launched, they fell, hook, line and sinker, into the clutches of fabled steel-king Charles Schwab, the flamboyant boss of powerful Bethlehem Steel. Schwab had supplied steel to BIW and was a frequent and spectacular visitor to Bath, arriving in his private railroad car, to stay at Elmhurst.

Schwab had a scheme to create a combine of all the biggest shipbuilders in America. He would form them into one gigantic shipbuilding trust or monopoly, and together they would corner all major shipbuilding contracts in the nation. Schwab would sell them steel.

Schwab formed a new company called United States Shipbuilding. He was head of it. And as directors he named John S. Hyde and his brother Edward Hyde of BIW; Henry T. Scott, president of Union Iron Works in San Francisco; Charles R. Hanscomb, president of Eastern Shipbuilding and former superintendent of BIW; and Lewis Nixon, president of Crescent Shipyard of Elizabeth, N.J. Others were involved in this monopoly scheme of Schwab's; but in the inner circle were three men with close ties to BIW — the Hyde brothers and Hanscomb.

The group was clearly out to get control of all major shipbuilding in the United States. They explained this away by saying their combine was necessary to meet foreign competition. But the combine would certainly have eliminated domestic competition, made a farce out of competitive bidding and set prices among themselves.

There were more financial shenanigans involved.

The prospectus to prospective buyers of stock in United States Shipbuilding said the company had contracts in hand totaling $36 million. This was absolutely fraudulent. The directors of United Shipbuilding knew the total contracts of all in the combine amounted to only $12 million. Yet these directors issued a balloon stock of $70 million.

Their scheme ran head-on into strong opposition from President Teddy Roosevelt, the trust-buster. Roosevelt was too powerful even for Charles Schwab and his swashbuckling pirate ways, Bethlehem Steel and the shipyard combine put together. The United States Shipbuilding trust was sunk, blown out of the water, by the White House and the Sherman Anti-Trust Act. But the bad news for BIW was that after it had pooled itself into Schwab's monopoly trust, it was not able to come out cleanly when the trust was broken up. Far from it.

Instead the family-owned BIW was still under the control of Schwab and Bethlehem Steel, and stayed there until February, 1905. Even as the Hydes were launching the battleship Georgia, BIW was under threat of being closed again, this time by Schwab who held $500,000 of BIW paper. And Bath was filled with rumors that Schwab would close the yard.

Then the clouds broke, sunshine for the Hydes came out in vinegary rays. Schwab sold back BIW to the Hydes for $275,000 and Hyde Windlass for $200,000. But the company had been milked almost dry. BIW had heavy debts, no working capital, big mortgages and almost no new business on the books.

Then Hyde landed a Navy contract to build the scout cruiser Chester, first to have the new turbine engines; 420 feet long, almost as long as the 438-foot battleship Georgia, five decks high and with a flank speed of 24 knots, four knots faster than the Georgia. Here was work enough to keep BIW's 800 workers busy for three years. Here was the acid test of whether BIW could rise from the seeming mismanagement or bad luck of the early years under the control of the second generation of Hydes.

The Hydes and BIW came through with flying colors. When the Chester was launched in 1907, she amazed the Navy by the excellent showing she made on her sea trials. Instead of the required 24 knots, Chester ran faster than 26.5 knots. When this news reached shore, the church bells at Bath rang out; and the BIW yard fired 26 resounding rounds from a cannon. The Navy money came in; the Schwab mortgages and other notes were paid off and the repute of BIW as a top yard soared.

New business poured in. Hyde, handsome, able and energetic, was proving himself a front-runner both in selling and delivering. He was bringing in government and non-government contracts, building both naval and commercial vessels, a mix which was making BIW and thereby Bath and the Kennebec prosperous.

Two big steel-hulled passenger vessels were built with a price tag of a million dollars each. They were the Camden and the Belfast, with 204 staterooms on the upper decks and 135 dormitory-type berths for men only below. For 20 years these two ships ran on the fondly remembered run, Bangor to Boston.

For the Maine Central Railroad, BIW built the railroad ferry Ferdinando Gorges, a sidewheeler with three railroad tracks on her main deck, so she could carry two locomotives and nine railroad cars across the Kennebec before the Carlton bridge was built in 1927.

Destroyer business from the Navy came apace. The Flusser and the Reid, speedsters which turned up 35 knots, were launched in 1909; three more went down the ways in 1910, the Trippe, the Jouett and the Jenkins; then bigger 1,000-tonners, the Cassin, the Cummings, the Wadsworth, the Davis and the Allen. These had a contract price of about $800,000 each. Business was good, and about to get even better. Hyde came back from Washington, D.C., with a contract in his pocket to build four "four pipers" at $1.1 million each.

Money rolled in. Jobs were plentiful in Bath, and wages at BIW seemed good to most Maine men. But no man prospered so mightily as John S. Hyde. BIW stock was owned wholly by him and his family. One night when talking about money and ships with close friends, Hyde was asked how much money he was making. He answered "Every third ship is mine." Translated, that meant his profit on every ship was about 50 percent of its contract price. And this was in the days before any corporate or personal income tax. Dividends of 100 percent were paid in 1909; 150 percent in 1910. By 1912, business was booming so much that BIW declared a 100 percent dividend in advance; and then sweetened it by paying extra dividends of 75 percent and 100 percent in June and December.

Hyde was by now one of the richest men in Maine, making his pile through his own work in his own shipyard, while still in his early 40s. He decided to spend some of his profits by turning his home into a showplace. He hired Maine's most noted residential architect of the days, John Calvin Stevens of Portland, and went to work.

He tore down the 70-year-old family home, built by grandfather Zina Hyde in 1842, and built a new Elmhurst. This huge brick Georgian mansion is standing today as the Hyde School, a private preparatory school, just a few blocks from the shipyard.

But John Hyde wanted more than a stunning showplace. He wanted a mansion whose price would be beyond the purse even of the famed Sewall family of Bath.

While the Hydes had made a name and a fortune, the Sewalls had done even better. The Sewall fleet of wooden ships and the Sewall house flag — a white S on a field of blue — had long been known and respected the world around. The Sewalls had begun their even more famous fleet, the Sewall ships of steel, the same year BIW had built its first steel gunboat, the Machias, for the Navy. Yet more fame kept coming to the Sewall name. Arthur Sewall, known across America as "the merchant prince," had been chosen to run for the vice-presidency of the United States on the Democratic ticket with William Jennings Bryan.

Now John S. Hyde would outshine the Sewalls with a mansion no Sewall could afford. So Hyde built the new Elmhurst complete with indoor swimming pool, ballroom, library, card room and a dining room so large that 60 guests could sit down to dinner. He sited his new brick showplace among 160 acres in Bath; and to set off the splendid house he established a model "home farm" and built great greenhouses to raise exotic orchids. He showered his wife with rubies and diamonds so big they could be easily seen and greatly admired by all.

Soon after this mansion was completed, in 1915, Hyde gave an enormous party to celebrate. Emma Eames, the Bath-raised opera singer who was a star of the Metropolitan Opera and known in all the opera houses of Europe, appeared. She sang Rachmaninoff's "How Sweet the Place," a fitting anthem to christen John Hyde's Elmhurst.

John Hyde married twice. His first marriage to a girl from Weyland, Massachusetts, ended in divorce. Then John Hyde married a local Bath girl, Ernestine Shannon. Her father owned and ran the Shannon House, sometimes called the King tavern. Ernestine Hyde, according to those who knew her, wore spectacularly big diamonds and extremely elegant clothes. She entertained lavishly for her husband at Elmhurst, giving very grand dinners for his business visitors as well as for the political and social bigwigs of Maine.

Illness hit John Hyde severely while he was only in his late 40s.

John S. Hyde's second wife Ernestine Hyde. (Maine Maritime Museum, Bath)

Elmhurst, the showplace mansion built by John Hyde with profits from BIW. It is now Hyde School, Bath.

After that, he spent much of his time at his house in St. Augustine, Florida, and there he died on March 20, 1917, five days before his 50th birthday, and three weeks before Bath-built destroyers entered World War I.

His widow and heirs sold all his stock in the family owned Bath Iron Works for $3 million. Thus Bath Iron Works as a family business lasted only through a father-and-son tenure. But in those 33 years since 1884, when General Hyde filed the incorporation papers of BIW, and John Hyde's death in 1917, father and son had launched a huge and memorable fleet of 75 ships into the Kennebec.

Ahead lay more years of spectacular shipbuilding, but they were offset with years of desperate crises and near collapse.

Ernestine Hyde was remarried to Henry Wright, a BIW draftsman, and died in France. Her body was brought home on the Deutschland in 1933. Hyde's son Jack and his wife Eleanor and their family moved into Elmhurst. His three daughters had friends in to swim in the pool; the tennis courts were busy; the butler Emile masterminded scores of dances, dinners and spectacular parties. Jack Hyde was a huge man in girth if not height. His weight fluctuated from as much as 350 pounds to as little as 270 pounds. Huge clothes closets in Elmhurst held hundreds of suits and jackets: his "fat" clothes, and his "thin" clothes and his "middleweight" clothes. For his weight changes up and down occurred so often and in such fast succession there was not time enough for new clothes to be made or old clothes to be taken in or let out to fit the changing waistline.

Despite his weight, Jack Hyde was an ardent and able golfer. He was a passionate and formidable bridge player, winning many Culbertson tournaments. He was a constant winner at backgammon and high stake roulette and card games. He also enjoyed alcohol. This, combined with overweight problems, triggered his sudden death in a Boston hospital only a short while after he had been driven there in a state of collapse from Elmhurst. His daughter Jane married Connie Fenn and died from some of the same ailments which hastened her father's death. His beauteous daughter Nancy suffered a tragic death by murder. Her marriage to Edmund Hoggard of Wenham, Massachusetts, ended. After the split, she met her former husband to talk over details of settlements. He pulled a gun and shot her dead, then killed himself. The third daughter Sally took the children. Elmhurst after Jack's death became a headquarters for Pine Tree Society for crippled children, and later became the Hyde Preparatory School.

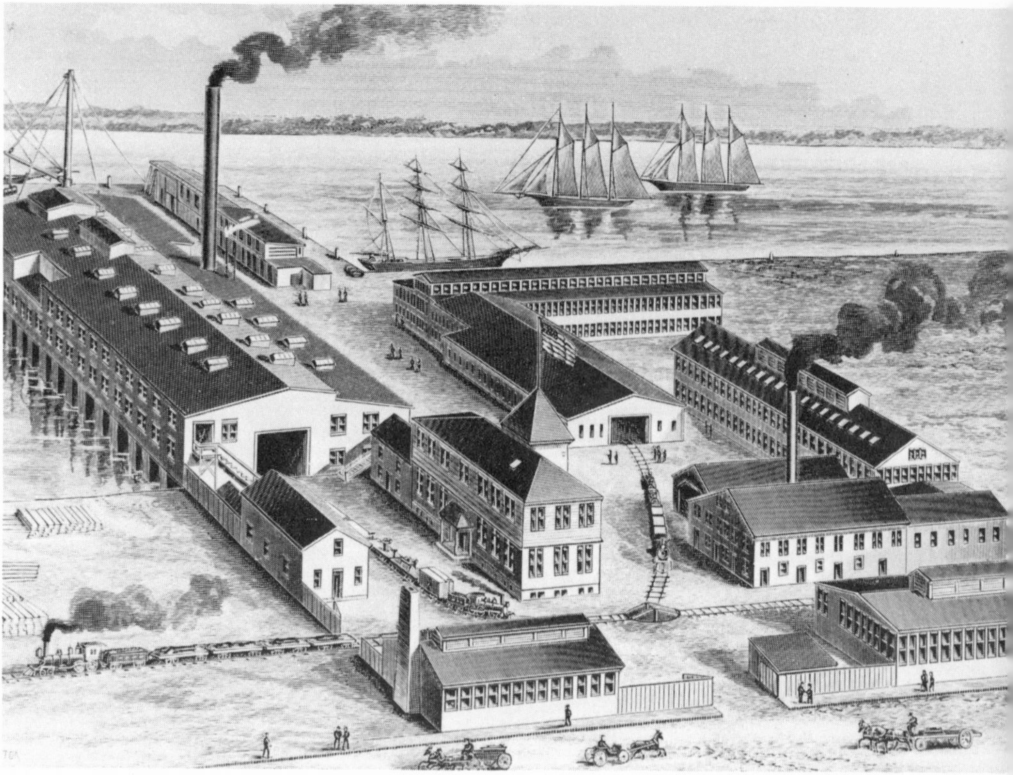

BIW yard, 1891, made for Gen. Thomas Hyde as a wood engraving by J.G. Conant Co., Boston, for cover of the first BIW catalogue. (Maine State Library)

Frigate gallery at BIW, 1982. U.S.S. Williams, Sprague, Estocin, Hall. (BIW photo)

Bath Iron Works yard, 1983, with seven Navy ships and one commercial ship. (BIW photo)

J.P. Morgan's yacht Corsair, delivered by BIW in 1930. (BIW photo)

Sugar barge launched by BIW 1982, passing Fort Popham at the mouth of the Kennebec River. (BIW)

The Bath-built Henry B. Hyde rounding the Horn, from the painting by Charles Patterson.

The yacht ARAS built by BIW in 1930s became the presidential yacht Williamsburg, used by Presidents Truman and Eisenhower.

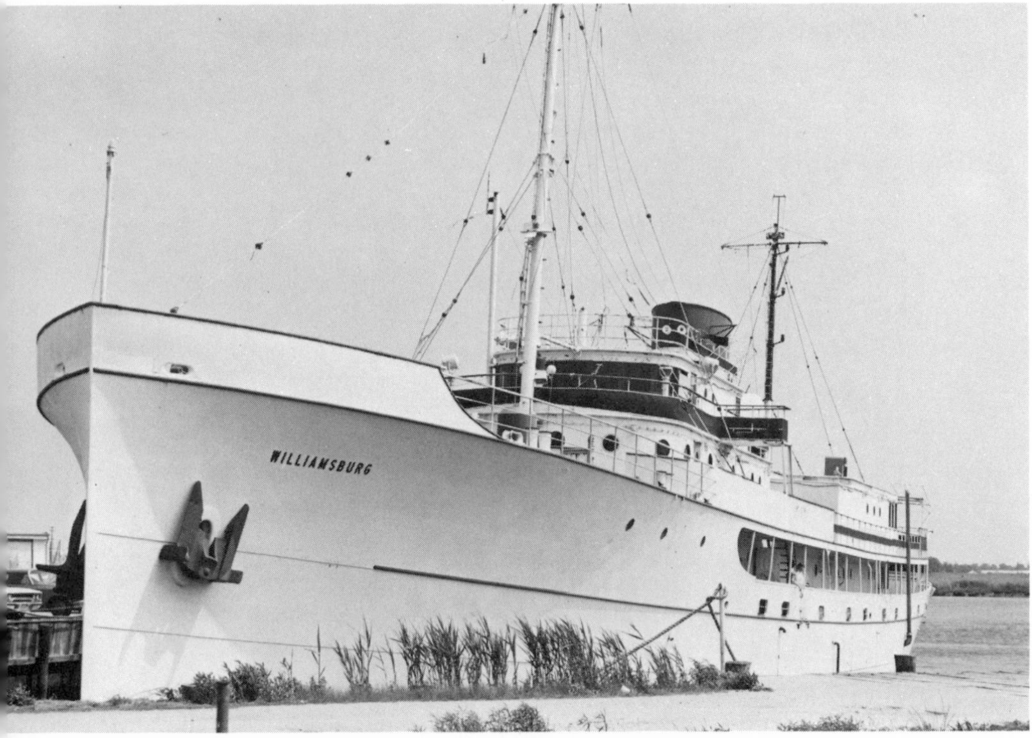

Presidential yacht Williamsburg (Keating photo)

William S. "Pete" Newell, president BIW, 1927-1945.

6.

Bankruptcy to Boom: 1920-1940

Newell Hits the Big Time

Decline came shockingly fast to the Iron Works after World War I. With the Disarmament Conference of 1922, navy shipbuilding ceased entirely for 10 years.

Navy contracts, recently so huge, dropped to nothing. Income to the yard was so small that BIW had to borrow $735,000 from the banks. Debt was increasing even as contracts fell off.

Men were fired. Employment dropped swiftly from 1900 jobs to 650. In the front office, the best brains were leaving. Death took John McInnes; engineering genius Charles P. Wetherbee left and chief supervisor John E. Burkhart followed him to Quincy.

In 1921 there were no dividends. A little work trickled in, enough to keep the yard open, but only barely. Six lightships were built during 1923 and 1924. Two steamers had been built in 1920 and 1921, but the yard had lost money on both. Money was so short in 1923 that BIW could not pay the interest due on its six percent bonds. At the end of 1924 the company went into receivership.

On October 1, 1925 came the final humiliation. Bath Iron Works was put up for sale at public auction. Theodore Friedburg, a speculator and scrap metal dealer from New York City, got BIW for $193,100. In liquidation, the bondholders got back about 10 cents on the dollar.

The son of Engineering Works manager William Newell, wrote:

> "The day after the auction Mr. Friedburg called on us at home, exclaiming what a beautiful house it was to my mother and what a shame she was about to have to leave it. His deal was this: father could have the plant for

> $20,000 more than Mr. Friedburg had bought it for the day before. You can imagine what the gentleman from New York was told!"

Bath Iron Works died a miserable pauper's death. Friedburg stripped the yard of all machinery and equipment that could be moved. He sold what he could, then turned what was left into junk scrap metal and sold that. The land under the yard and the buildings which remained standing and rotting, Friedburg sold to a utility, New England Public Service Co. Eventually pie plates were made in one building, leased by the Keyes Fibre Co. of Waterville. They had a subsidiary, Rex Products, inside making pie plates where once ships had been built.

William S. "Pete" Newell, after 25 years at BIW, was licking his wounds in New York at a job with Cox & Stephens, naval architects, who were designing yachts for the millionaires of the mid-1920s. He left to accept the best-paying job he had ever held — general manager of the New York Shipbuilding Co. of Camden, N.J., one of the three largest shipyards in the United States.

When Newell heard that his old love BIW was making pie plates, the news drove him to find a way to bring that yard and the Bath shipwrights back to useful, productive life again. He went for advice to his old boss Charles Wetherbee, now president of another big shipyard. The wise Wetherbee doused his one-time assistant and long-time friend's dream with cold water: "You have no men, no staff, no capital, no market and the plant is stripped to its bones — you can't spin a thread!"

Newell went to talk with Archibald Main, a man born to shipbuilding on the banks of the Clyde in Scotland who had spent 27 years in American yards and become a leader in American shipbuilding. Main was fired by Newell's dream of bringing the once prestigious and profitable BIW back to speed.

Together Newell and Main, with William Truss, organized the new Bath Iron Works Corporation in 1927. But it was a shipbuilding corporation on paper only. They had to get the yard first and then bring it back to producing ships, but they had almost no money.

Newell went to Walter S. Wyman in Augusta. Wyman was president of Central Maine Power and an officer of New England Public Service Co., which now owned the yard.

"Will you lease me the plant at a rent I can afford?" asked Newell.

Wyman had just built the new Wyman dam at Bingham. CMP was generating plenty of power but needed customers. Wyman saw a flourishing BIW would be a fine future customer. Wyman also knew a lot about starting on a shoestring. He had started the little Messalonskee Electric Co. on a shoestring and built it into Central Maine Power Co. Wyman agreed to lease Newell the old BIW plant at $17,000 a year, with an option to purchase at a reasonable price.

(Wyman came out of that deal a winner. Within four years he was selling BIW $50,000 worth of power each year. In World War II, BIW was buying a million dollars a year of power from CMP. Today BIW is buying many million dollars worth of electric power.)

Newell and Main were convinced they could build millionaires' yachts in the American yard at Bath better than they were being built in European yards, and do it at a competitive price. He took his scheme to Joseph A. MacDonald, president of Henry J. Gielow Inc., naval architects who specialized in the design of luxury yachts. Gielow agreed to lend BIW startup money in exchange for stock. At about this time Newell landed his first contract to build a yacht — a 240-footer for Ernest B. Dane of Brookline and Seal Harbor — to be called Vanda. Dane had admired the quality of BIW joiner work years earlier, aboard a small steamer at Mt. Desert. Ever since then, he had wanted his yacht to be built by those craftsmen. It happened that Gielow was the architect for Vanda.

On such lovely little coincidences of good luck and good timing was BIW rescued from another miserable death. Newell persuaded Dane to advance 15 percent of the construction cost of his yacht. This provided a small amount of cash in hand. For the balance, Newell asked Gielow. They went to the Harriman National Bank; Gielow borrowed $200,000 and turned it over to Newell. But there was a safeguard; in return for the $200,000 Gielow took 50 percent of the common stock of BIW (thereby hangs a tale which will be told). After 90 days, however, Newell returned half the money, saying he faced too many temptations to spend it rashly in fast upgrading of the broken-down yard.

To get the needed machinery and equipment they had to have, Newell and Main went to auctions. It was a lucky break for them that the great Philadelphia shipyard of William Cramp & Sons was facing liquidation. There are few things worth less than a shipyard that is losing money. Consequently prices are extremely low when a bankrupt shipyard must auction its equipment. So the auctioneer was receptive when Newell and Main came to buy; there were mighty few buyers. According to the account of John, his son, Newell bought bending floor slabs at scrap prices, along with a carload of sledges, dogs, half moons, chains, tongs and wheezers thrown in free. The auctioneer wanted 25 percent down. Newell did not have it, but gave his personal check for 10 percent, and then had to borrow the fare back to Bath from a friend.

With a lease on the yard from Wyman, loans from Gielow, a railroad car of equipment from the Cramp auction, a down payment from Dane and a contract to build his yacht, Newell now needed men, shipwrights, to work in his yard. He spread the word he was hiring old BIW hands. He got them cheap, too. They agreed to put in a 54-hour work week for a 48-hour wage. Before long there were 300 men working on Vanda. She was launched in 1929, 240 feet of luxury, with a dining salon 35 feet by 17 feet, paneled in black walnut and an owner's stateroom bigger than the master bedroom in most homes, measuring 25 feet by 15 feet.

Under construction next to the Vanda was an even bigger luxury yacht, a 266-footer for H. Edward Manville, the asbestos king. (Ironically, as this is written BIW is involved in a major lawsuit concerning asbestos poisoning among its work force during the years long after WW II). She was the Hi-Esmaro, and because she would be used often by Manville's daughter who had married Count Folke Bernadotte of the Swedish royal family, the Bath carpenters were kept busy emblazoning replicas of the Swedish crown over beds in her staterooms. Her plumbing was gold-plated. On the eve of the Great Depression she cost a million dollars to build. But none of her luxurious fittings stopped her from being sunk by Japanese bombs off San Cristobal Island, near Guadacanal, in World War II.

A third luxury yacht, Paragon, for J. H. Davol of Providence, R. I., was also under construction. Then came the most spectacular yacht of them all, the famed Corsair IV, built for J.P. Morgan, II. She was launched April 10, 1930, shortly after the catastrophic market crash of 1929. Corsair measured 343 feet long, with a beam of 42½ feet and draft of 18 feet. Her two engines put out 6,000 horsepower, and gave Corsair a speed of 18 knots. She had 6 guest staterooms, and teak paneling in her salons. Her crew numbered over 60 men and women. Just 15 months after the contract had been signed, the $2½ million yacht ($30 million today) was ready to launch.

Morgan and his guests arrived in two private pullman cars from New York City. At Brunswick a special locomotive picked up Morgan's two cars and brought them to the rail siding inside Bath Iron Works. Morgan forbade entrance to the throngs of press reporters and photographers. So they rented seats in the windows of nearby homes and shot their pictures from there or from the Carlton Bridge.

Morgan was hugely delighted with the looks and performance of his immense yacht and after sea trials wished to keep going. Newell, however, had a few changes he wished to make and the Corsair was brought back to Bath. On that sea trial trip, Morgan, who owned U.S. Steel, asked Newell why he had not used steel from his plant instead of buying it from Lukens.

"Your company had no faith in me after seeing BIW's financial statement," replied Newell. "But when I went to Lukens they said that when I wanted steel they would furnish whatever I needed and that I could pay later." Morgan agreed that under those conditions he too would have done business with Lukens.

When asked why all the doorknobs aboard Corsair were gold, Morgan answered. "The brass ones always need polishing." Corsair, like so many luxury yachts, saw Navy duty in World War II. After the war she was made into a cruise ship to carry 80 passengers. In November 1949 she hit and broke up near Acapulco, Mexico. But her huge turbines were salvaged and brought ashore where they were used to provide power and light for the town of Acapulco. Few towns can brag of getting power from the engines of J. P. Morgan's yacht.

BIW also built the 150-foot yacht Black Douglas for the grandson of William Roebling, the man who built the Brooklyn Bridge. And the Aras, built 243 feet long for Hugh J. Chisholm, the Oxford Paper Co. king, whose plant was in Rumford, Maine. This Aras was bigger and more luxurious than the Aras built for Chisholm by BIW in 1924. After World War II, the Chisholm yacht became the presidential yacht Williamsburg.

Also built in the early 1930s were the yacht Helene for Charles E. Sorensen of the Ford Motor Co; Seapine for Mrs. Frank H. Goodyear of the tire family; Caroline for Eldridge H. Johnson, who'd made his money as president of the Victor Talking Machine Co., one of the early record-makers of America. She was second in size only to J. P. Morgan's Corsair, being 279 feet long and equipped specially for scientific exploration of the giant stone monoliths on Easter Island in the far Pacific.

Newell's tie-in with the yacht designer Gielow was certainly proving mutually advantageous. But as if all these luxury yachts were not enough on the edge of the Great Depression, BIW built five more 190-foot yachts with price tags then of $500,000 each — and built them on speculation! They sold four; the would-be owner of the fifth got wiped out in the stock market crash. And there was BIW with a half-million dollar luxury yacht on its hands. The Navy took it for $100,000 after it was more than 90 percent finished; and then gave it to Britain to use as a patrol boat in the early days of World War II.

While building the sybaritic pleasure yachts, Newell got news from Boston that Frank O'Hara (whose fine fishing fleet now runs from Rockland) was in the market for trawlers. When Newell walked into O'Hara's office on the Boston waterfront, seeking the business for BIW, he was told he was too late to bid for the job. "The bids are to be opened here at noon tomorrow. You can't make your drawings and designs and bid in time."

But Newell met the deadline by taking the specifications and hightailing across Boston to Massachusetts Institute of Technology. He'd been a student there and knew his way around the marine engineering school. He hired a team of students to work beside him non-stop and went to work. The deadline-beaters worked through the night at drawing boards, making the necessary tracings while Newell did the cost estimates. By mid-morning the job was ready and Newell rushed back to the O'Hara office in time to file his bid before the noon deadline. BIW won, even though it had no money to post a bond. That contract led to building 18 fishing trawlers, business which BIW had to have to keep alive during the lean 1930s.

Even so, the Great Depression almost wiped out Newell and BIW. When the stock market crashed, BIW stock plummeted to $1 a share, and still there were few takers. Newell even tried to peddle stock in the company to his shipyard workers to obtain cash. Desperate for cash to meet the payroll, he went to his local bank, the Bath Trust Co. Rupert H. Baxter, brother of Maine Governor Percival Baxter, was president and William B. Mussenden was treasurer. They lent BIW $50,000. When the state bank examiner found out, he raised hell. But Baxter told the bank examiner, "I'll loan our money to anybody I please. None of your business!" The loan was repaid. The Bath Trust Co. became the lead bank in BIW loans for many years. Newell later became a director of the bank.

The next money squeeze almost sank BIW. The yacht designers, Henry Gielow, the firm which had bankrolled the startup of Newell and BIW with a loan in 1927, were strapped for money. They went to their bank, the Harriman National, to borrow $100,000, and as collateral put up the big block of BIW common stock, which Gielow still held. Then on Bank Holiday of March 1933, the Harriman Bank closed its doors, never to reopen. Among their frozen assets was the controlling interest in BIW. Neither Newell or BIW had the cash to buy it. But Ross W. Judson, a Detroit automobile man with a genius for picking up speculative equities cheaply, and with a kindly feeling toward Newell and BIW, finally bought that BIW stock from the defunct bank. This gave Judson control of a shipyard, a business he did not know. So Judson offered to transfer to Newell enough of his stock to give control of BIW to Newell and his top associates — provided they would all agree to stay with the company. Judson took a risk in buying that almost worthless BIW stock from Harriman Bank; but he ultimately made a 3500 percent profit on his speculation.

At Judson's suggestion, this old stock was retired (BIW had been capitalized at only $150,000) and in 1936 a new stock issue of 500,000 shares with a par value of $1 was sold to the public at $12 a share. In the next 20 years, BIW paid $36 in dividends on each of those shares, declared a 5 percent stock dividend, and the market value of a share in BIW rose from $12 to $48 by 1955.

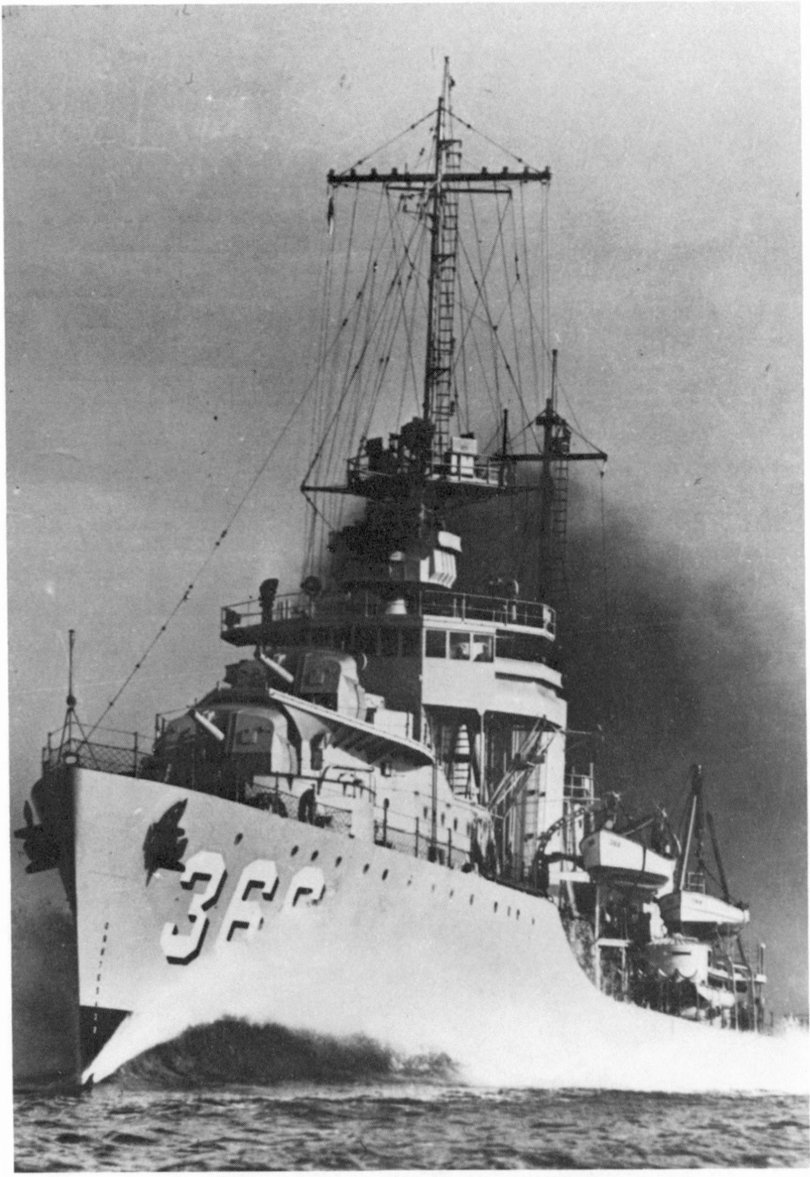

U.S.S. Drayton delivered by BIW 1936.

7.

The War Years: 1940-1954
Destroyers & Liberty Ships

In the disarmament decade from 1920 to 1930 almost no Navy ships were built. Forty percent of the shipyards in the United States went broke. Almost any type of ship was a glut on the market. In the fall of 1922, the government sold 226 wooden ships to a San Francisco man for $750,000. They had cost $300 million to build. He paid an average of $3,318 per ship, whose average price had been over $1.3 million.

Closer to home, in January 1931, nine four-masted ships owned by New England Maritime Co. were sold at auction for $13,425. They had cost $2 million to build. A four-masted schooner at $1,500! This was the bleak backdrop against which BIW was reborn in 1927 on a shoestring.

When the Navy in 1932 finally asked for bids on five destroyers, Newell took a risky dive into the bidding. It was a risk because Newell had no design or cost experience on Navy ships since he had been chief of engineering at BIW when the yard built destroyers for World War I — more than 15 years earlier. Nevertheless he put in a bid for two of the five, knowing the yard was ill-equipped, knowing he faced a penalty of $2000 per pound if his ships should fail to meet fuel consumption limits set by the Navy, and a penalty of 50 cents a pound if his ships exceeded a specified weight, and a further penalty of $300 a day if he failed to meet delivery dates.

Newell gambled. When BIW turned out to be low bidder at a price of $2.6 million, the competition protested that BIW was incompetent to build complicated warships. But Newell landed the job to build the Dewey — and then wondered if his bid was so low that his newborn yard would go broke. When the Dewey was finished, she was delivered on time and met all specifications.

In 1933, Franklin D. Roosevelt became president. As a Navy enthusiast and one-time secretary of the Navy, FDR ordered more destroyers built, and he wanted to spread the work in depressed areas. Bath certainly qualified. So, using funds from the Public Works Administration because the Navy Department didn't have enough, FDR saw that BIW got orders for two more destroyers, Drayton and Lamson, at $3.5 million each.

By the time Hitler was overrunning Europe, Congress was frightened by the glaring weakness of American defense. In 1940 Congress passed the then gigantic appropriation of $1.3 billion to build a fleet of 15 battleships, 59 cruisers, 173 destroyers, 87 submarines; and declared that half the business should go to private yards, but that profits should be limited to 10 percent of the contract price.

Work poured into BIW. By 1943 more than 12,000 people, including 1,300 women, were working in the shipyard, where in 1933 Pete Newell could not meet a payroll for 300.

More than the existing yard at Bath was needed to help meet the wartime demand for ships. When France fell in July 1940, Secretary of the Navy Knox sent Newell a telegram: "Take immediate steps to expand your facilities with view greatly enlarged shipbuilding program. Speed is of the essence."

With nothing but that telegram as a contract, Newell bought tracts of land in East Brunswick, three and a half miles from the BIW plant and spent $1.5 million building warehouses there to stockpile material. He had the job finished by December 1940, while other yards which had received similar telegrams from Knox, were waiting for firm orders. Said Newell: "You can't stop to scratch fleas when the wolves are after you!"

Newell grabbed ideas for speeding production from any source, including St. Patrick's Cathedral on Fifth Avenue, New York. Walking past it he was amazed to see workmen using pipe scaffolding. BIW had always used wood. He talked to the foreman, found out that pipe scaffolding was faster to erect and take down section by section, and then could be reused. He took the idea to the men in the yard at Bath. The old timers laughed. But when Newell told them it had, in effect, the blessing of the Pope, BIW workers agreed to try it. And that is how pipe scaffolding came and stayed at BIW.

BIW was bursting at the seams. Newell bought the Maine Central Railroad land adjoining BIW and built more facilities there to build more destroyers faster.

There was desperate need for cargo ships as well as warships. Hitler's submarines were devastating the transatlantic shipping lanes, and the Allies were in danger because of lack of cargo vessels.

This led to the strange wartime marriage between Todd Shipyards and BIW to build Liberty ships. But where? Newell had the answer: South Portland. His answer didn't come out of a hat in wartime. It had its origin years earlier, when Newell saw an artist's rendering of a mind-boggling futuristic mammoth vessel. He was in New York City, visiting at Gibbs & Cox, naval architects, where he had once worked. A friend there let Newell look at the artist's conception of a new kind of warship they were designing for Russia in 1938. It was wild; 200 feet longer than the biggest battleship afloat; able to launch and retrieve submarines from her bowels. One problem was that no yard in the world was big enough to build such a monster.

That is when lightning struck Newell. He sent an office boy out to buy a chart of Portland Harbor. He showed the chart to Gibbs, saying an enormous natural drydock could be built in South Portland simply by pouring concrete to keep the sea out, building the gigantic ship, then opening the doors in the concrete dam to let in the sea, and floating the ship out. Newell went back to Maine, bought an option on the land in South Portland and set to work designing a basin shipyard there. That was in 1938. Then in 1939 Russia signed a nonaggression pact with Hitler, and that put an end to Soviet negotiations with Gibbs & Cox about designing the leviathan. Newell stowed his idea and his drawings in a cupboard.

Then came the urgent British contract to build 60 ocean-class cargo ships, to be designed by Gibbs & Cox and built by Todd.

That is when the old idea was reborn. Todd and BIW teamed up to form the Todd-Bath Iron Works Shipbuilding Corp. Newell began digging ship basins in South Portland, the first in American history.

It was a huge job. First, to build the coffer dams 400,000 cubic yards of earth had to be dug out; and a place found to put it. Then 50,000 cubic yards of cement had to be poured to make seven basins, each 500 feet long and 75 feet wide and 25 feet deep, in which to build the cargo ships. Each basin had to have enormous steel gates, built in 10-ton sections, to keep out and later let in the sea to float out the ships.

Four months after this work had begun, the government demanded another basin yard like it, with six ways.

Building ships at breakneck speed was only part of the job. New shipyards had to be built at the same time. And workers trained simultaneously.

In 16 months, Newell and his teams had doubled the size of Bath Iron Works in Bath; and increased its capacity from building eight destroyers at once to building thirty-one; they'd built two huge new shipyards and basins at South Portland and there they had turned out thirty 10,000-ton ships for the British and 84 for the United States. As for the work force, it had expanded to 12,000 in Bath and gone from zero to 30,000 in South Portland. Records were broken. On one memorable day of mass launchings, August 16, 1942, two destroyers were launched at Bath, five cargo ships and one Liberty ship were launched at South Portland. Never in one day in one state had so much sea power been launched.

Here, lest they be forgotten, are the records of those astonishing shipbuilding years. Bath turned out 82 destroyers between Pearl Harbor and V-J Day. (In the same period all the shipyards in the Japanese empire turned out only 63 destroyers). All Bath ships were delivered under their own power. No other yard in the northeast did that. Further, only one of the 82 destroyers missed her delivery date — and that was by just two days, due to foul weather.

The South Portland yard launched 274 ships; 30 British freighters and 244 Liberty ships.

Let two stories symbolize the feats of the workers. Riveter Henry J. Dionne and his gang broke the world's record on August 15, 1942. Dionne drove 3701 three-quarter-inch rivets in 7 hours, 37 minutes; then he stopped for a quick drink of cold lemonade, and that floored him. Had he skipped the drink and worked 8 hours, he probably would have driven 4,000 rivets.

The other story concerns the women who by the thousands worked in Bath and South Portland. One woman building destroyers at Bath lived 30 miles away on a farm in North Whitefield. There she milked 18 cows and bathed, dressed and fed a sick husband before driving the back roads, ice-slicked and unsanded in winter, to her 8-hour shift at BIW; then she drove back 30 miles at night to repeat her farm and household chores.

Bath built 82 destroyers at a total cost to taxpayers of $435 million; an average cost of $5.3 million each.

After the war was over Congress made an exhaustive study of war profits by private shipyards. It reported: "The two companies showing the highest average rates of profit on their costs are the Bath Iron Works and the Electric Boat Co."

But at the same time it was making top profits, BIW delivered its ships more cheaply than other yards. Delivery price of BIW's 1630-ton destroyers averaged $300,000 less than other yards; and on the 2100-ton class destroyers, Bath delivered them at $700,000 less than other yards. Had the 82 BIW destroyers been built elsewhere, the total cost would have been $48 million more — the equivalent of nine destroyers.

When the war was over, seven of the top officers at BIW retired: Pete Newell, president; Archibald Mains, vice-president; Roland Hill, procurement; Sidney L. Eaton, treasurer; E. Everett Price, naval architect; Rear Admiral William P. Robert, USN retired, assistant to Newell.

Newell had developed a handy deafness. Until the war began, one of his civic duties had been heading the Bath Water District. He knew every pipe in the system. When he was 50 years old he put on a diver's suit and went down to the bottom of the Kennebec to inspect a broken main. As a result, he lost his hearing and had to wear a hearing aid. This gadget he turned off when he wanted to concentrate in his office; or when he wanted to sleep on trains and planes; or when he was bored with small talk.

After his retirement Newell lived ten years. He traveled a lot; first to witness the original atomic bomb tests at Bikini Atoll, as an observer for President Truman. He spoke to 130 groups in New England about the terrible new force he had seen. (His son John later became a leader of the group in Maine opposed to nuclear energy).

Newell died on Easter morning, 1954. A letter to his son John from the Chief of Naval Operations, Robert B. Carney, said:

> "There were few men in the industry who enjoyed the degree of the Navy's respect and affection that our service accorded your father. We all knew him as a man who turned out a fine product — it was always the dream of us young destroyer officers to serve on or to command a Bath boat.
>
> "We knew him as a man of complete integrity whose word was a gilt-edged bond and whose adherence to the terms of his contracts and verbal guarantees was inflexible.
>
> "And those of us who are old enough knew him as a charming personality and a very delightful friend."

John R. Newell, his son, became president of BIW in April 1950, and continued until 1965. Then the Newell connection with BIW stopped. Like the Hyde family before them, the Newells ran BIW for just one father-and-son span.

o sections of BIW's 800 foot drydock arrive at new Portland repair facility, Oct. 1982. (Gannett files)

Gov. Joseph E. Brennan (L), talks with Bath Iron Works President William Haggett (C) and Chairman of the Board John Sullivan (R) following announcement that BIW would build a 47 million dollar shipyard and drydock in Portland in 1983. (Gannett file photo)

8.

The Managers Move In: 1967-1983

Congoleum Buys BIW

Four Maine men — two Hydes and two Newells — sired, raised and ran Bath Iron Works for 80 years, from the 1880s to the 1960s.

Then in came the professional managers from away; and with them an influx of money needed for modernization and expansion through the 1970s and the 1980s.

As a result, BIW has lost some of its strong Maine flavor. But at the same time it now has gained a backlog of more than $2 billion of contracts in hand by 1983. It has expanded, again, to a repair facility including a huge new drydock in Portland — more than 800 feet long. This expansion was financed to the tune of more than $40 million in a complicated way by the State of Maine, the City of Portland and BIW or — in the final analysis — its parent conglomerate called Congoleum. Congoleum is today the parent company of BIW. The Maine-born-and-bred Bath Iron Works is now the subsidiary of an out-of-state corporation.

First sign of this approaching deep-seated change came in 1964, when two men from away named Kyle and O'Boyle bought heavily into BIW stock, and soon thereafter joined the board of BIW. They were William D. Kyle of Milwaukee and John W. O'Boyle from Texas.

Strange things began happening to BIW stock. For unseen reasons, its price took sudden spurts on the stock exchange, jumping from $30 to a peak of $70 a share.

By 1967 Kyle became chairman of the board of BIW. A holding

company called Bath Industries was created and BIW was made a wholly owned subsidiary of it. At the same time Hyde Windlass also was made a wholly owned subsidiary of the new Bath Industries.

But the financial statements looked bad. When the 1966 annual report was issued, it showed losses of $16.67 a share; as a result the share price dropped precipitously on the market.

The day-to-day management of BIW was now in new hands. After John Newell's retirement as president in 1965, an outsider, James F. Goodrich from Todd shipyard, was named the new president. Goodrich held that position for 10 years. After he left he became undersecretary of the Navy under President Reagan.

In 1975, another new president from away was appointed, John F. Sullivan Jr. Sullivan came to Bath from the auto parts business. He had no shipbuilding experience. But he had a reputation as an astute manager, with an uncommon ability to get the best work from people.

Goodrich and Sullivan were sharp contrasts in personalities. Goodrich was small, dapper, bird-like and gregarious. He enjoyed meeting people and made an easy, affable speaker at public functions such as ship launchings, Chamber of Commerce dinners and before congressional committees.

Sullivan was the opposite. Stocky, a typical handsome Irishman in looks, Sullivan seemed uncomfortable on public occasions and was uptight as a public speaker. But inside the shipyard, he quickly lived up to his reputation as an astute, competent manager, able to get the best work out of each department. His most visible hallmark was his insistence on a clean and neat-looking shipyard, which he felt strongly was an outward sign of Bath's quality workmanship. Often, wearing his hard hat and rumpled suit, he would prowl the yard on inspection trips. His abilities as a first class manager soon showed, outshining his lack of previous shipbuilding experience.

Within six years, by 1981, Sullivan was moved up from president to chairman of the board, but he retained his operating power as chief executive officer. William E. Haggett, who had long worked at BIW and had been Sullivan's Bath-born assistant, was named president. Haggett was a suave speaker and front-man, in many ways the embodiment of the successful extrovert business man with long Maine roots. As an indication of his agreeable public personality, Haggett was briefly boomed as a possible Republican candidate for governor of Maine. The idea lost its appeal to Haggett when he was promoted to president of BIW in 1981.

In May 1983, Sullivan announced he would retire as BIW's chairman and chief executive on July 1, 1983 and as vice president of Congoleum. Eddy G. Nicholson, president of Congoleum, was slated to succeed Sullivan as chairman of BIW. Sullivan, aged 59 at his retirement, joined BIW in 1975. At that time, BIW had 3,500 employees and a $125 million backlog of business. Eight years later, at Sullivan's retirement, the BIW workforce was up to 8,500 and the backlog of business was up to $1 billion.

During Sullivan's time, BIW delivered 12 guided missile frigates to the Navy, every one of the delivered ahead of schedule and under budget.

Haggett was named to succeed Sullivan as chief executive officer on July 1, 1983.

These changes in top personnel were reflections of major financial changes that had been happening but about which only a few people in Maine had detailed knowledge. Here is a short summary of a complicated series of financial maneuvers.

On September 3, 1968, the holding company Bath Industries which owned BIW, and which had been created by Kyle and his associates the previous year, bought and merged with Congoleum-Nairn, a company far bigger financially and far better known than Bath Industries. But by this action Congoleum became a subsidiary of Bath Industries and stayed in that subservient position until 1975.

In 1975 these significant changes occurred. The name Bath Industries was dropped and a new holding company with the umbrella name of Congoleum was formed; with BIW and the Congoleum-Nairn floor covering company becoming subsidiaries of it. In the same year Byron C. Radaker and Eddy Nicholson came in as executive vice presidents of Congoleum. Kyle was chairman of the board of Congoleum. On the surface matters stayed this way for five years.

Then in 1980 Eddy G. Nicholson, now president of Congoleum and Radaker, now chairman, and director of a dozen financial institutions, including First Boston Corp., bought control of Congoleum through offering a high price for the stock on the open market. This buy-out was supported by a number of other financial institutions.

Congoleum shareholders gained greatly as a result. They were offered $38 a share — a price Congoleum stock had never reached — to sell their stock, which was quoted at only $24 a share on the open market.

Congoleum, largely owned by a number of insurance companies

with ties into First Boston Corp., became the owner of Bath Iron Works.

Fears ran rampant in Bath and Maine. Fear first that men who had no experience in shipbuilding might ruin BIW as a shipbuilder of high repute. And fears that a conglomerate run by financiers in distant cities would pick the meat off BIW and then toss the bones away.

The opposite happened. BIW now had access to the increased cash flow necessary to allow more capital purchases needed to place it in a better position in competitive bidding and performance. Navy contracts came rapidly; big ones for ever more sophisticated and more expensive ships. The reputation of BIW as a shipbuilder grew stronger each time the yard delivered guided missile frigates ahead of schedule and below contracted cost. This became a habit and soon a trademark of BIW, at a time when other shipyards were running far behind their delivery dates and running far ahead of original contract costs.

The abilities of BIW management teams certainly had a lot to do with this performance. But most of the credit belongs to the work force of more than 7,000, which, in the Maine tradition, gave more than full value for the wages paid them — a contrast to other shipyards.

Nevertheless, work strikes were called or threatened every three years between 1967 and 1973, when union contracts came up for renegotiation. The strikes never lasted long enough to cripple the yard or delay ship deliveries. Then before the 1976 negotiations began, Haggett, the Bath-raised president, proposed a typical Maine solution toward one part of the labor problem. Before the fourth strike was called, workers were given an annual week's spring vacation with pay — a week off to go fishing, repair the barn, put in the garden or paint the porch. After this concession, a more friendly atmosphere induced more amicable negotiations over wages and hours.

More contracts for naval and commercial ships came in, due largely to BIW's record of delivering quality ships on time and under cost estimates. With the cash resources of Congoleum behind the yard, BIW's continuing ability to buy the best in equipment and in brains increased its competitive edge. Employment rose to 8,000 by the 1980s. BIW was recognized as the biggest single employer in Maine. Its wages were above the Maine average. Its blue-ribbon reputation was again world-wide, both for naval and commercial construction.

Then in 1981 came a testing point, almost a breaking point, in relations between BIW and Maine. It developed over expansion, money and loyalty.

Top management at BIW and its parent Congoleum wanted to grab the chance to expand — to handle the multi-million dollar contracts for repair, modernization and overhaul of very big vessels, vessels too big to navigate up the Kennebec River to Bath. To bid on these contracts, BIW needed deeper water and a mammoth drydock.

Boston made tempting offers to BIW to expand in Massachusetts by taking over the existing idle yards and idle drydock in that city.

Boston seemed to have the inside track. Not only because the required facilities were in place there, but also because of close links between the First Boston Corp. and Congoleum, the conglomerate which owned BIW. If the First Boston Corp. could exert the right pressure in the right places on Congoleum to get Congoleum to bring BIW's new ship repair business into Boston, then First Boston might gain useful "I.O.U.s" in the financial district of Boston, its home turf.

The deal was close to consummation before Maine woke up to what was going on and realized that its hallmark shipbuilder was on the verge of expanding operations not in Maine but in Boston.

There can be little question that Maine had been snoozing at the switch. State government seemed unaware of what was happening. Maine awoke to the reality in a near panic at the thought of losing to Boston all the future jobs, money and prestige involved.

But Maine also felt hurt. Hurt because its own BIW was on the brink of making a huge expansion into another state without cutting in Maine on its plans or asking Maine to make a counteroffer. Maine had been the birthplace of BIW and Maine workforces had been the making of its success. Now it seemed Maine was being jilted because of the wiles of the painted ladies in Boston. Blame for this was laid at the doorstep of Congoleum, which was depicted as a souless conglomerate from away which now gave orders to the native-born BIW.

Almost at the last minute, the State of Maine and the City of Portland, with its huge, deep harbor and available waterfront land, made BIW a counteroffer. The State proposed a massive public bond issue to help finance a BIW deepwater facility in Portland. Portland proposed issuing city bonds to help pay for waterfront improvements. Legislation was rushed through the State House and the City Council authorizing a referendum, a public vote, on the issuance of bonds. The proposal was for a three-way package involving state funds, city funds and BIW funds, which together would keep BIW and the future jobs generated by a new repairyard and drydock in Maine.

Suddenly opposition, stronger and far better organized than anticipated, rose up against this public financing of a private corporation.

The opposition was spearheaded by Common Cause. This organization, which then had only about 2,000 members in Maine, had a name made magic by the fact that Archibald Cox, hero of the opposition to Nixon's Saturday Night massacre, was the well-known president of Common Cause.

Common Cause argued that the taxpayers of Maine and Portland should not be panicked or dragooned into subsidizing any private business, especially the multi-million conglomerate Congoleum. For the first time, many Maine people woke up to the fact that their pride-and-joy, BIW, was just a subsidiary, controlled and financed by an out-of-state conglomerate; and their qualms were skillfully fueled by Common Cause. The fight took on the excitement of David and Goliath contest.

Common Cause took many Mainers by surprise with its argument that it was a violation of the Maine constitution for the state to use public money to finance a private business in this fashion. Their argument, well covered in newspapers, press conferences, television shows, carried considerable weight and inflamed more passion on both sides.

Into the fray on the side of issuing bonds for BIW stepped many of Maine's foremost political and business leaders. A committee to save BIW for Maine raised money and spent it lavishly on advertising campaigns in newspapers, on radio and television. But little Common Cause fought back; and a surprisingly large segment of Maine joined with Common Cause. Maine was treated to an emotional as well as legal battle between what seemed to many as the might and wealth of BIW combined the Maine Establishment pitted against the righteousness of Common Cause fighting for the taxpayer. To others, Common Cause seemed a noisy, self-righteous, anti-Maine group which cared too much for legal technicalities and too little for future jobs for Maine working people.

At the peak of the battle came the vote by referendum in November 1981. When the ballots were counted, Maine voters overwhelmingly supported the bond issues both by the State and by Portland to help finance the expansion of BIW in Maine. Nevertheless about one-third of Maine voted against the issue; especially those who lived far from Portland and disliked the dominance this city in southern Maine exerted over the rest of the state. Matched against this was a reservoir of goodwill to the old Maine shipbuilding firm whose name was a symbol of Maine seafaring tradition. Yet during the fight before the referendum, news stories and Common Cause had emphasized that this good old Maine firm was now simply a part of an unloved and unknown conglomerate called Congoleum. The warmth of Maine's generally good feeling toward BIW cooled.

Overriding all the arguments, however, was the dominant fact that Maine people were hungry for more good-paying jobs; and Portland, with its large number of voters, was hungry for a spectacular big new maritime operation on its decaying waterfront which would spark that area of the city into new life. These feelings more than anything else led to approval of the controversial bond issue.

Even after Maine people had voted to approve the bond issue, Common Cause was not ready to quit the fight. It fought its case through the Maine Supreme Court and lost it. For a while, Common Cause talked of appealing to the U.S. Supreme Court, but eventually abandoned that course.

As of 1983, the drydock is nearing completion. BIW bought a surplus drydock from the Navy, towed it from Norfolk to Maine and installed it on the Portland waterfront. In April 1983 BIW/Portland won a $70 million contract to overhaul three Spruance class guided missile frigates. BIW was also the top U.S. contender bidding on a $100 million dollar overhaul of the S.S. United States as its first job in the new drydock. If successful, more than 1,000 people are expected to be at work on it in 1984.

Kennebec Men & Memories

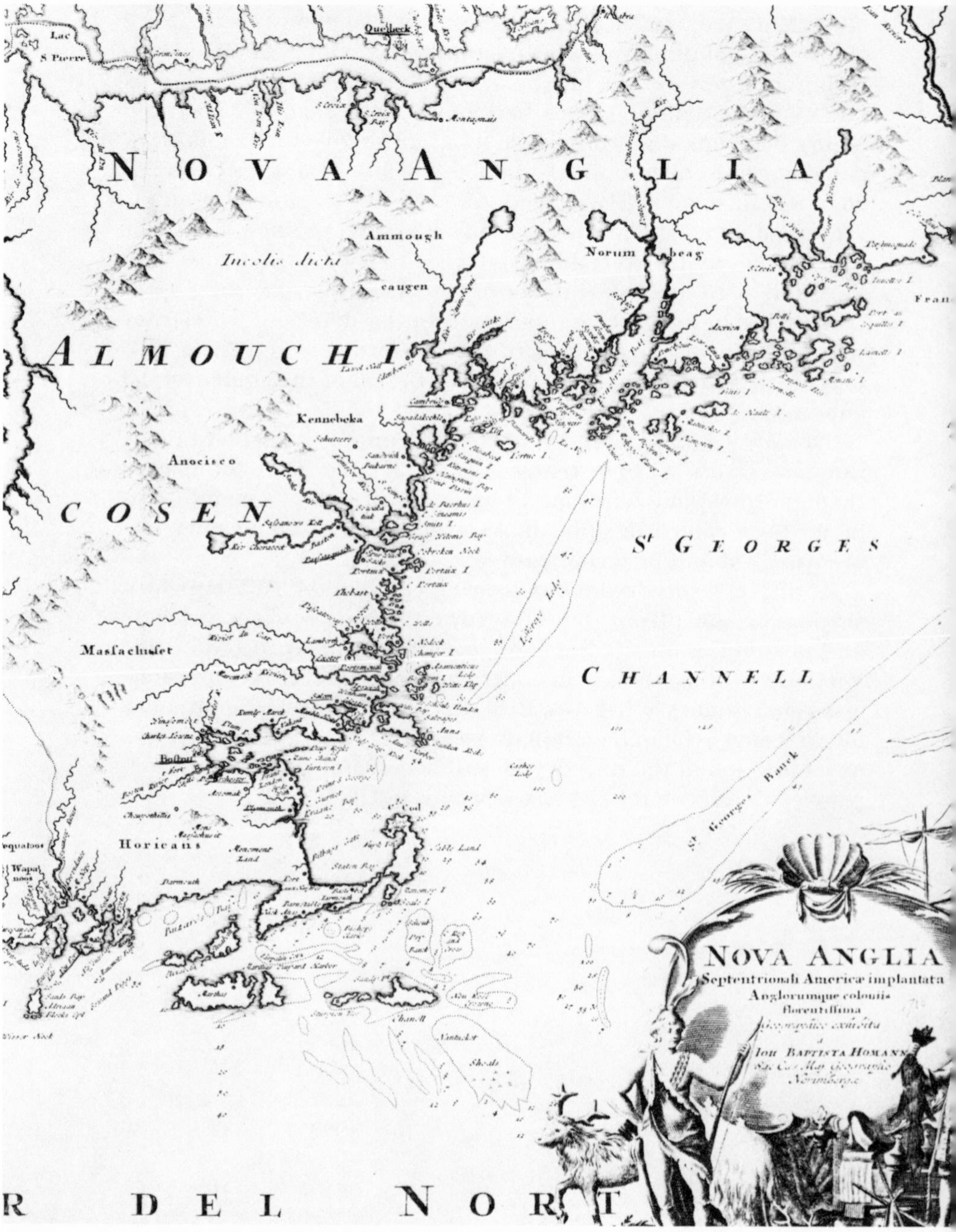

9.

First American Colony: 1607

First Murder on the Kennebec

Getting into the Kennebec River from the ocean can be devilish. I remember too well the first time we did it in a small boat. We were heading west from Monhegan, aiming to spend the night on a mooring off the Portland Yacht Club at Falmouth, tucked deep behind the sheltering islands of Casco Bay. But the weather turned bad and by the time we were coming up to Seguin Light, we choose to head for shelter in the Kennebec River.

We had a bad time getting inside. The tide was rushing downriver and a strong wind was blowing upriver. We were caught between the opposite forces. That ride into the Kennebec was so unpleasant it stays vivid in my mind after 18 years. Since then, we've gone into the river many times and seldom had trouble, because now we are careful not to turn in to the Kennebec when a strong tide is running out.

Possibly on the day in August 1607 when English ships arrived they hit the wrong tide and wind combination too and got bumped about badly. The Gift of God, under Capt. George Popham, and the Mary and John, under Raleigh Gilbert, had already been hit by a storm outside Seguin before they turned into the Kennebec.

And if they'd also hit the bumps of an ebb tide and southwest wind, they too might have been eager to anchor in the first protection and get ashore. After all, these 120 sailors and colonists had been at sea three long months. They left England at the end of May, and now it was almost mid-August.

These were the first settlers in New England. They began building their colony close to what is now Phippsburg. Today there is little left to show where these first colonists tried to establish roots. But the diaries and plans they left show a fort and 50 other buildings.

They had chosen a bad site. When they landed in August, it may have seemed lovely. But when the gales of October blew, they suffered. When the cold came in November and December — and that winter of 1607-08 was especially cold — they suffered more. More than half of the 120 left and sailed in disgust and disappointment for home and England aboard the Gift of God on December 13, 1607.

Their leader, George Popham, fat, old (almost 80), died, and leadership passed to the fiery Raleigh Gilbert, nephew of the famed Sir Walter Raleigh. There had been fights and bloodshed between the first colonists and local Indians. So when the colonists' food grew short and their clothing inadequate for winter snows, the Indians were in no mind to help the shivering band of white, discontented colonists. Yet the handful saw winter end and spring arrive, and that surely raised their sunken spirits. Then their second leader, Raleigh Gilbert, got the news that his brother, Sir John Gilbert, had died in England and Raleigh was needed at home to run the family estate. When he decided to leave, so did the others. One year and one month after the first American colonists settled on the banks of the Kennebec, the last of them left. The Popham colony had failed.

To excuse their failure, they took back to England such doleful tales of winter in Maine that nobody would make another attempt to settle on New England for a dozen years. Then the Mayflower arrived at Plymouth with the Pilgrims.

The Mayflower carried fewer people, 102 compared to the 120 at Popham. But in the Mayflower there were women and children, families with faith and unity and determination. These qualities were not among the male only settlers at Popham. According to one contemporary account "that company was composed of the vagrant and the dissolute."

Soon the bad name these failed colonists had given to the Kennebec was forgotten. Other pioneers found the river filled with fat fish, made friends with Indians who would trade valuable beaver skins for worthless beads, found stands of timber for building homes and boats.

The Pilgrim Fathers from Plymouth had a sharp eye for profit. And money and profit brought them to the Kennebec. The Plymouth colony, almost starving to death in its second winter of 1622, had sent a boat to the fishing settlement long established at

Damariscove Island, off Boothbay Harbor, seeking food supplies. So well-established were these Maine settlers by then that they fed the Plymouth colony and charged them nothing. After that, boats from Plymouth came regularly to trade at Damariscove and Monhegan. While in the area, they certainly poked up the Kennebec to make fur-trading deals with Indians. And pretty shady some of those deals were.

The tricky trading may be excused by the fact that the religious colony at Plymouth was hard pressed for cash to make payments to London bankers. To finance the Mayflower expedition, they had borrowed money in the City of London. The bankers thought the expedition to the New World so risky that they charged 51 percent interest on the money they lent the Pilgrims.

The best cash crop to pay yearly installments of 200 pounds was furs. The Indians along the Kennebec had the best supply of the finest beaver skins. Beaver skins in London fetched 20 shillings each. In 1625, Capt. Edward Winslow of the Plymouth colony bought 700 pounds of good beaver skins from Indians on the Kennebec.

William D. Williamson in his "History of Maine," reports:

> "The Plymouth company opened trade in a new article called wampum, which her people were pursuing with great profits. It consisted of white and blue beads, long and large as wheat-corn, blunt at the ends, perforated and strung; possessing a clearness and beauty which rendered them desirable ornaments . . . within two years after wampum was first brought into this region, it was found to command a more ready market among the tribes than any other commodity."

To keep the profitable fur trade on the Kennebec to themselves, the Plymouth Company in 1627 applied for and received in London an exclusive patent to the Kennebec trade. By 1628 they had established two trading houses; one at the mouth of the Kennebec, another and bigger one upriver where Augusta now stands, at Fort Western. They were ready to fight, even to murder, to protect their profitable franchise by which they were trading cheap beads for valuable beaver skins.

It was worth protecting. The pilgrims could buy for two shillings enough wampum beads to trade for 100 pounds worth of fur from the Indians. A good beaver hat in London fetched many pounds.

In 1634, records show that 20 hogsheads of beaver were taken from the Kennebec trade by the Plymouth Company. A hogshead was a barrel big enough to hold 140 gallons. This translated into at least 140 beaver skins per hogshead, so that year alone they took out 2800 beaver skins.

When a free-booter John Hoskins (or Hocking) tried to clip off a bit of this profitable fur trade for himself, he was murdered. From his murder comes the first record of the Pilgrims killing for financial gain. Involved in the murder was one of the most fabled Americans from our early history, John Alden. It happened this way.

John Hoskins came up the Kennebec in April 1634 from Piscataqua, in a boat owned by his employers, Lord Brooke and Lord Say. But Hoskins was venturing into territory controlled by the owners of the Kennebec Patent, and he was warned off. The next month, Hoskins was back again and this time he went upriver as far as Fort Western. There, representing the Plymouth Company, was John Alden, the same John Alden who had been first man to step off the Mayflower, the same John Alden to whom Priscilla had coyly said, "Speak for yourself, John."

Alden warned Hoskins off again. Hoskins refused to leave, and sat provocatively in his boat moored just off Fort Western. Alden then told the fort commander, John Howland, to go out with some men and cut Hoskins's lines and force him down river. They cut one of Hoskins' three cables. Thereupon Hoskins grabbed his gun, swore at the three men and said, "Touch another line and death is your portion!" The men cut another line. And Hoskins shot one of them dead. The gunfight was on. And quickly Hoskins himself was killed.

Relatives of Hoskins swore out a warrant against John Alden, who was arrested in Boston. The case became big news throughout New England. A political fire flamed up with the slogan, "When men cut throats for beaver, it is time to have a general government!"

The Massachusetts General Court authorized the prosecution of John Alden. A special advisory tribunal studied arguments at length. After long deliberations, the court ruled:

1. The New Plymouth Company, which Alden was representing, did indeed have legal exclusive rights to fishing and fur trading on the Kennebec and that Hoskins was an unauthorized intruder.
2. Killing Hoskins was a violation of the Sixth Commandment.

3. Under the circumstances murder was "excusable homicide."

Alden made public apologies and expressions of regret to the Hoskins family. The Massachusetts tribunal sent a stern letter to the New Plymouth Company, saying;

> "We could, for the death of Hoskins, have dispatched a man-of-war and beat down your houses on the Kennebec about your ears. But we have thought it preferable to let the magistrates of Massachusetts to justice."

There ended the trial of John Alden for murder on the Kennebec in 1634.

Rot crept into the trading posts' operations in the next decade. Maybe they seemed too far away, too hard to reach, for the administrators. Boston was growing fast. There was too much profit to be made nearby to spend time, money and good men on the Kennebec trading posts. Discipline there slipped, so that not single intruders like poor Hoskins, but bands of outlaw traders began to infest the river and broke the grip of the Plymouth Company. There was no power to send them packing.

The Indians began to trade with whomever offered them a good deal. The fur trade at the posts fell off. By 1650 the New Plymouth Company decided to get rid of the franchise it had fought so hard to get exclusively only 23 years before. It leased out the entire franchise for 50 pounds a year, for three years, to an investment group of five, headed by Gov. Bradford. They tried to start afresh by convening a major meeting along the Kennebec to get everyone's agreement to a charter of law and order. But only 16 men showed at the meeting; and thereafter very few followed the proposed charter.

The rot continued. Soon the franchise wasn't worth even 50 pounds a year, and the price was reduced to 35 pounds. Then, the rent was dropped to ten pounds yearly; but there were no takers. The Plymouth Company sold its patent outright for 400 pounds to John Winslow, Edward Tyng, Thomas Brattle and Artepas Bois. For that money, these four got a deed to 1.5 million acres; to the land reaching back 15 miles on either side of the Kennebec all the way from the mouth to the head water of the tide at Augusta.

In the 700 square miles, the white population numbered fewer than 300 souls.

The Kennebec and its people sank into near oblivion for the next 100 years.

Today, if you come upriver slowly, not trying to make a destination at a specific time, you may see the ghosts of 300 and more years ago along the banks.

Ghosts from that night in 1676 when Indians slaughtered nine people on Arrowsic Island. Two men named Thomas Clark and Thomas Lake had been the first land developers on Arrowsic and had laid out a town in lots, intersected with wide streets. Arrowsic and Parker's Island had by 1670 become the population center, with 50 families. They became targets of Indian attacks, perhaps made in reprisal for having been cheated. Cheating triggered one of the worst Indian attacks, which ended with widespread murders and burnings.

That harrowing night of August 13, 1676, began upriver close to Woolwich, with an attack on the Indian trader Richard Hammond. The Indians said Hammond had plied their brothers with rum till they passed out and had then stolen their furs. So they came back for blood and revenge. They murdered Hammond, burned his house and went on to kill his neighbors, Samuel Smith and Joshua Grant, and took 16 others prisoner.

Part of the attack group split off and headed down river by canoe to Arrowsic. They landed in stealth in the middle of the night and watched from behind rocks until the sentry on duty at the garrison wall left his post. Then the Indians poured through the fort gate. The Arrowsic families awoke in terror and fought hand-to-hand with the Indian raiders.

Captains Lake and Davis and others fled to a canoe and tried to paddle over to Parker's Island nearby, for help. Lake was killed by a musket shot, Davis wounded so he could neither flee nor fight. He hid in the rocks for two days. All in all nine people were killed and 26 taken into captivity. The garrison house, the fort, the mill, the out-buildings, the homes, all the work of years, were burned to the ground.

The alarm spread quickly to Sheepscot, to Newcastle, Damariscotta and Pemaquid. All inhabitants fled by boat, finally meeting for safety out on Monhegan Island, thoroughly terrified of more attacks. The men worked around the clock to fortify Monhegan. They slept only after posting a guard of 25 men each night. They let no vessel leave or enter the harbor. Finally after a week, one boat was sent to the mainland to bring back household goods. Scarcely had that boat made it back to Monhegan than the settlements at New Harbor and Pemaquid were put to the torch.

In this one month, Indians ravaged and torched most of the settlements along the coast, and the refugees fled as far away as Boston.

When news of the massacres reached Boston, 400 troops were sent to Maine; and an Indian war raged here for another year.

By the time a peace treaty was signed at Casco in 1678, losses on both sides had been great. At least 260 whites were known killed, and perhaps other hundreds of deaths were unrecorded; dozens of settlements had been burned and farm animals destroyed. Losses of Indian lives were probably 10 times greater, amounting to 3,000, by some estimates.

Fear and desolation clung to most of the Kennebec for the next 30 years. Not until 1714 did settlers come back to Arrowsic, and then only because the General Court declared it a fortified town and sent militia to protect it. One of the first to come was William Butler Sr., from Scotland, who bought 350 acres on what is called Butler's Cove. He built a house, later made it into a tavern and rented office space to a traveling lawyer named James Sullivan. Sullivan must have been on the move most of the time, for his practice ran from Pemaquid to Portland. His name and face became so widely known that he was later made governor of Massachusetts and wrote "Sullivan's History of Maine." But the families who resettled here were soon to face an even worse war with the Indians.

It began in 1722, when a war party in 20 canoes kidnapped nine entire families on Merrymeeting Bay, on the Kennebec. Next they attacked Georgetown and burned Brunswick. The General Court declared war upon the Indian tribes, voted to keep 1000 men under arms, with 400 of them to range between the Kennebec and Penobscot rivers. A bounty of 15 pounds was offered for every scalp taken from a male Indian over 12 years, and 8 pounds for every woman or child taken captive. Arrowsic (Georgetown) managed to repel the worst of an attack by 400 Micmacs on the early morning of September 10, 1722. The 26 families kept out of harm's way by hiding in the fort. But the Indians killed 150 head of cattle (a good ox was worth about 20 pounds sterling) and burned down 26 homes and buildings.

This Indian war raged till 1725. About one-third of the Abenaki tribe was destroyed. About 200 white men in Maine were killed or captured. Costs of the war amounted to over more than a quarter million pounds sterling, a disproportionate amount of which was borne by the people living in Maine.

The Sewall family have been front-runners throughout the history of the Kennebec. Here is a 1780's portrait of Dummer Sewall, father of the clan.

10.

Early Georgetown: 1716-1816

Settlers fight, then flourish

Just before you cross the Kennebec via the Carlton Bridge at Woolwich, you'll see a road to Georgetown, 12 miles downriver. In the summers of the 1980s, you'll see a dozen cars parked at the turning, with families in swim suits inside, eating ice cream concoctions from the big Dairy Queen. Most of them have been to the beach at Reid State Park, a part of Georgetown, and have been swimming in the Atlantic off one of the biggest sandy beaches in Maine.

The road in summer is busy. But year-round, fewer than 500 people live in Georgetown. Far down the finger peninsula, Georgetown today is too remote from the shopping center of Bath, 12 miles up the winding road.

But 250 years ago it was the other way round. Georgetown was the hub where the action was, and Bath was known as "Twenty Cow Parish." The census in 1764 showed Georgetown with 1,329 people, almost three times as many as live there in 1983. Georgetown, defended by a fort, was on a rising wave to prosperity. Bath was Georgetown's "second parish." Bath was not a town in its own right until 1781, when it split off. By then Georgetown had been the official center of the lower Kennebec since 1716, when it was incorporated as the 10th town in Maine. The Governor of New England, Samuel Shute, whose brother Lord Barrington was in the English Parliament, came to Georgetown in August 1717, to hold a peace conference with the Indians. He handed out Bibles in the hope of converting them from being the Catholic allies of the encroaching French. Georgetown was the key outpost of English New England. To encourage more settlement, any one who would move into the region from Massachusetts was offered 100 acres of good land and free transport of their families and household effects to Georgetown.

Governor Shute believed wholeheartedly in the idea of pacification and colonization by encouraging family life in this outpost. He set aside 250 pounds a year to pay a minister to settle in the Georgetown area and bring in a young schoolmaster. He budgeted another ten pounds a year to buy "books and curiosities to distribute among pupils according to their merits."

Four ministers came and left in quick succession. The only one to leave a lasting mark was the Rev. Ezekiel Emerson, who ministered here 40 years until his death at age 80, in 1815.

Samuel Penhallow, in his "History of the Indian Wars of the early 1700s," wrote that Doctor Noyes of Boston, one of the Plymouth proprietors, built a stone fort at the head tide where he ran a profitable fish business.

> "Being patronized by some fishmongers in London, Dr. Noyes entered largely into the sturgeon fishery. In some years he laded 20 vessels with many thousand kegs of salted sturgeon which were prize delicacies in London, esteemed equal to any that ever came from Hamburg or Norway. Noyes also shipped to London, vast quantities of pine boards, planks, hogshead, barrel staves and all kinds of lumber."

The ledger of a Georgetown tavern keeper, who ran a general store in the back, gives a workaday picture of how the money went and what it bought in 1800, when John Adams was president of the United States. Reporting supplies sold for a local funeral, the ledger records: "one yard of crepe gauze, black, 58 cents; one gallon of rum $1." On the night of September 6, 1802, the ledger records this summary of a man drowning his sorrow. "One glass of rum, .04 cents; two glasses of rum, .07 cents; one pint of rum, .14 cents; your wife entertained, when she came to fetch you, .50 cents."

Though survival was hard, some of these early Kennebec people lived to ripe ages. An entry under 1716 reports that Jonathan Preble on Arrowsic Island lived to the age of 73, dying in 1768. His son Joseph died aged 80, in 1808.

Towns upriver from Georgetown began to grow. By 1753 Bath had become a parish. The next year Fort Western was built; in 1759 the town of Woolwich was incorporated; in 1760, the counties of Lincoln (reaching to Canada) and Cumberland were incorporated. (Before this, York was the only county in the District of Maine.) And in 1760 David Trufant, called King David, was appointed the first customs collector at Bath. In 1764 Dummer Sewall came to Bath and was the first postmaster of Bath and lived to age 94, dying in 1832.

But Bath, later the kingpin of the Kennebec, was not incorporated as a town until February 17, 1781, and became the 41st town in Maine. Dummer Sewall is credited with suggesting the name. The town grew swiftly. The Bath Academy was established in 1805, and by 1820 Bath had four churches, two banks, each capitalized at $100,000, and two weekly newspapers. By 1828, the shipping tonnage of Bath was 36,291 tons, and the boatyards were launching 8,000 to 12,000 tons yearly. Population in 1822 reached 3,100. By 1832 the kindly people of Bath were rich enough to load the brig Eastern Star with a cargo of food for the suffering inhabitants of the Cape Verde Islands. The town was raising $600 a year for schools and taxing dogs at $3 a head. By 1836 Bath could boast 24 roads, and by 1844 had a railroad link to Brunswick on the Portland & Kennebec Railroad.

In 1848 Bath became a city.

At Georgetown, fishing and shipping had been growing. By 1820 the people of Georgetown owned almost 200 small vessels. At the fish docks, they were landing 450,000 pounds of codfish and hake, plus 40,000 pounds of salmon and 6,000 barrels of smoked fish.

"Georgetown is a place of more celebrity than any other except Falmouth and York," reported William D. Williamson in 1832 in his "History of the State of Maine."

But Maine was facing tough times. The British had invaded the Penobscot, landed at Bangor and seized Castine. English sails were sighted off Pemaquid in 1814. And the war scares reached into Bath, which feared an attack up the Kennebec. Major General King of Bath issued orders for his entire militia to rally under full arms at Wiscasset. General Sewall called his troops to full readiness. Currency was removed from the vaults of the Bath and Wiscasset banks. The treasury of Massachusetts (which included Maine till 1820) had been drained to finance the ill-fated Penobscot Expedition. Blockades had depressed Maine shipping.

After peace came in 1815, a wave of political dispute swept through Maine. Should Maine seek independence from Massachusetts? The choice was put out to a vote in all towns. The towns would also choose delegates to a constitutional convention in Brunswick. If the public votes counted there showed a majority of five to four in favor of separation, then the 185 delegates would draw up a Maine constitution.

But when the votes were counted that September day of 1816 in Brunswick, the outcome was a shock. There were only 11,969 yeas compared to 10,347 nays. Not enough for Maine to become a state. The delegates, most of whom favored independence, tried to stretch the legalities and proceed with drawing up a Maine constitution. But the General Court of Massachusetts saw what they were up to, and dissolved the convention.

Maine had suffered greatly in the 1814 war; its territory had been occupied by the British; the memory of Indian attacks were still fresh. Prices for food were high, necessities scarce. On top of all this, now came political strife. "The altercations of political parties, so spirited, so obstinate and so long protracted, had become extremely tiresome and disgusting to all unaspiring men," reported Williamson.

On the top of this came the dreadful winter of 1815-16, the coldest and severest in history; and that was followed by an icy-cold spring and summer. Crops failed. No corn was raised. On June 8, 1816, snow covered the ground beside the Kennebec. Farmers by the thousands chose to sell out and head west to Ohio. There was no money in general circulation. And for the four years 1820 to 1823, food was scarce and high priced and money was almost non-existent. Barter rather than cash became the common means of exchange. If cash was used, laborers were paid 50 cents a day, with work lasting from sunrise to after sunset. Kitchen help got 25 cents a day. But flour cost $5 a barrel; corn was 60 cents a bushel and potatoes 20 cents; chicken was four cents a pound; cheese almost 10 cents a pound, and hardwood was priced at $3.00 a cord.

Maine, with a population of under 300,000, lost between 10,000 and 15,000 settlers in this panic to sell out and go west.

11.

The Survival of Sarah Porterfield: 1741

Ordeal of an Irish girl

This is the story of the endurance and survival of Sarah Porterfield, a 19-year old girl from Ireland, who arrived at Georgetown, at the mouth of the Kennebec River, in 1741.

Her story comes from her own lips. She told it to a female friend when she was 76 years old, who wrote it down and passed a copy to the Rev. Henry White. He printed the story in 1854 in his book "Incidents in the Early History of New England." A photocopy of those pages was given to me by James Stevens in 1983. It reveals better than any other record I have found the amazing will to live, survive and make a new life which was a necessary hallmark of women who helped settle early Maine.

There are very few accounts of these remarkable women. And this one came to me in such an ordinary, everyday way that I will tell how it happened, because it is an example of centuries of Maine continuity in the same place by the same pioneer families.

I was in the Yellowfront market in Damariscotta buying dog biscuits when I bumped into Jim Stevens, a boat builder from East Boothbay and a local history buff. I told Jim that I had been reading old books which often referred to a plague which had swept through coastal settlements around 1740, and I asked if he knew more about it. Jim said that one of his early ancestors had encountered that plague, when she first arrived in America. Her name was Sarah Porterfield. And he would send me her story. Here it is, as she told it:

"I was born in Ireland, in the county of Donegal,

Aug. 13, 1722. I had pious parents, who instructed me in the Christian religion, and set good examples before me. When I was about nineteen years old, my father went to Pennsylvania, in America, and finding a plantation suitable for his family, he wrote over for my mother and the children to take passage in the first vessel, and come to Pennsylvania. Accordingly, my mother, with three daughters, took passage on board a large ship, which was going with passengers to Philadelphia on July 28, 1741, we sailed from Londonderry, Capt. Rowen being commander. For some time after we sailed, we had pleasant weather, and every thing was agreeable, excepting our sea-sickness. The ship's company daily assembled on the quarter-deck for prayers, which were performed alternately by four or five of the passengers, to the great satisfaction of many on board.

"When we had been about three weeks at sea, a mortal fever broke out, and spread through the ship's company. In this melancholy situation we were reduced to great distress. It is enough to make one's heart ache, to think of our condition. Not one was able to help another. My mother and her children were preserved and restored to health. Thanks to God for such a mercy, when so many were daily dying around us.

"But God, who knoweth all things, and never does any wrong to his creatures, did not suffer us to rest here. Sorer trials were appointed for us. When we had been ten weeks at sea, we were visited with a violent storm, in which our ship was much wrecked, and we were all very near being lost. The captain at that time thought we were near land, and expected every day to make it, and to get into port soon. But God had different purposes in view. The violence of the storm drove us to the eastward. The sea raged greatly. Our masts gave way, and we were in a distressed situation, even at our wit's end. When we cried unto the Lord, and he heard us, and came down for our deliverance. O that I could praise the Lord for his goodness, and for his loving kindness unto us!

"At that time the captain thought proper to put all hands on allowance, as he did not know where the ship was, or how long we should be continued in our present situation. His reckoning was out, and he knew not where to steer his course. One biscuit a day, a small portion of meat, and a quart of water, was all our allowance. This was continued for ten or twelve days; then we were put upon half allowance, excepting the water, which was continued the same. Ten days after, we spoke a ship, which supplied us with provision; but our allowance was not increased. The storm was now abated, and we were relieved from some distressing fears.

"October 28, we made land on the eastern coast, found it to be a desolate island, or neck of land, inhabited only by a few Indians. The ship was anchored, and we remained a few days on board. The captain and others took the long-boat, and went, hoping to find some French inhabitants, but returned without success. We were then ordered to land on this island. Accordingly, many boatloads of people were landed, and scattered round the island, without any provision. The number of people could not, I presume, be less than a hundred. We were told that the last boats should bring us some provision, but were disappointed. No provision was sent us. Oh, the distressed situation! some crying, some almost distracted, not knowing what to do. Death seemed to stare us all in the face, and very soon marked out many for his victims.

"After we were landed, twenty or thirty of the passengers set out to look for inhabitants, but were never after heard of. Probably they all perished. The captain, mate, and seamen left the ship and went in search of inhabitants. After a few days' sail to the eastward, they fell in with land, and came to a place called New Harbor, about thirty miles east of the Kennebec River. Getting two small vessels there, they came back for the plunder of the ship, which had been cast upon a small island, and broken to pieces. They tarried until they had collected what plunder they pleased to take, with which they returned to New Harbor, taking with them a few of the servants and passengers that were on the island. These were sold for their passage, but in this way delivered from their distressing situation. The rest of the passengers were left in the most melancholy circumstances; but a kind Providence furnished us with something to support nature. We found some mussels on the beach, which with sea-kelp and dulce, we boiled in a pot we had brought on shore, and were nourished by them. This was all the food we had for as much as two months. A distressing time! But God supported me even at that time, and gave me hopes of relief, which I ever maintained in the very darkest hour. Every day, more died around us. It was observed that the men failed sooner than the women, and that a greater proportion of them died. There was scarcely one to help another, as every one had sufficient to do for himself. The provision for the day was to be sought in the day, as the manna was in the wilderness.

"The Indians soon visited us, and added much to our distress, robbing us of all they could find, which we had brought from the ship. In a severe snow storm, we hung our clothes on trees to shelter us. The Indians came and took them down. When I offered to resist them, one drew his hatchet, and attempted to strike me. I drew back, and left them to take what they pleased. Among other things, they took our pot, in which we boiled our mussels, which increased our distress. At length, I providentially thought of a sauce-pan, which some of the passengers had. I went and found it on the ground, the owners all being dead.

"Some further particulars deserve to be mentioned. I was landed in one of the first boats. As my mother and sisters were landing, one of my sisters died. All being in confusion and trouble, there was no one to bury her but myself. I performed that service with great composure. I then had to take care of my mother and other sister, who were somewhat helpless. God gave me strength, so that I was enabled to do something for them, as well as for myself. For some time we appeared like a very thick neighborhood, being divided into separate companies. Our company consisted of nine persons.

"When the boats were landing, as I stood on the beach, a child, about two years old, was put into my arms. I looked around to see who was to take it from me, but found no one that would own it. I inquired, Who takes care of this child? A little boy, about twelve years old, answered," Nobody, ma'am, but I." How I felt, knowing that this child's parents had both died in the ship! I was obliged to lay down the child, and leave it to the care of Him who had the care of us. The boy and child were soon after found dead, lying together. A most sorrowful sight!

"I went to see a cousin of mine, who lay at a little distance, in a feeble state, unable to rise. I asked her whether she had anything to eat. She said, yes, her shipmates gave her mussels when they got any for themselves; but added, she could eat some boiled dulce, if she could get any. I told her I would get her some tomorrow. On the morrow, returning to see her, I found her dead, and several more by her. Walking along the shore, I found a boy, about seventeen years old, sitting very disconsolate, with a book in his hand. I said to him, 'What do you do here?' He answered, 'I am looking for the captain, who is coming to carry me off the island.' I said to him, 'Did he promise you that favor?' 'Yes,' he said. 'Well,' replied I, 'don't depend upon it, for I don't believe he will ever come here again.' Upon this, he wept bitterly; but I could not persuade him to give up his hope, and do something for a subsistence. In a few days he was found dead, with his book open under his head.

"The people began now to die very fast. There was no travelling any where, but dead bodies were found, as few were buried. All were so weak and helpless, that they had enough to do to keep life in themselves. In this distressing situation we remained until every person, of whom we had knowledge, on the island, was dead, excepting my mother, my sister, and myself. At that time our fire went out, and we had nothing to strike with. Several snows had fallen, but soon melted away. Another snow fell when we were in such distress for want of fire. This scene was of all the most hopeless; nothing to cover us but the heavens, and nothing to eat but frozen mussels. In about one day after our fire went out, my mother died, and there she lay, a lifeless corpse by our side. We were not able to bury her, or do anything with her. My sister began to fail very fast, and her spirits were very low. I laid me down beside a tree; to rest my head against it, but soon thought I must not lie there. I rose, and went down to the beach, got some frozen mussels, and carried them to my sister, who ate them. We then both sat down beside a tree. Now my courage began to fail. I saw nothing to expect but death, yet did not wholly give up my hope of deliverance. There we were, two distressed sisters, surrounded by dead bodies, without food or fire, and almost without clothing. I had no shoes to my feet, which were much swollen by reason of the cold. The ground was covered with snow, and the season was fast advancing, it being nearly the middle of December; so that we had every reason to expect that we should soon share the fate of our companions.

"But at that time God mercifully appeared for our relief, and thus showed himself to be the helper of the helpless. To our great surprise, we saw three men on the island, who, when they approached us, appeared no less surprised to find us living. I took courage and spoke to them. Having related to them our distress, one of them asked me if it were not better to be servants, than to die on the island. I said, yes. They then asked me several questions, which I answered as well as I could. They appeared pitiful, told us that they had come from New Harbor with two vessels for plunder, and offered to take us on board. We gladly complied with their invitation, and were hurried to the vessel. As I was rising from the frozen ground, by the assistance of one of the men, I put out my hand to take a small bundle, which I had preserved through all our difficulties, and which contained some clothes and books, especially my Bible. Seeing me attempt to take it, the men promised to take care of it for me. Trusting to their honor, I left it with them, but never saw it more. I also desired to see my mother buried before I left the island. They engaged to see it done; but I have reason to fear they never performed the engagement.

"After we were on board, they treated us very kindly. The captain gave each of us a spoonful of spirit and half a biscuit. This was the first bread we had tasted for two months. When collecting the plunder, the people told us we should have whatever we claimed as belonging to us in the ship. This was more than we expected. After plundering the ship and stripping the dead, they sailed. Then I saw the last of my miserable abode. In five days we arrived in New Harbor. Our new friends then appeared disposed to take advantage of us, and to sell us as servants to satisfy themselves for their trouble in saving our lives. This was a trial almost insupportable.

"But to our great comfort, a man came on board, who was from the same place in Ireland from which we had come. He was kind and pitiful, and endeavored to comfort us. God then appeared for us, and raised up a friend, who came and took us to his house, and there tenderly entertained us, bidding us to be of good cheer, for he would not suffer such ruffians to take advantage of us. This gentleman gave us every consolation in his power, and conversed with us in a very Christian manner, which was affecting and comforting. He proved very punctual in fulfilling his promises.

"We tarried with him, until we had so far recovered, as to be able to work for our living. This gentleman wrote to my father in Pennsylvania, informing him of our situation, and did all he could to forward the letter as soon as possible. This was about the last of December, 1741. In the mean time he provided good places for us. My sister was sent to live with a friend of his, at a place since called Boothbay; and was very happily situated. Soon after she went there, a happy revival of religion took place among the people. I trust that she was made a subject of the work. I tarried at New Harbor through the winter. The next spring, I came to this place, (Georgetown) and was employed in a family where I enjoyed the privileges of religion, as well as very kind treatment. Both the man and his wife were professors of religion, and were greatly animated by the good work which was going on in the place. At that time, there was manifest a general attention to religion. Having no minister, the people met together every Sabbath, and frequently on other days, for the purpose of worshipping God in the public manner, by prayer, singing psalms, and reading instructive books. In this way their meetings were made both agreeable and useful.

"Some time in the summer, my father came to visit us. He intended to take us with him to Pennsylvania. But before his arrival, I had an offer of marriage, which my situation seemed to urge me to accept. In November, 1742, I was married. My father tarried with us through the winter. The next summer he returned to

> Pennsylvania, where he spent the remainder of a very long life, as I trust, in the service of God.
>
> "I lived very happily with my husband thirty years. We had eight children, two sons and six daughters. When I review God's dealings with me, in the various scenes of life, I am filled with wonder and amazement. Great has been his goodness, and great my unworthiness. I view him as my covenant God, who foresaw these trials, and was graciously pleased to prepare me for them, by taking me into covenant with himself. He has upheld and supported me under all my trials, so that I have abundant reason to say, He has ever been a present help in time of need. I have reason; as it seems, more than any one on earth, to acknowledge God's goodness, which has been so abundantly manifested towards me, even from my youth.
>
> "I am now seventy-six years old. My anchor of hope has been, for many years, cast within the veil. My faith rests on the Rock of Ages, against which the gates of hell can never prevail. Though winds and waves have often beat heavily upon me, my anchor never has been, and I trust never will be, moved. Not withstanding the various trials of my life, I have never been left to renounce my hope, or to murmur against God, but would justify Him in all he has laid upon me, considering his mercies to be much beyond all my afflictions. For his mercies have been new every morning; great has been his faithfulness every night. And now unto Him, who has wrought all my deliverances, both spiritual and temporal, be ascribed the whole praise of my salvation. Amen."

The name of the ship was Grand Design. The ship was 90 days on the ocean, from Ireland to day of shipwreck. Sarah survived on the shore, with the company dying about her, for almost 60 days, through the cold of November and December, until her rescue and arrival at Georgetown.

12.

The Rock that Burns:

Coal comes to Maine: 1826

John Waite, a sea captain out of Portland, and Luther Oliver, a Kennebec river pilot, never knew each other, and would be surprised to find their names linked in a book written 100 years after they were dead.

In 1826 Capt. John Waite sailed into Portland from Philadelphia with a routine cargo except for two personal items. One was a hogshead lashed to the forward deck. The other was a crate measuring 4x4x4, stowed below. These were family presents and he had them loaded onto a wagon at the wharf and taken to his house.

Waite's crate when pried open revealed an open grate stove, and the hogshead which had been lashed to the foredeck, contained coal. Once Capt. Waite had the two working together, his house was quickly overrun with neighbors, flocking to see him "burn the rocks."

Eighteen years later in 1844, Capt. Luther Oliver piloted a two-masted schooner, the Sarah, up the Kennebec to Gardiner. He was mighty curious about a peculiar part of the cargo aboard. He asked the skipper for permission to take a sample home.

When Capt. Luther Oliver got home to Bath after docking the Sarah at Gardiner, he showed the samples to his neighbors.

Later he told the story of that day;

> "Coal was such a curiosity that I hadn't the slightest idea what it was like, so when I left the craft, I asked the skipper for a few pieces to take home to show the folks. A circus couldn't draw a more curious crowd. Not one in the place had seen a lump of coal before."

No coal had been burned along the Kennebec until 1846. Ever since the first white settlers had landed down river at Popham, 237 years earlier, men had been burning wood or charcoal for warmth, for making steam, for blacksmith's forges. There were no iron stoves until Benjamin Franklin designed and made the one which still bears his name. Only one room in most houses was heated, by an open wood fire on cold nights. In Maine winters, the temperature in every other room was close to freezing.

Capt. Waite's "burning rocks" caused such a sensation among Portlanders in 1826 that the next year he sailed home from Philadelphia with 60 tons of coal and plenty of stoves to sell. By 1853, 11,000 tons of coal were being unloaded in Portland.

Coal power was slow in getting to Maine. But once here it caught on quickly, changing ships and shipbuilding on the Kennebec, changing the cargoes ships carried, as well as changing home life in the towns along the river.

In Bath, a high rolling group of adventurous businessmen formed the Bath Gas Light Co. in 1853, startling the residents on that October night when they turned on 14 street lights. By 1858, Bath was getting about 2,000 tons of coal a year, mostly in small lots of under 200 tons. Two locomotives on the Kennebec and Portland Railroad began burning coal, though the others stayed with wood.

But soon the demand for coal was growing so big that a special coal dock was built just north of where the Carlton bridge now stands. By 1875, the Bath newspaper reported eleven vessels arrived into the coal dock within a few hours of each other, unloading 5,193 tons of coal. On an August day, 1885, four large schooners were unloading coal at the same time for the Maine Central Railroad. In 1886, 46,000 tons were unloaded at Bath. Only 15,000 of those 46,000 tons stayed in Bath; the rest was shipped out to inland customers by rail. Records from 1891 show that 1,570 railroad cars filled with coal left Bath's coal docks. Bath became second only to Portland as the biggest and busiest coal port in Maine.

This had led to changes at the coal dock. For almost 40 years, men working in the holds of schooners had been shoveling coal into tubs, which were then hauled by pulleys up to an elevated runway. The tubs ran down the runway by gravity into the coal yard and the loads were tipped into barrows. More men wheeled the barrows of coal into storage sheds. Thence it was later transferred by hand into rail cars. It was so slow and inefficient that in 1889 Oliver & Morse, stevedores, installed a stem hoist system and were then able to speed unloading to the rate of 36 tons an hour.

Perhaps the biggest revolution caused by coal on the Kennebec was in the size of the ships that could now be built and sailed.

Plentiful, cheap coal led to plentiful, cheap steam power; and steam power led to bigger schooners. With steam power to lift sails and anchors, it became feasible to raise and lower bigger sails and to lift the massive anchors needed for bigger ships.

The first steam-powered three-master in Bath was built by Goss & Sawyer in 1879, the Charles A. Briggs for Capt. Jacob B. Phillips.

First four-master was built the next year, again by Goss & Sawyer, again for Capt. Phillips, the William L. White. The biggest was the Bath built Frank A. Palmer, 2014 tons, launched 1897. Eventually 460 four-masters were built on the Atlantic coast, the last in 1928.

There is a beautiful symmetry and historical tidiness to that last four-master. She was launched, unnamed, Nov. 27, 1920, at Bowker's yard in Phippsburg, close to where the Virginia, first vessel built by white men in America, was launched in 1607. The last four-master deserves a small obituary here. She was bought by Capt. Charles H. Barnes of Saugus, Massachusetts, and he christened her for his wife, Laura Annie Williams. Barnes sailed her along the Atlantic coast as a general cargo vessel until 1930, when he sold her to Capt. James L. Publicover who used her to haul wood pulp from Nova Scotia to New Haven, Conn. On Jan. 17, 1939, loaded heavily, she grounded out on Tuckernut Shoal in Nantucket Sound. Coast Guard boats tried to free her, but on the second afternoon of trying to haul her off, her seams opened, and the master and crew of six were taken off the unsafe vessel. By the third day, her deck was under water and then pounding seas broke her to pieces.

As always, the cry was for bigger and bigger versions of a good thing. Coal freight was up to $2 a ton. A busy four-masted schooner could carry 3,000 tons and earn $6,000 a trip and make 30 trips a year. So if four-masters were good, five, six and even seven masters would be better. So the first five-master on the Atlantic seaboard was built at nearby Waldoboro in 1888, and named the Governor Ames. But she did not do well. She was dismasted on her maiden voyage in a November gale off Cape Cod. That put an end to five-masters for a while. It was 10 years before the next five-master was launched, the Nathaniel T. Palmer, 2,440 tons, built at Bath.

In all, 56 five-masters were built, all but four of them in Maine.

Then came the move up to six-masters. The first on the Atlantic was built in 1900 at Camden and named the George W. Wells. Two months later, Percy & Small at Bath built the Eleanor A. Percy. Some said the Atlantic was not big enough for two such monster sailing ships. For in 1901, when there were only two six-masters in the world, these two collided with each other on a summer night off Cape Cod. Both made it safely to port.

Only nine six-masters were ever built on the Atlantic coast, all of them in Maine and seven of them built by Percy & Small of Bath. The last and greatest was the Wyoming, 3,720 tons, launched in 1909, for the Winslow fleet. She once carried a record cargo of over 6,000 tons of coal.

The only seven-master was the Thomas W. Lawson, built 1902 at Quincy, Massachusetts.

The demand for ever bigger coal schooners had a self-destruct mechanism built into it. Due to the weight of the huge cargos and the length of the ships (six masters were up to 330 feet long) big coal schooners were inherently weak structurally. Hindsight shows that over 250 feet in length created too much strain on a wooden hull. The huge six master Wyoming, needed to be recaulked every few years. And recaulking her 300 feet and 3,370 tons of ship cost 5,000 man hours of work. Not only was such maintenance costly, but the operation of these huge sailing ships required big crews, despite the help from coal-powered steam engines for hoisting sails and raising anchors.

The handwriting was on the wall in 1900 when the Pennsylvania Railroad ordered eight coal-carrying barges from Bath Iron Works. Each barge would be able to carry 3,000 tons of coal with a crew of only four, whereas a schooner able to carry 3,000 tons of coal, required a crew of 16. Freight rates were soon halved, dropping from $2 to $1 a ton.

The end came quickly. The news is contained in the 1905 report of the U.S. Commission on Navigation:

> "In 10 years, the number of American sea-going schooners has declined from 2,152 to 1,523, a loss of almost 30 percent. They have been supplanted by sea-going barges rigged with masts so they can use sail in an emergency. Back in 1894, there were only 65 such sea-going barges, aggregating 62,821 tons; by 1904 there were 236 such barges, aggregating 247,702 tons."

Along the Kennebec, another era was ending. By 1908, there were only four active wooden ship builders left in Bath. The new age of steel ships was coming.

Independent Ice Co.'s huge ice storage houses on the Kennebec.

Ice harvesting on the Kennebec. Horse teams clear the snow before cutting begins in 1890s.

13.

Ice Harvests: 1870-1900

Cold Water Crop

Easiest, cheapest crop in the world to raise is Kennebec River ice. No need to clear land, plow, till; no need for seed, fertilizer or weeding. Just sit back and wait for winter, and ice one or two feet thick, and clear as crystal, will cover thousands of acres of the Kennebec. Harvested and shipped, ice was a fine cold-cash crop worth millions of dollars for 30 money-making years, 1870 to 1900. The Maine ice crop of 1890 peaked to 3 million tons, stored in 244 ice houses; and close to 25,000 people and 1,000 horses worked in Maine's ice business, state wide.

Like many a good business, the selling of ice from the Kennebec started by a fluke.

In 1824 Capt. William Bradstreet wasted in anger a long, profitless winter. His brig Orion was locked in the Kennebec by ice at Pittston and he could not budge. As soon as spring break-out started, Bradstreet was impatient to get out and start hauling cargo for cash. His first loading port was to be Baltimore, so he'd be heading out the Kennebec empty.

That's when he had the brainstorm to fill his empty hold with ice. Huge chunks of ice surrounded his Orion. He had them hoisted aboard and stowed. His cargo cost him nothing. But in Baltimore, he sold it for $700. The heat of summer was already making people pant and food spoil in Maryland, and they were willing to pay good money for Kennebec ice.

Word about the $700 paid to Bradstreet for ice that cost him nothing spread and the news fell on fertile minds. The next winter the brig Criterion sailed out of Bath for Cuba with 160 tons of ice.

Mainers had long used ice themselves, and sold it in local trade. In Boston, the first international ice man was smart-trader Frederick Tudor. After peddling 130 tons of ice to the folks down in hot

Charleston in 1805, well-to-do people who'd scarcely seen, let alone used, ice before, Tudor signed a contract in 1812 to deliver ice to Cuba. But the trade was small because ice was still strange and suspect. For example, when Tudor carried a cargo of ice into New Orleans, the creoles rioted at the sight of it, refused to unload it, and threw the entire cargo into the Mississippi. But by 1833, international trader Tudor was selling his ice as far away as India. About one-third of it melted on the way; another one-third melted into the bilges as he sailed slowly through the heat of the mouth of the Ganges. But the remainder was a hit in Calcutta. During the 1830s, Tudor came to cut ice on the Kennebec. Rufus K. Page built the first big icehouse at Richmond to store ice. But most of the trade was still local. The big out-of-state ice dealers were getting their ice from the Hudson in New York and rivers in Massachusetts, closer to the big city markets.

Then in 1860 the ice crop on the Hudson failed. It was too warm in New York for a good ice crop. But on the Kennebec the ice was 15 inches thick, crystal clear, and plentiful. Into the Kennebec came the big iceman from the Hudson River, James L. Cheeseman; and he promptly cut 30,000 tons of Kennebec ice. His customers admired its crystal clarity and the way it stayed cold so long.

The ice rush was on. Out-of-state operators poured money, men, icehouses, ships into the Kennebec.

By 1863 so much ice was stored in the newly-built ice houses at Gardiner that it would have needed 300 schooners to haul it all to market at once.

Cheeseman took his profits, but he did not run. In 1868 he sold out to the Knickerbocker Inc. Co., a giant firm in New York, and then he promptly moved across the river to Pittston. There he built a dozen of the biggest ice houses seen in these parts, each 700 feet long, each able to store 70,000 tons of ice.

The canny Cheeseman had hit the market right, and more out-of-staters followed him and Knickerbocker into the Kennebec. By 1869 the Charles Russell Ice Co. at Boston, Cochran-Oler Ice of Baltimore and Great Falls Ice of Washington, D. C., were all operating their own ice cutting, storing and shipping operations on the Kennebec. They sent out 225 ships carrying 65,000 tons of ice to customers in Philadelphia, Baltimore, Washington and New Orleans.

Ice fever was raging on the river. More than 60 ice companies were in hectic competition, running their own ice cutting teams of men and horses, their own ice storage houses and their own fleets of chartered ships to carry ice cargoes.

Consider the ice houses themselves. They were a weird form of architecture which bloomed fast and outrageously along the river, and then died slow ignoble deaths.

In the stretch of river between Woolwich and Augusta stood more than 45 ice houses. Mrs. Blanche Everson in her book "Tidewater Ice on the Kennebec," gives details of the lumber required to build the Modoc ice houses at Richmond, which consisted of six storage rooms under one roof. These ice houses were each 150 feet long, 192 feet wide. To build one of them, says Mrs. Everson, who grew up thereabouts, required 700,000 feet of long, heavy lumber; 385,000 shingles; 15 kegs of wrought spikes; half a ton of bolts.

James Hall, a local roofer, used over two million feet of long lumber in a single year to build icehouses. As for the shinglers, the speed and quantity of their work was incredible. For example, one very big icehouse required over a million shingles.

To build these icehouses, most within a short few years, kept an army of workmen busy and behind them scores of sawmills, and behind the sawmills the work of hundreds of men and teams of horses and oxen felling and moving trees.

Icehouses were fire hazards. Despite tens of thousands of tons of ice inside them, more than 13 big icehouses went up in a torrent of flame. What started these giant conflagrations beside the river is hard to discover now; hot embers from a watchman's pipe; sparks from a stationary donkey engine; an overturned lantern. But these enormous structures, made entirely of wood, lined between double walls with tons of sawdust for insulation, and with high roofs, usually blazed out of control and burned to the ground. Vessels at the loading docks fled for safety to mid-channel.

Thousands had winter jobs, thanks to the ice; they were able to earn cash money in months when gardens produced no food and children needed boots and coats, clothing which couldn't be made at home.

Wages for working the ice were small; 15 cents up to 25 cents an hour. The work day was 10 hours long.

The work was bone-chilling. In winter on the river, the temperature often dropped to zero and sometimes went to 30 below. Making it feel far colder was the knifing north wind whipping down the river corridor. Men wrapped their feet and boots inside layers of burlap bags. They huddled inside sheepwool coats, wore old newspapers between shirts and chests. Because they were handling ice and working by the river, many men never got dry, certainly never stayed dry.

At the peak of ice harvesting — dead of winter — more men were needed than could be hired from the Kennebec Valley. Many Maine men would refuse to work at the wages of 15 to 25 cents an hour, in the perishing cold. So hundreds of immigrants, often newly arrived Italians, would be brought from Boston, New York and other cities to work in the ice harvest on the Kennebec. It is saddening to picture men from sunbaked villages of southern Italy, newly arrived in this country, unable to understand English, being dumped on the Kennebec in December or February and ordered to get out on the frozen river and cut ice.

To house their workers, ice companies built 20 or more company boarding houses close to their ice storage houses. These were big two-story buildings of wood; on the ground floor were communal rooms for eating, smoking, preparing food; upstairs were open dormitories with 100 or more crude bunks in an unheated, unprivate warehouse for weary men. The loneliness of them, the stench of them, perhaps never being warm enough to get out of their dank clothes for two months or more, the fights, the gang terrorism, are not hard to reconstruct.

Hundreds of other men preferred to pay a bit more and board out in private homes. Many local farms converted attics, sheds, barns into dormitories and took in boarders, often 12 men to a house. It meant loads of extra work for the women of the house, because if you took in boarders, you fed them, too. That was part of the bargain. And the bargain price was 50 cents a day, including meals for very hungry men. Yet with 12 boarders, a family could gross $42 a week. So hundreds of families along the river did it.

Prices then were six cents for a quart of milk; 20 cents for a dozen eggs — and the price for ice in 1870 was up to $10 a ton, delivered to the boat.

Horses, strong pulling horses, were an important part of the river scene. Hundreds of horse teams had to be fed, stabled. Blacksmiths, working at their forges, were as vital a part of the operations as carpenters; blacksmiths had to repair and often make the specialty tools, picks, saws, tongs used in harvesting ice, as well as fix horses' harnesses, marine hardware and the thousand hinges on the icehouses.

More than 3,000 people worked in one way or another during the winter months of ice harvest. And the harvest kept getting bigger and busier.

In the winter of 1869-70, when the weather was so mild in New York and Massachusetts, the ice cut on the Kennebec jumped to 300,000 tons. Since the average vessel was loading only 300 tons, almost 1,000 vessels were needed; and traffic on the river was immense.

The Kennebec was now a major ice supplier to the world. Kennebec ice was traveling around the globe; its clarity was known and admired from London to Calcutta to Canton. On such long journeys, effective insulation was essential to prevent most of the cargo from melting away. Wood shavings and sawdust became hugely in demand. One large ship carrying 2170 tons of ice required 200 cords of shavings and sawdust for insulation. Before the ice boom, shavings and sawdust had been throwaway items. Now sawmills discovered a new way to prosperity. As the price of sawdust rose, shippers looked to other materials; for a while they used hay; at one time they used coal dust; at another they wrapped the great blocks of ice in brown paper.

In 1874, the ice crop on the Hudson was blighted by yet another very mild winter. Again the Kennebec's fortunes rose. Ice shipments jumped to 590,000 tons; almost double the 300,000 ton record set in 1870, only four years earlier. By 1886, shipments topped the million-ton mark and stayed over a million tons a year for the next decade.

Ice, which cost nothing to raise, was producing a wintertime harvest of millions of dollars.

The end of the great ice boom came swiftly but not mercifully. A Bath native with family ties close to the river and the ice trade, hastened its end. Charles W. Morse had cornered the market. His Consolidated Ice Co. by 1897 controlled 80 ice storage houses along the Hudson with a combined capacity of 3.5 million tons. That was more than enough to see his customers through a winter if there should be no ice cut at all on the Hudson. But Morse wanted more. By 1899 Morse had merged his Consolidated Ice Co. with the other giant in the field, Knickerbocker Ice. Then he gobbled up others and he formed the American Ice Co., which gave Morse a virtual monopoly on all major markets.

In two short sentences on January 16, 1901, the Bath Enterprise summed up the end of the story; "The only ice operations on the Kennebec now are for the local trade. The ice trust will harvest their whole crop on the Hudson."

The ice trade was dead on the Kennebec, and soon was dying everywhere. The advent of electric refrigeration was the nail in the coffin.

But the rich villain was Bath-born Charles W. Morse.

Logging camp, 1890s. Note the ax sharpening, the cookie in apron, long saws at center right, and hovel for horses. (courtesy James Vickery collection)

14.

Kennebec Logs & Steamers: 1800-1924

One sleeting, freezing winter afternoon I sat in the public library at Bath, looking through Bath newspapers from 100 years ago, trying to picture life along the Kennebec then.

One small item from the Bath Daily Times of April 7, 1884, gave me a picture of sights on the Kennebec River a century ago. Here it is:

> "In the month the tug Seguin was launched, the in-and-out traffic on the Kennebec was 892 vessels . . . 755 schooners, 86 steamers, 39 sloops, 7 barks, 3 brigs."

I put an earlier reel of microfilm copies of the newspaper on the machine and searched for a similar item about river traffic above Bath, on the stretch to Augusta. I was lucky to spot this one from July 1880:

> "Yesterday a passenger on the steamer Henry Morrison counted 27 schooners at Bath; 13 more between Bath and Richmond; 55 more between Richmond and Gardiner; 16 more between Gardiner and Hallowell; two more at Augusta . . ."

He had counted a total of 113 vessels in one day tied to wharves, loading and unloading cargo and passengers in that stretch upstream between Bath and Augusta.

Compared to those days, the Kennebec is naked today. What a joy it would be to be transformed in a time warp back to those days for just one afternoon, and to see the river alive and crowded with handsome craft. Yet the days of river traffic are not so very long ago.

Many of Bath's great-grandmothers fell in love on Kennebec River steamers. River romances got a boost in 1871 when Capt. Guy Goss built a pleasure barge called Yosemite, which cruised the river on summer nights, towed by a tug. On the decorated barge there was music and dancing, singers and entertainment, and dinners were served while romances began on the forward deck. This recreation became so popular that in 1896 Charles Morse transformed a 60-foot scow into a Cleopatra-like pleasure barge. Morse laid down a dance floor, protected the open decks with colored awnings. This pleasure barge, reported the Bath Independent, "provided ample room for one hundred soles (that's how the paper spelled it) to stroll in time to harps and violins. Suspended overhead are tables which are lowered for lunch. And there are plenty of hammocks in which to rest on a summer afternoon and evening."

The river had its share of rowdies, too. Bath residents protested loudly and in unison against another class of pleasure boat from Hallowell which used to steam downriver with men "drunk and swearing loudly into the night, inflamed with liquor and ale."

In early springtime, as the snows of winter melted, the river filled with a different kind of traffic — the massive log drives. For 250 years men had driven logs downriver, on the flow of snow and water. While snow lay deep, axe men had first felled huge pines for the masts of the English navy. The snow cushioned the fall of trees more than 100 feet tall and worth big cash prices. Snow, sluiced to make a sliding ice surface, provided the "grease" to move these monsters to the river shore. Once in the Kennebec, the fast flowing freshet of snowmelt moved the logs downstream to the sawmills and loading ports. The sawmills harnessed the power of the river to run their saws.

For the first 100 years, pine was the prime tree crop. When pine got scarce, then spruce was cut. Spruce bled, and its resins began to kill fish and stain the clear waters of the Kennebec. And later, when the spruce got scarce, the lumbermen began cutting every kind of tree to satisfy the demands of pulp mills. As this change occurred, the logs dumped into the river became smaller and smaller. Instead of massive trees, the length diminished to a few feet. These logs sank by the thousands and lay in deep piles on the river bottom. The papermills dumped millions of gallons of toxic wastes into the river. They transformed the Kennebec from a clear and clean river abundant with shad, salmon and sturgeon, into a foul smelling, poisoned river, stained dark brown. After almost 250 years, log drives were forbidden by law and the last log drive on the Kennebec went downstream in 1976. Industries and towns spent over $150 million on waste treatment. The Kennebec's recovery from death by poison is told in the last chapter of this book.

James Tibbetts of Woolwich rafted logs on the Kennebec for three-quarters of the 19th century. Born in 1817 on the family farm beside the Kennebec at Woolwich, Tibbetts was 94 — and still living in the same family farm — when on his birthday that year he spoke about his memories of log rafting. He told about working on rafts managed by a crew of six men. Those rafts consisted of 1,500 to 2,000 logs set crosswise to the current, enclosed by ropes tied to wooden wedges driven into the outside logs. Tibbetts and the crew would steer this monster down river all day, through currents, around bends. At night, they'd tie the raft into a sheltered bank and bunk down. They'd eat supper and grab their sleep ashore in the open.

As Tibbetts grew older, the rafts became a mite more comfortable. Raft houses were built on them, 30 feet long, 14 feet wide and 8 feet high. The crew slept, ate, sheltered inside these on the downriver drive. By the 1870's, steam power was a common use and tugs hauled or guided log rafts from astern.

A kingpin among the men who ran these tugs was Capt. Andrew T. Wyman, born in Phippsburg in 1835. He went to work on the river as a cookboy when he was 14. More than 60 years later, Wyman was still working on the river with his small steam tug Kapeela. The year he turned 75 years old, Wyman and Kapeela hauled 39 rafts containing 48,606 logs. That was far below his average, for Wyman was slowing down a bit at age 75. He figured that during his last 35 years on the river, he towed over 2 million logs, an average of more than 57,000 a year. These rafts were towed parallel to the current, instead of crosswise, the way Tibbetts had done before the days of steam, when men alone guided these enormous rafts of logs.

River-driving was probably the most dangerous job on Maine

rivers. It required all of a man's courage, and often that had to be buttressed with a rum bottle.

Movie makers in their early days liked to include a terrifying log driving sequence in their epic. Robert Pike, in his fine book "Tall Trees, Tough Men" tells of the movie company which came to film a sequence on the Kennebec. They were hot to get a sequence of a riverman riding logs over a sluiceway at the side of a dam. Their own stuntman refused flatly to try it. So they tracked down Spider Ellis, one of the native sons who was surefooted as a cat, and offered him $5 to do the trick. Two days' pay for two minutes work attracted Spider and he did his ride in front of the cameras. To get a still more exciting sequence, the movie makers offered Spider $10 to ride another log through and this time to fall off into the white water. He took the $10, climbed onto his log; but rode it safely through. To the angry movie maker he explained, "You see, I've never fallen off a log in my life. I just can't do it for less than $25!"

One of the worst log jams in history happened on the Kennebec in March 1896. Logs by tens of thousands were in the river above Augusta, jammed there because the ice had not gone out below Augusta. When the ice let go, the log jam broke loose and roared downstream; bridges were knocked out; roads and railways went next; homes and trees were washed away. Mills and factories were flooded. The streets of Augusta and Gardiner were piled high with logs. Snow and gales hit the Kennebec Valley for five days in succession, atop the flood waters. For seven miles above Swan Island the Kennebec was a wild thing packed solid with wreckage of bridges, logs, lumber, houses, trees. In Hallowell, the raging water reached second story windows.

But there was an easier way to come down the Kennebec.

A hundred and fifty years ago you could ride the steamboat from Gardiner to Boston for only $4, a 14-hour trip, with three meals included in the price.

Steamboating on the Kennebec began in 1835 with the first direct run between Gardiner and Boston aboard the steamer New England. But she was short-lived. On the night of June 1, 1838, on her way to Boston she collided with the schooner Curlew off Portsmouth and sank. Curlew was able to rescue all passengers and take them into Portsmouth. But the first steamer on the Kennebec-Boston run was a total loss within three years of her first voyage under Capt. Nathaniel Kimball.

The money-making potential for freight and passenger transport was so promising that local interests built and launched a successor, named Huntress. She was a swift and handsome vessel, making so much money and so much news that the grasping hand of Commodore Cornelius Vanderbilt, no less, reached out to take the profits for himself.

In 1840, Vanderbilt outfitted the steamer Augusta and put her on the run from Hallowell to Boston. In an effort to steal business from Huntress, Vanderbilt hoped his new boat would make the run much faster. But Augusta turned out to be a slow and rolling tub, and could win no customers from the Huntress.

Furious, Vanderbilt decided he'd build a boat so fast and so luxurious that no one could hold a candle to her. Determined to defeat the Maine men who dared challenge him, the Commodore christened his new boat Vanderbilt. He challenged Huntress to a race, thereby attracting widespread attention from Boston to Augusta. Heavy bets were laid on the race all along the seaboard, even by the Commodore.

Both steamers were wood-burners. The local crew of Huntress scoured lumberyards for the best wood to get the maximum power from their boilers. And the very best they put into a special pile, to use if the race got tight.

Neck and neck the two boats left Boston heading for the Kennebec. Vanderbilt took the lead across Boston harbor; but at the Boston Light, Huntress drew alongside; by Easter Point Huntress was ahead by a boat length. All night the two steamers ran neck and neck, passengers on deck, laying bets. Through the night each could see lights on the other. The crews worked without rest. Next morning Huntress and Vanderbilt were still jockeying for the lead as they turned into the Kennebec. They raced neck and neck upriver as far as Merrymeeting Bay, just above Bath. As word of the close race spread, crowds came to the wharves of every river town to watch.

Then as the two boats raced past Merrymeeting Bay into the final stretch past Richmond and into Gardiner, the crew of Huntress turned to their secret weapon, the pile of special wood. The crewmen filled their fires with it and opened the drafts wide. Up and up went the steam pressure to and then beyond the red danger line on their gauges. They risked blowing up their boilers. Huntress forged ahead, and kept increasing her lead in the final miles. To the resounding cheers of crowds on the river banks and the mob waiting at the wharf, Huntress pulled into the dock a full mile ahead of Vanderbilt.

Her clocked time from Boston to Gardiner was 10 hours and 45 minutes. She had set a record which stood for 60 years.

An angry Vanderbilt acted like a robber baron. He bought Huntress. Then he told the former owners they could buy her back for $10,000 more than he had paid. "If you give me $10,000 profit, then I will withdraw from the Kennebec. If you refuse, I'll put Huntress under the Vanderbilt flag and you'll never build another to beat her, and you'll go to the wall for lack of business."

The local men raised the money and bought back Huntress. Vanderbilt took his $10,000 profit and left the Kennebec. Huntress performed well on her Boston runs, and tasted another moment of news and glory in 1847 when she was chosen to carry President James K. Polk, some of his cabinet and Maine's bigwigs from Portland to Gardiner for Polk's visit to the state capital in Augusta. After the festivities, Huntress carried them all safely and swiftly back to Portland.

Ten years later, in 1857, a local group of investors spent $100,000 for a New York shipyard to build the palatial Eastern Queen, able to carry 800 passengers to Boston in comfort and elegance.

During the Civil War, she carried a Massachusetts regiment to Annapolis; then she became flagship to the fleet of 75 vessels which together landed 12,000 troops at Roanoke Island. Faced with so much strength, the Confederate forts there surrendered the next day.

After the war, competition rose as business on the Kennebec increased. A group of investors, headed by Edward K. Harding of Bath — a front man for the real owners, Spear, Lang and Delano of Boston — launched the Daniel Webster. In response, the Kennebec company spent an amazing $180,000 to build Star of the East, 244 feet long, 35 feet wide, able to carry 1,000 passengers, and with handsomely appointed and paneled public rooms and cabins. Cabins were finished in cherry and walnut, with ash for decoration; stairways were of mahogany with brass finishings. Steam heat and electric light added to comfort. In the splendid dining salons there were starched white table cloths, embroidered napkins, and elaborate menus. String orchestras played at mealtime.

Sidewheelers and steamers poured from shipyards almost like rabbits to serve the Maine coast. There were sailings from Bangor, Camden, Rockland, Boothbay, Bath, Augusta, Gardiner, Portland. Vacationers and businessmen alike used and enjoyed the steamers for fast, pleasant, cheap transportation. But competition led to price wars. For a time the fare from the Kennebec to Boston dropped to one dollar, then, briefly, to 25 cents.

Thousands who had never set foot on a boat, who had never glimpsed the ocean, who had never traveled out of Maine, took the steamers to visit big, bad Boston. They poured to the wharves, bought cheap tickets and had the time of their lives.

When these splendid steamers outlasted the peak of business in Maine waters, they were sold to work on the Hudson, on Long Island Sound and on Narragansett and Boston Bays. They changed their names and their runs many times in their lifetimes. As the years went by, some went slowly down hill. Their once glorious looks, immaculate paint and fine woodwork became seedy. But in their heyday these steamers and sidewheelers were beauties. Every day a thousand or more passengers rode them in both directions between Maine and Boston. Above all, these vessels were money-makers for the companies which owned them. Some had room for 2,000 passengers with staterooms for 400.

Their names are remembered still: Kennebec, City of Bangor, City of Rockland, Camden, Belfast, Katahdin, Forest City, Sebanoa, Wiwurna.

How dreary is the way to Boston now! Driving the Turnpike, pressing through Route 128, often with only a radio for company is a miserable way to travel compared to going by sea aboard a Kennebec steamer.

I like to picture the excitement, the feel of going on a voyage, as the Maine passengers went up the gangplanks, headed for Boston. They followed a steward carrying their bags through passageways, down magnificent staircases to their cabin; gongs sounded for dinner and they watched for friends or pretty women being shown to their tables; they lounged in the bar, chatting with new acquaintances or strolled on deck to watch the sea, feel the salt spray or pick out landmarks along the shore; they came into Boston harbor, fascinated by the shipping traffic and stood enthralled as they watched the backing and filling, the throwing of lines, the tricks of the trade as the ship captain brought them safely alongside. The going to bed, the sleeping in a cabin to the throb of engines, the awakening to the roll of the sea . . . all these pleasures seem immense and enthralling compared to a boring drive by car today.

The passengers might, of course, face fog, storms, even accidents. There were scores of accidents at sea aboard these coastal steamers — collisions, groundings, damage by gales, sometimes the loss of life. In that great storm of November 26, 1898, the Portland, built in Bath, went down on her way to Boston, with a loss of 176 lives. Yet even this enormous tragedy did not seem to put a crimp into the traffic using coastal steamers.

On September 2, 1923, the City of Rockland left Bath for Boston in fog. She moved slowly down the winding river. Perhaps her speed was too little to combat the strong current toward the mouth of the river. She hit hard on the Dix Island Ledge and drove her bow hard aground. In the dining rooms china, silverware, glasses of wine and water, and passengers too, were thrown to the deck; water poured in fast through two big holes, putting the generators out of action, thereby plunging the ship into darkness. Captain Brewer surveyed the damage and gave the order to abandon ship. Coast Guard boats from nearby Popham answered his SOS. All passengers were taken off, sheltered in Popham for the night, then ferried upriver to Bath the next morning. Time and again, tugs and the Coast Guard tried to move the City of Rockland off the ledge. Finally, but not till September 25, on the fourth attempt, did their efforts succeed. The City of Rockland was towed to Boston. Inspection proved she was too badly damaged to be repaired, and on October 29, 1924, this fine old Kennebec steamer was towed out to sea, burned and sunk off Little Misery Island.

This disaster virtually marked the end of the Kennebec-Boston run after almost 90 years. Begun in 1835, steamers and sidewheelers had enjoyed a long and profitable life. The man who for a while cornered coastal shipping all the way from Bangor to Galveston, Texas, was the Bath native son, Charles W. Morse, who became the most notorious financial pirate to come out of Maine.

15.

Saga of a Scoundrel: 1856-1933

Charles W. Morse

When the High School carries your family name on it, that bestows an aura of respectability few other things can match.

The High School in Bath stands imposing on a hill, its facade impressively decorated by long, white columns. Emblazoned on it are the words "Morse High School."

Dozens of times, as I drove by, I had admired the building; had imagined Morse may have been a city father, who had served pompously and long on the City Council; or the adulated coach of winning basketball teams; or maybe a rich old codger who in prosperity wanted to make public thanks to the town where he had learned his three Rs.

Wrong. Though Morse High School was first built in 1903, the finest in Maine, and was the gift of Charles W. Morse, he was far from respectable. Morse was among the greatest scoundrels ever raised in Bath, at least in the way he handled other people's money.

Morse was raised close to the Kennebec River; and later the river lined his pockets with millions.

Morse's father, Capt. Benjamin Morse, had been among the best known tugboat owners on the river, and he had interests in the flourishing ice trade, too. On October 21, 1856, his son was born and christened Charles Wyman Morse. This boy grew up in his father's waterfront office, aboard his tugboats. After graduating from Bath schools, he went on to nearby Bowdoin College and graduated from there in 1877, aged 21. But because he had worked in his father's shipping office, doing men's work, not just a youngster's after-school chores, he had acquired a sound savvy of how to turn one dollar into two.

After college, young Morse became the bookkeeper in his father's business. By 1881 Bath seemed too small for him and he left for Boston's State Street. By 1897 Morse was making his fortune on Wall Street. In his first year in New York, the country boy from Bath made $50,000.

Morse's move into the big league came when he formed his own Consolidated Ice Co. (The Kennebec ice business was booming, with 60 icehouses shipping close to a million tons in almost 1,000 ships.) No sooner was this flourishing than Morse showed his genius as a financial manipulator, brilliant at merging companies to form monopolies. He merged his Consolidated Ice with competitors to form the giant American Ice Co. in 1899. A financial writer paid Morse a compliment of a kind: "This was one of the earlier and more flagrant instances of corrupt and over-capitalized promotion in the annals of the American trust movement."

Morse capitalized his American Ice Co. at a whopping $60 million, when he was not yet 44 years old, and overnight he was called "The Ice King." His new company held a virtual monopoly on all the ice sold in Boston, New York, Philadelphia, Baltimore and Washington.

Within 24 hours after Morse had his monopoly, he jumped the price of ice 100 percent. On May 1, 1900, his trust announced ice in New York City, which had sold at 25 to 30 cents, would from then on cost 60 cents for a hundred pounds.

There was a public outcry, led by the New York Journal and Advertiser. Newspaper reporters began investigating the big stockholders in American Ice. They unearthed the scandal that among them were New York's Mayor Van Wyck, Tammany Boss Richard Croker (successor to Boss Tweed) and Tammany henchman Charles W. Murphy, superintendent of docks. A lawsuit was begun. Testimony soon revealed that Morse had not only let Mayor Van Wyck buy stock in the American Ice Co. at half of par value, but that Morse had lent the mayor the money to buy it. In return, the City of New York excluded Morse competitors — the independent ice companies — from selling ice on the city docks or other city property.

Voters kicked Van Wyck out of office at the next election. The stock market price of American Ice dropped through the cellar. But Morse did not get burned. Quite the reverse, he made another bundle. By a series of weird manipulations, Morse formed a holding company, the Ice Securities Corporation, and then sold out, coming away $12 million richer. However, ordinary stockholders in his American Ice saw their liquid assets melt away before their eyes.

After he had manipulated his hometown ice from the Kennebec into a fortune for him and failure for others, Morse picked another hometown target. Kennebec coastal shipping became the next money tree that Morse would shake.

The canny Morse, now approaching 50, ran two horses to pull his cart this time; banks teamed up with ships, while Morse pulled the reins. His method was to penetrate individual firms in the same field, then combine and pyramid their assets in a swift, bewildering series of maneuvers. Then he criss-crossed his banking and shipping interests, so the banks financed the shipping, while the shipping bolstered the banks. Morse meanwhile floated shares in his syndicates, hugely over-capitalized.

This ploy began by Morse getting control of coastal shipping in Maine; mostly the lines plying between Bath and Boston, Bangor and Boston, Portland and Boston. With the northeast under his control, Morse spread south and then to the Gulf of Mexico. Within a few short years, Morse had control of almost all coastal shipping from Bangor, Maine, to Galveston, Texas. In 1900, his nickname had been "The Ice King." By 1907 his nickname was "Admiral of the Atlantic Coast."

Now his ambition spread from sea to land. He was out to gain control, pirate-fashion, of the coastal railroads as well as the sea lanes. He threw Wall Street into a turmoil, and President Teddy Roosevelt, the trust-buster, into a fury.

That fury hit a boiling point in 1907 when Morse offered $20 million to the New Haven Railroad for its Long Island Sound lines. Determined to kill Morse's scheme, President Roosevelt promised immunity from further government interference to President Mellon of the New Haven railroad if Mellon promised never to sell to Morse. Thwarted by Roosevelt, Morse turned his guns on banks, and then the copper market.

The banks which privateer Morse set his sights on, boarded and almost sank, included the Bank of North America and the Mercantile National Bank, plus ten others in New York. The Bath Trust Co. in Maine, which Morse controlled, had to close temporarily. Then Rupert H. Baxter bought out Morse's controlling interest and became its president in 1910.

His co-conspirators in the banking capers were F. Augustus Heinze, a copper speculator, and E. R. Thomas, a young man whose main accomplishment was inheriting a lot of money. These three tried to corner the market in copper, milking the banks to buy copper stocks and then repaying the banks with shares in copper companies which they had bought early and cheaply.

Thereby Morse drove up the paper value of those copper stocks.

Then this bubble burst. Copper prices collapsed, and Morse stood accused by his partner in the caper, Heinze, of secretly unloading his shares in copper at the peak and triggering the collapse, which left others holding the bag.

That collapse of copper prices, of course, put the banks which held so many copper shares into deep financial trouble. The Bath Trust Co. had to close briefly.

That latest caper by Morse angered the blue-blood bankers on Wall Street. Many of them had long criticized the dicey dealings of this man from Maine, which had been giving the more respectable money men a bad name. They had been out for his scalp since the glare of exposure spotlighted him as the balloon artist in the great American Ice caper, back in 1900. Following that, Morse had stepped hard on establishment toes when he cornered control of coastal shipping from Bangor to Galveston; and his brazen offer of $20 million to buy out Mellon — one of their very own — had brought the President of the United States into the heart of Wall Street on a trust-busting crusade.

Just as bad were the personal pecadillos of Morse which had hit the newspapers in one of the most muck-raking stories of the time. In 1903 Morse's family went to court to annul Morse's second marriage, to the divorced wife of a Pullman car conductor.

Morse had married Hattie Bishop Hussey of Brooklyn on April 14, 1884, soon after he had arrived in New York. She bore him four children and died probably in 1897. Her children, in their teens by 1903, presumably felt their inheritances might be threatened by their father's second marriage in 1901 to Clemence Cowles Dodge, the divorced wife of the Pullman car conductor. So they sued to have the marriage annulled. The story made lurid reading; and one of the lawyers in the case, Abraham H. Hummel, was sentenced to a year in jail.

For these reasons, the Wall Street establishment turned onto Morse with claws out. They set up a "vigilance committee" of 15, and delivered an ultimatum to Morse to sell out his bank shares and stay forever out of banking.

But Morse had more trouble coming. Henry L. Stimson, then United States district attorney for New York, investigated the financial troubles of the Bank of North America. In the course of this investigation, Stimson got an indictment and then a conviction of Morse for making false entries in the books of the bank and for misusing bank funds. In November 1908, Morse was sentenced to a 15-year term in the federal penitentiary at Atlanta.

"This fat, squatty little man with the masterful, inquiring eyes," wrote a contemporary journalist, "had either not played the game the Wall Street way, or played it too well." Morse was taken off to prison January 2, 1910, to serve 15 years. He left, screaming to reporters that "the administration wanted a scapegoat;" that "there is no one on Wall Street who is not doing what I have done;" and that "the system wanted a victim." He served 2 years, getting out of the Atlanta penitentiary with a presidential pardon from President Howard Taft. Morse worked his pardon caper this way.

First he tried every avenue to get a pardon, but Taft adamantly refused to consider it. Then Morse hired Harry M. Daugherty as his lawyer. Morse paid $5000 as a retainer to Daugherty (later attorney general under President Harding and jailed in the Teapot Dome oil field scandal) and promised $25,000 more if Daugherty obtained his release.

Daugherty tried every trick in the book, including having a team of doctors examine Morse. They came back saying that the prisoner was fit as a fiddle. Daugherty sent another medical team, this time army doctors. They told President Taft that Morse was suffering from many ailments, including Bright's disease, and could not live out the year.

President Taft signed Morse's pardon. Morse quickly fled to Wiesbaden, Germany — supposedly for medical care. But Morse had overlooked the matter of the $25,000 fee due to Daugherty for getting him out of jail.

Before long the White House received information that Morse had hoodwinked the doctors. He had drunk a combination of chemicals and soapsuds just before the medical team examined him and reported to the president that Morse was a dying man. The soapsuds and chemicals had produced the symptoms upon which the army doctors had based their diagnosis. Later, Taft charged that he had been hornswoggled and told the New York Times that the case "shakes one's faith in expert examination." Morse returned from Europe, presumably paid Daugherty the $25,000 and was quickly back into new schemes for manipulating money.

Before Morse went on trial and was sent to prison, he is said to have made certain arrangements with Walter Reid, a fellow businessman in Maine.

To ensure he didn't lose all his fortune as the result of his trial, Morse asked Reid to hold certain assets for him in Reid's name. Reid agreed, and Morse turned over title of some of his ships to

Reid, with the understanding that Reid would turn them back to Morse later.

When Morse got out of the Atlanta penitentiary, he asked Reid for his ships to be put back in his name.

"What ships? what ships, Charlie?" Reid is said to have replied.

This is the Reid whose name, like the name of Morse, is honored today in the Bath region. Reid gave most of the waterfront land and magnificent miles of sand beach which today is called Reid State Park.

Reid had been a banker in Waterville, the mortgage and loan officer who handled this land. While in this position, Reid himself acquired title to this oceanfront land, which he so loved when growing up as a child. After he acquired part of it, he built a house there, and as opportunity arose, bought more and more adjoining land. His family, which inherited it, eventually gave much of the land to the state. It is now enjoyed by many thousands of people in summer and called Reid State Park.

Morse went back to the arena where he had started as a boy in Bath — to shipping. By July 1915, his Hudson Navigation Co. was already being sued for — what else? — unfair competition. Six months later Morse was back in the headlines, this time with a grandiose plan to form a gigantic American shipping combine (or monopoly) to rule the Atlantic. He pyramided the idea into a holding company called the United States Shipbuilding Co., which was made up of 16 subsidiary companies, each owning one ship. Later the U.S. Government would indict and charge Morse with using the mails to defraud prospective buyers of stock in United States Shipbuilding.

But before that charge was leveled, World War I offered Morse an even greater opportunity to make money, and he grabbed it. He finagled contracts from the Shipping Board to build 36 ships. Against these contracts, Morse borrowed money from another government agency, the Emergency Fleet Corp., with which to buy shipyards and equipment.

Eventually 22 of the 36 ships were built. But in the postwar investigation by the Justice Department into "war frauds," Morse again found himself in deep trouble. He was accused of misrepresenting his shipbuilding facilities in order to obtain contracts; of diverting government money to his own pocket instead of using it to build ships; and of failing to return to the government any of the excessive profits he had made from the contracts.

When news of the impending indictment reached Morse, he fled to France. But his old lawyer Harry Daugherty was now Attorney

General in the Justice Department, and sent Morse a cable ordering him to return and face charges.

This and other court cases against Morse dragged on through the 1920's. In one case, the government won a judgment of $11.5 million against Morse.

But by 1926 Morse was too ill, in fact, to stand more trials. He was sick in body and mind. On September 7, 1926, he was declared mentally incompetent to handle his own affairs, and placed under guardianship by the probate court of Bath.

"I remember him as an old, frail man, hunched in a wheel chair," says a former neighbor in 1983. "His male nurse would take him out for airings. He was bundled in laprobes and scarves. But he had an eye for women. The old man would whistle like a wolf at anyone in skirts, from 15 to 70."

Morse spent six years in Bath, incompetent and sick. After getting pneumonia and suffering several strokes, he died in Bath on January 12, 1933.

But the Morse High School carries his name.

Charles W. Morse, (1856-1933), the Bath-born millionaire who became a financial scoundrel, was sentenced to the Atlanta penitentiary and for whom the Bath High School is named. (Maine Maritime Museum, Bath)

Arthur Sewall, (1835-1900) the merchant prince of shipping, who was nominated as Democratic candidate for vice president of the United States on ticket headed by William Jennings Bryan in 1896. (Maine Maritime Museum)

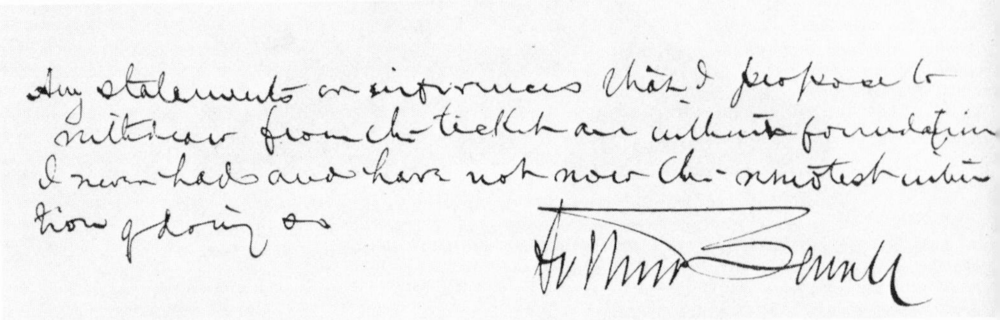

Any statements or inferences that I propose to withdraw from the ticket are without foundation. I never had and have not now the remotest intention of doing so

Arthur Sewall

Arthur Sewall's handwritten statement denying he would withdraw from the ticket. (Maine Maritime Museum, Bath)

The first and only ramming ship, U.S. Katahdin, built at Bath Iron Works for U.S. Navy by John S. Hyde before World War 1. Pictures show Katahdin on surface and partially submerged to ram an enemy ship. This wild idea was never tested in action. (Maine Maritime Museum, Bath)

City of Rockland, launched 1900 from Wm. McKie Yard, East Boston, served on the Kennebec-Boston run. Length 247 feet, she carried 2,000 passengers in luxury. She suffered many mishaps, including a severe collision with her sister ship City of Bangor. On Sept. 2, 1923, she was wrecked on Dix Island in the mouth of the Kennebec, was later burnt at Little Misery Island, off Salem, Mass.

City of Rockland hard aground.

River steamer Penobscot

Eleanor A. Percy, the first six-master launched on the Kennebec by Percy & Small, 1900.

Racing yacht Ranger, built 1933 by BIW for William Vanderbilt, won the America's Cup and won more blue ribbons than any racing yacht of her class.

William D. Sewall, founder of the Sewall fleet

108 & 112 DAYS
TO SAN FRANCISCO
The Popular First-Class Clipper Ship
LOOKOUT
SHERWOOD, Master, at PIER 12 EAST RIVER.
This favorite Clipper being well known to the trade as first-class in every respect, will fill quick. All Freight intended for her should be sent immediately alongside.
SUTTON & CO., 58 South St., cor. Wall.
The Ships of this Line are the best up, and dispatched quicker than any other from ew-York to San Francisco.

Advertisement for clipper ship, 1870s.

Ships and Sailors

Henry B. Hyde and the tug Seguin, off Seguin Light at the mouth of the Kennebec River. (Ganne file photo of painting by Patterson)

16.

What's the Difference?

Clippers and Schooners

Ships of many kinds sail through this book.

What's the difference between them? Let's start with clippers, the loveliest of all. These beautiful, sharp-pointed, swift ships have left an indelible love in their wake. But, like other extraordinary and expensive beauties, their years of glory were short. Only seven years. About 90 clippers were built along the coast of Maine in seven years, 1850 through 1856. Their heyday ended with the financial crash of 1857.

The demand for speed, speed and more speed created the clipper: speed to the California gold rush with the 49ers; speed to the Australian gold rush; speed to the China tea trade. Getting there first often meant big profits; getting there two weeks later after the market price had dropped meant lean pickings.

To keep a sense of proportion about clipper ships is hard because of their beauty and legends. But in 1850, when Maine yards launched 326 vessels only three of them were clippers. In 1851, the clippers were up to 9. In 1852, Maine launched 20. In 1853, Maine yards built 33. In 1854, Maine yards built 15. In 1855 and 1856, Maine launched five fast clipper ships each year. By 1857, the great depression had killed the clipper ship era.

Another fact will keep the clipper ship legend in proper proportion to the truth. In 1856, U.S. shipbuilding reached a peak and Maine led the nation. Maine launched 216,000 tons of ships that year; and less than 5,000 tons of them were clipper ships; less than three percent of the tonnage.

But when Maine built clippers, they were the best, most beautiful and fastest clippers on the ocean. Red Jacket, built in Rockland in 1853, raced through January storms on her maiden voyage from New York to Liverpool in 13 days, one hour, 25 minutes, dock to dock. This record for sailing ships has stood for more than 130 years. The Flying Scud, launched in Damariscotta, logged an incredible 449 nautical miles in a single day. This meant that this 1,713-ton sailboat was averaging about 19 miles an hour for 24 hours. Flying Dragon, from Bath, made it around the Horn to California in 97 days — a 15,000-mile course.

The Nightingale, named for Jenny Lind, whose figurehead decorated the bow, was the most beautiful clipper ever built, when she was launched from South Eliot, Maine, in June 1851. She raced to the Australian gold fields; raced to China for tea; raced to California. Unhappily she picked up "the taint of a musky ship." She did a shameful stint as a slaver.

Her owners paid $75,000 for this Maine beauty. As soon as she was launched they issued a challenge to race any ship, British or American, to China for a prize of 10,000 pounds sterling. No ship accepted her challenge.

What's a schooner?

The small schooners were the errand boys, the pickup trucks of the sea. These sturdy, vessels were the links — more reliable than stage coaches — between sea towns in a fast developing America. They carried the supplies to a growing and moving population. It didn't matter to the schooner skippers what the cargo was, or how much of it there was. These coastal schooners were the United Parcel vans of 19th century America. But they had a fine ancestry stretching back most of 200 years before that.

To understand better the daily necessity of these small Maine built schooners, let me quote some schooner traffic figures from the year 1835. Fifteen years after Maine became an independent state, when Maine's population stood at only 330,000, 574 schooners from Maine arrived in Boston, 328 arrived in New York and 99 arrived in Philadelphia. That adds up to 1,001 schooners from Maine arriving at three cities in 1835.

But most schooners worked locally. You'd find them in every cove, round every bend of the coastline. They carried eggs, cheese, hens, potatoes, dried fish, lumber, bricks, hay, cordwood. A few were floating general stores, catering to island populations; one in Penobscot Bay was a floating shoemaker and harness repairer. They turned a good profit too. For example, one day in April 1844 on the wharves at Belfast, 10,000 cords of wood were piled and 50 schooners stood off, waiting to be loaded. A skipper would pay $2 a cord in Maine and sell it for $4 a cord in Massachusetts.

These schooners were small two-masters, averaging about 100 tons.

Here again, the economic pressure was to build them bigger. If small schooners made money, bigger schooners would make more money. Thus came the change from two- to three-masted schooners, and then to four-; and still later to five- and even six-masters. As the masts multiplied so did the tonnage. The two-masted 100-tonner finally was blown up to the huge four-poster. The biggest four-masted schooner ever built in Maine was the Frank A. Palmer, 2,014 tons, launched at Bath. By 1900 Percy & Small of Bath had launched the six-masted Eleanor A. Percy, of 3,401 tons.

The profit motive then as now favored design which would cut back on manpower — reduce the crew, and lessen the payrolls at sea.

So the schooners, even the big schooners, had a more simplified sail plan and simpler rigging. For example, on a full-rigged ship, there were 204 running lines. To set the topsail meant handling eleven lines simultaneously. But on a schooner, you could run up the mainsail with only three major lines — and these were helped along by steam power.

The importance of not only less manpower but also less skilled manpower was enormous. Crews were scarce; skilled sailors were rare as gold nuggets on any dock in the world. In the United States, sailors who had not risen to a command by the time they were 25 or 30, usually quit the sea. Most crews on U.S. ships were not Americans, but a mixed bag of many nationalities. (See chapter on Crews and Bucko Mates.)

Compare the specific cases of the Shenandoah and the Eleanor Percy. The Shenandoah, a four-masted bark of 3,258 tons, with 12,000 square feet of sail, was built in Bath by Arthur Sewall & Co. in 1890. She was so beautiful under acres of canvas that 6,000 people came to see her launched. The United States government put her picture on the licenses of all shipmasters. But Shenandoah had to have 33 men in crew.

The schooner Eleanor A. Percy, virtually the same tonnage, needed only 15 men.

As a rule of thumb, schooners could be manned with one man for each 250 tons, whereas square riggers needed three men.

Then came the barges. Barges looked ugly; but their profit on the bottom line looked beautiful to the owners.

In less than a lifetime, Maine ships went downhill, from clipper ships to barges. In 50 years, shipyards which had built the most beautiful clipper ships and Downeasters which sped across oceans under acres of canvas, descended to building barges and ocean-going tugs to pull them.

The reason was, of course, money. The prime purpose of building or owning any commercial ship, from a lobster boat to a supertanker, is to make money.

The money-making Morses of Bath were the first to make the tow-and-barge into a large highly profitable operation. They didn't wake up with a brilliant new idea one creative morning. They were pushed into it by force of the figures in the office account books.

Capt. Benjamin W. Morse, father of the Wall Street "bad boy" and multi-million-dollar pirate Charles W. Morse, (featured in an earlier chapter), had been edging into the ice and shipping business. His son, while at school in Bath and at Bowdoin, worked in his father's office learning the figures. Father and son were quick to see the profits to be made from tugs and later barges. So Capt. Benjamin Morse began the Kennebec Towing Co., bringing boats up and down river at a fee of $75 or more, often with several in tow. But the company books also told the other side of the story. As Morse shipping expanded, Morse ships were paying out large sums for being towed in and out of other ports to which they were carrying ice, coal and lumber.

When the boy grew up into Charles W. Morse, the financial genius, he bought up the Knickerbocker Ice Co., changed the name of the Kennebec Towing Co. to the Knickerbocker Towing Co., and spread its operations. The big money flowed into it. They soon had a virtual monopoly — something Charles Morse sought in every business he touched. When a thousand boats were coming up and down the Kennebec, his towing business brought in lots of profit. But the books showed that at the other end, Morse ships were paying out too much for being towed into distant ports.

Morse's answer was to tow his cargos all the way. Enter the barges. At first, Morse bought worn-out schooners, stripped them of rigging and masts and increased their cargo capacity. He'd use one tug to haul three such vessels, and he needed only three or four men to man these schooner hulks. Soon the account books proved the tug - and barge combination was the most profitable way to go. And Morse went.

His company began building three big ocean barges. In 1889 they launched Independent, 2,254 tons. A neighboring Bath yard, Kelly & Spear, turned out eight barges a year from 1885 to 1889.

New England Shipbuilding, another Bath yard, turned out nine barges and Rogers made four barges.

Operating costs dropped. Tugs, unlike schooners, were never tied up in port, unloading. They dropped off the barges they had brought in tow, picked up other full ones, and left.

Freight prices dropped. Cost of shipping a ton of coal was cut in half from $2 to $1 and then to 60 cents. Cost of moving lumber from the Carolinas, where they cut it, to Philadelphia, where they used it, dropped from $5.50 to $2.40. Tugs and barges were in — until they too met a still lower-cost innovation; fast steam colliers able to deliver 7,000 tons of coal in quarter the sailing time of a barge under tow.

Then suddenly, schooners got a new lease on life. The outbreak of World War I created a demand for everything that could carry cargo. Freight prices skyrocketed. Coal freight which was 65 cents in 1914 rose to $5 by 1917. Then with peace came world-wide depression in shipping.

But the one Maine type of vessel which truly dominated all others around the world for a half century was the Downeaster. What were Downeasters?

The William B. Frye, a Bath-built vessel, under full sail.

The William B. Frye sinking after being torpedoed by a German submarine.

17.

Downeasters:
Glory of Shipbuilding

Downeasters: those were ships which epitomized Maine shipbuilding at its finest and most productive. Downeasters made Maine-built ships and Maine-bred captains admired the world around.

The Maine Downeaster was born in order to carry the wheat crops of California.

Maine and California were far more entwined than most of us realize today. The California gold rush of 1849 triggered the speed and beauty of the fast Maine clipper ships. For a few glorious years, they were the sailing marvels of the world.

Then the bumper crops of wheat in Califorina from the 1870s to 1890s triggered the hey-day of Maine's handsome Downeasters, so admired in paintings today. This California wheat had a quality of special importance to Maine shipbuilders: It could survive in 15,000-mile voyage from San Francisco to Liverpool and arrive in near perfect condition. That was the prime reason Maine built hundreds of Downeasters.

Here are the dimensions of that reason. In 1860 only 1,087 tons of wheat were exported from San Francisco. But by 1865, the California wheat crop was up to 43,302 tons, worth $1,750,000. The next year wheat export value was more than $6.7 million, almost a 400 percent jump. By 1875, exports were up to 360,000 tons; and by 1880 they reached 488,000 tons. By 1882, more than a million tons of grain and almost a million barrels of flour were leaving San Francisco. And leaving by ship. That year 559 ships were needed to haul California wheat, mostly to Europe. The flags of seven nations flew on the grain fleet — and 423 of them were American. Maine-built, Maine-captained Downeasters led the pack.

William Hutchinson Rowe in his excellent book, "The Maritime History of Maine," gives this definition of a Downeaster;

> "A full rigged wooden ship, canvas spread, often with 25 full bellied sails, built in a Maine shipyard, most often captained by a Maine man."

The expert Howard I. Chapelle in his "History of American Sailing Ships" wrote of the Downeasters:

> "Some of these vessels were without doubt the highest development of the sailing ship; combining speed, handiness, cargo-capacity and low operating costs to a degree never obtained in any earlier square-rigger."

Chapelle was paying tribute to the workmanship of boatyards all along the Maine coast. In 1875, Maine yards delivered 80 percent of all square-rigged ships built in the United States. (The last was built in Phippsburg on the Kennebec in 1893.)

Grain was not an easy cargo. To carry it required a tight, fast ship, sturdy and strong enough to withstand storms coming round the Horn, and gales they'd endure crossing the Atlantic. So Downeasters were built strong to withstand the punishing seas. Hulls were often 16 to 20 inches thick, with white oak ribs and planking of thick pitch-pine. Keel and keelson together formed 12 feet of thick solid timber. Knees to brace the beams were of the strongest wood to be found — native hackmatack. Bolts were of copper.

Yet, with all their toughness, Downeasters were handsome ships. Their lines were not as hollow or sharp as those of the true clipper ships. Because they carried far more cargo, the vertical rise from the keel was flattened out, and more gradual. Yet their trim bow lines, flowing into the deck, were as pretty as a clipper's.

Maine had special pride in her Downeasters, from the day they were launched to the day they docked in foreign ports.

Take the day in September 1878 when the Cushing & Briggs yard in Freeport launched the John A. Briggs, Freeport's largest ship. Schools closed. Stores closed. The Maine Central ran special trains. Island steamers filled their decks with thousands of spectators. The bay near Freeport was a kaleidoscope of sails from hundreds of local craft. Visitors from inland came by oxcart and carriage. The governor of Maine, Alonzo Garcelon, was there; so was James A. Garfield, up to make a presidential campaign speech in Yarmouth. In all, more than 7,000 people cheered the massive new Downeaster into the water, a bigger crowd by far than those which come to see the Navy's guided missile ships launched today at BIW.

Skippers set high standards for the good looks as well as good performance of their Downeasters. Capt. David H. Rivers, aboard his Bath ship, the A.G. Ropes, reports on his shipkeeping on an outward voyage across the Pacific:

> "We have scrubbed all the paint work, cleaned and oiled all the decks, and the top of the houses . . . and are pumice-stoning the ship on the outside and tarring the rigging . . . Because there is about $25,000 worth of sails, spars and rigging above the ship's deck and I think these things worth looking after, we have the yards scraped bright . . . I have had the pins and sheaves of every block in the ship brought to the poop deck for my inspection . . . I have had every bit of rigging brought aft and passed every foot of it through my own hands . . . We have begun painting the whole ship today, white inside, and I have had the lower masts pumice-stoned so they are as smooth as a table top."

When a Maine Downeaster sailed into any foreign port, men on the waterfront or on other ships knew by looking at her that she was a Maine boat.

> "With the flowing lines of her hull accentuated by black paint and little or no ornamentation, her masts and spars of natural wood, scraped, varnished and squared as with a tape line, her deck houses shining white and the decks scrubbed and oiled so as to equal them in whiteness, and without a line out of place from stem to stern, no yacht was ever more ship-shape than a State of Maine Downeaster."

So wrote William H. Rowe.

For the owners (and captains usually had at least a small share of ownership too) the Downeasters proved handsome money-makers. On average (which includes total losses) owners earned 15 to 20 percent on their money. The profit of course was free of tax, either corporate or personal.

Some ships and some owners made far more, especially those risk-takers who paid the yard to have their ship built, bought her cargo, sold her cargo and sometimes insured themselves.

The Sewalls always seemed to make money with their ships; but few ships did as well as Carollton. She cost about $81,000 to build. Immediately after she was launched at Bath in November 1872, she was chartered for the booming trade to San Francisco for $32,000. There, she sold her cargo at a good profit, and loaded with wheat for Liverpool. That 15,000 mile trip earned $40,000 for her owners. In Liverpool, the Sewalls sold her for $96,000, which was $15,000 more than her launch price. On their $81,000 investment, the Sewalls had grossed $190,000 within a year.

The men in Searsport who owned the William H. Connor kept her working constantly for many years, wound up making 600 percent on their investment.

The safety record of Downeasters was good, even though the long routes they sailed were dangerous. One reason, according to marine historian Basil Lubbock, was that owners did not scrimp on the upkeep of these profit-makers:

> "No pinch-penny policies ruled the Downeasters. Repairs were promptly made, and sails, spars and ropes replaced with the best the market afforded as soon as they showed the least sign of wear."

Lubbock went on to praise the food, the "preserves," the salt beef, even the hardtack — which may have been going too far. His praise, however, was bitterly contradicted, as we shall see in the next chapter, by accusations made in The Red Record, newspaper of the new Seaman's Union.

One safety achievement beyond dispute was recorded in the official papers of William Bates, United States commissioner for Navigation. Bates estimated that from July 1881 to July 1884, 423 American wooden vessels were employed in the California wheat trade and that there were but two losses. That amounts to a loss of .5 percent, an extraordinary safety record.

Yet the Downeasters suffered. Crews endured or perished, beset by storms, brutal treatment, sickness and plague. Pay was meager, food was drab and monotonous at best, often abysmal. Often most of the crew had been dragged aboard, drugged or drunk. Most had no sea knowledge. They worked in surly anger, but there was no escape from themselves or their ship. Violence, mutiny, even murder were frequently reported in the bare terse words of the captain's log. No one knows how much brutality went on, never reported. A sailing vessel on a distant ocean was an isolated, constricted world of its own, ruled by a captain whose sole concern usually was the safety of his ship and cargo, with small care for the crew. The crew, so often shanghaied out of a waterfront bar or whorehouse by agents who got a price for delivering bodies aboard, had no recourse except to jump ship in an alien land when they reached port. Some told the Red Record of barbaric punishments. But by the time their accounts were published, the events were long passed, the ship and captain long gone on another voyage. Along with this black side, were tales of heroism, superb seamanship, rescues and even amazing bonds of compassion and love.

They deserve books to themselves. But here are a few short examples of exploits, good and bad, from a handful of the hundreds of Downeasters which sailed to the loveliest and most scurrilous ports of the world a hundred years ago.

Fire broke out aboard the Hornet off the west coast of South America. She was a Downeaster built in Freeport, and under the command of Capt. Josiah Mitchell. Fighting the flames the crew lost the battle. Some were burned to death. The ship became a funeral pyre. Fourteen of the crew and Mitchell got off into a lifeboat, ill-equipped.

These 15 men in an open boat crossed 4,000 miles of the Pacific to the Hawaiian Islands. The voyage took them 43 days and nights, with full share of brutal weather, heat and cold, gales and high seas, shortages of food and water, all exacerbated by body sores and mental traumas. But they made it, the longest open boat journey on record — longer, even, than the ordeal by the survivors of the Bounty mutiny.

In another case, survivors built their own boat from wreckage. Capt. Issac W. Keller of Rockland and his crew aboard the Elizabeth Kimball were driven aground and wrecked on the barren ledges of Easter Island in the far Pacific. There, among the 300 ton monliths of ancient stone gods, they salvaged planks from their vessel and built a new 10 ton schooner. They sailed her for 2,550 miles to Tahiti, a passage of 24 days.

There is the macabre and doleful picture of the return of the Phineas Pendleton. After her launching in Brewer, Maine, this vessel sailed the world for 19 years without touching at an U.S. port. When she finally came home, she arrived with her lower masts painted black, in mourning for the captain's three children who had all died of diphtheria off Peru.

Rounding the Horn, off the tip of South America on the way to and from San Francisco, was always a hard passage. Few ever had it harder or longer and survived than the crew of the Edward Sewall of Bath, under the command of Capt. Richard Quirk. Battered by gales, snow, sleet and ice, the ship clawed her away for 67 days, trying to make passage around the Horn and failing.

During those 67 days, Capt. Quirk steered 54 different courses, zig-zagging, crossing, circling, back-tracking 25 times and covering 23,407 miles before he finally got his vessel to San Francisco. This voyage from Philadelphia to California had lasted 293 days. A good passage took about 100 days.

Quirk's log showed that several crewmen broke legs. He made very little of it, saying they were not sailors in the first place.

When Maine skippers found themselves and their ship in terrible trouble, they improvised ways to get out of it. This ability to invent and make do is still the hallmark of Maine skippers.

One Searsport captain, William H. Blanchard, lost his rudder and steering post in a gale coming down the South Atlantic, heading for the deadly Cape Horn, and the crossing into the Pacific. Blanchard hove to, set his crew to work, rigged a jury rudder and improvised a steering gear. Then he sailed round the Horn with this rig, made stops to unload and load cargo at several west coast ports and then sailed back to New York on his homemade rudder and steering gear.

Another Searsport captain of the same stripe was Capt. E.D.P. Nickels. His Downeaster, May Flint, was hit hard by a cyclone and damaged to the point where many captains would have abandoned her. The cyclone had torn away most of three masts. Passing ships sailed close to offer assistance or to take off the crew. Nickels waved them away and set to work. For two weeks his ship wallowed sailless in the ocean, while the crew improvised new masts. Then, satisfied he had done all he could, Capt. Nickels hoisted his new spars, ran up the old sails and sailed the May Flint across thousands of miles to safe harbor in New York.

The young wives of ship captains also performed amazing feats of seafaring. When Capt. William York of the Don Quixote was washed overboard, his wife navigated the ship to port.

But the most romantic and awesome tale concerns the young and beautiful Mary Brown Patten. When her husband fell very ill, she took command of his 216-foot clipper, Neptune's Car, and ran the ship for more than 50 days and nights. When the mate mutinied and tried to kill her and take command himself, Mary Patten put her pistol to his head, marched him below decks and threw him in irons, where he stayed.

There are scores of stories of women at sea doing man's business well in dire emergencies. But because the story of Mary Patten caught the attention of the newspapers of 1856, more details are available today.

Mary Patten was 16 years old when she married 24-year-old Joshua A. Patten in Rockland. Mary went to sea with her husband in 1855, grew fascinated by ship's business and asked her husband to teach her how to navigate. The next year, her husband was given command of the 216-foot clipper-ship Neptune's Car. They sailed from New York for San Francisco in July 1856.

But trouble started soon, when the first mate named Tarker refused to stand his watch. Young Capt. Patten stripped him of rank, and took over the mate's watch as well as his own. By the time they were sailing down the South Atlantic coast off Argentina, the weeks of double duty took their toll. Patten collapsed. His wife put him to bed. His fever soared. His eyesight failed. He turned delirious just as Neptune's Car was heading into the tumultuous seas and gales of Cape Horn. The second mate did not know how to navigate. The first mate had been locked in the hold, by order of the sick captain.

Mary Patten, now 19 years old, took command of the clipper.

Gales hit hard. She ordered all sails dropped and Neptune's Car waited bare-masted off the Horn for three days, while the restless, worried, captainless, mateless crew wondered what to do about the 19-year-old girl on the quarterdeck. The gale let up, Mary Patten raised sail and Neptune's Car made safe passage around the Horn into the Pacific.

But the ship was still thousands of miles from her destination of San Francisco. Mary Patten set her course fixedly on California. One day, First Mate Tarker got free from his cell and tried to assault Mary so he could take over the ship and change course to nearby Valparaiso. Mary Patten hit him over the head, knocked him down and unconscious with her pistol butt. Later she marched him back to the cell and padlocked the door.

For the next 50 nights Mary Brown Patten did not get out of her clothes. She ran the ship, cared for her ranting, blind, fevered husband, and steered for San Francisco. She was also visibly pregnant, even under her oil skins, and the crew knew it. But she was the only person aboard who could read and write and navigate, except for her delirious husband and the mutinous mate locked below.

Neptune's Car, commanded by Mary Patten, sailed safely into San Francisco harbor on the 136th day out of New York.

Her story made great newspaper copy across the nation. San Francisco papers raised money to send Mary and her sick husband home by steamer to the East Coast. When they arrived first in New York and then in Boston, newspapers were again eager to print details of her remarkable story.

Mary Patten was a heroine around the world. Newspapers everywhere picked up the story of her amazing voyage.

And to cap it all, on March 10, 1857, in Boston, she gave birth to a son, Joshua.

The underwriters of Neptune's Car sent her a fine letter of appreciation and esteem, enclosing a check for $1000. Some newspaper readers wrote letters to the editor pointing out to the underwriters that the ship and cargo Mary Patten had brought to safe port were worth $350,000.

Her fame faded fast. Sadness closed in. Her young husband died in the Somerville Lunatic Asylum. Mary Patten herself became ill with typhoid fever and tuberculosis and sank to poverty as she tended her baby. The ladies of Boston raised $1,399 to help her. A blind man in London who had read newspaper accounts of her exploits sent her $100. In her 24th year of life, Mary Patten died. Her four-year-old son was sent to live with his grandparents in

Rockland, Maine. Two plain gravestones in Woodlawn Cemetery near Boston stand side by side; "Mary Ann Patten, born April 6, 1837, died March 17, 1861." And "Joshua A. Patten, born April 20, 1827, died July 26, 1857."

There is no mention of Neptune's Car.

The Young America from painting by Ron Goyette.

18.

Guano:
The Foulest Cargo

Men after money dig in horrendous places to find it. Today, we dig deep under oceans for oil or seek it in empty deserts. We dig deep holes in Africa for diamonds and gold. And we go down deep and at peril into the belly of the earth for coal.

But one of the most horrendous, foul smelling places man has ever dug for money is on a group of three tiny islands in the Pacific, off the coast of Peru, called the Chinchas.

There, men dug for guano, droppings from sea birds. The stuff was piled 40 to 80 feet deep when the money-seekers began to dig and ship it out as fertilizer in 1851. And they dug and shipped for 21 years before getting to the bottom of these bird droppings.

Guano proved more valuable than gold from the California gold rush, which had fevered money-seekers two years earlier in 1849. And this money-mine of guano lasted longer too.

In the 21 years between 1851 and 1872, 10 million tons of guano with a value of almost $30 million dollars a year was shipped out from those three rocks jutting up into the Pacific. And Maine-built sailing ships carried the cargo. It was the foulest cargo ever hauled, except for slaves.

Millions of tons of guano coated these three islands as the result of an equation in nature.

First came the Humboldt current, running along the coast of Peru. The warm temperature, the salinity, the algae, the microscopic multitudes of life sustained so richly by the qualities of the Humboldt current attract more fish to feed there than in any other body of water that size in the world.

Many millions of these fish are tiny, just the right size for sea birds to feed upon. Because the fish are here for dinner, sea birds by the millions flock here to eat. After millions of sea birds have eaten millions of fish come the droppings. For reasons not known, some early birds chose to let their droppings go on the Chinchas. Then millions of like-minded birds followed suit, and the Chinchas became the lifetime toilet for excreting birds. Drop by dropping, the excrement piled up until it reached heights of 40 to 80 feet.

Then some uncredited man somehow found out that guano made good fertilizer. And fertilizer was exactly what was needed by farmers to increase crop production for growing populations in Europe and America. The guano began to find eager buyers in Holland, England, and the Atlantic states of America and elsewhere.

In 1865 2,000 shiploads of guano were taken off these tiny islands.

The sublime and the ridiculous met one day in the anchorage between the north and central islands; 200 square rigged sailing ships waiting in the broiling sun to load 2,000 tons each of bird shit.

It was a foul and odiferous cargo for ships to carry, the same ships which carried grain from California, coal from Philadelphia, ice from the Kennebec. The crews despised it. Not only was the stench sickening, but as the cargo was poured down chutes into the holds, it would send up clouds of guano dust. That dust would envelop the entire ship and those downwind. Decks, cabins, clothes, food, eyes, hands, nostrils, throats, lungs — all were coated in a film of acid, irritating, bird excrement.

Perhaps the worst job in the world fell to the poor souls mining guano, digging and moving it by the ton everyday.

A vivid description of that awful labor was given by William H. Rowe in "The Maritime History of Maine."

> "The guano was dug by Chinese coolies together with a few peons and criminals from Peru. For these unfortunates the system was one of absolute slavery, the worst and most cruel in the world. Under the blistering sun and all but naked, be he strong or weak, each must dig and wheel to the 'manqueras' or large enclosures at the edge of the cliffs, at least five tons of the dust each day."

These islands were in effect burial grounds for the coolies and prisoners sentenced to work there. Uncounted thousands died from the work which made them breathe ammonia fumes and dust, which penetrated their lungs and every orifice of their bodies.

But the export of guano was a monopoly of the Peruvian government that poured wealth into the treasury, with plenty to line the pockets of government officials on the side. Shipmasters had to buy a license in order to be able to buy a cargo of a specified amount.

After millions of tons of guano had been shipped out, year after year, the massive deposits at last grew thin. So ships began going to other guano ports and nitrate ports along the coastline of Peru. These were dangerous waters, with no protected anchorages. Tremendously strong northly gales swept down the coast of South America for thousands of miles with nothing to weaken their force until they hit the ships at anchor. Frequently these "northers" were followed by huge and destructive tidal waves.

Even worse than a "norther" and a tidal wave were the earthquakes. On the night of May 9, 1877, an earthquake catastrophe caught 13 Maine ships at anchor off the coast of Chile.

At 8:30, the earthquake shook the land. Houses ashore were tumbled. Mountains broke apart. Huge boulders were loosened and came careening down the hills, touching off mountain slides. These demolished the waterfront. Soon the towns were devastated by fire and flattened by quakes. The 13 Maine ships at anchor shook and trembled and bucked on their anchor chains from the violence. Crews rushed topside to see what was happening to the world. And were terrified by the sight of mountains falling into the sea and the towns burning.

As the quake subsided, some alert skippers could hear the warning; the noise that sounded like distant thunder but wasn't. Then with a roar, the monster was upon them, a giant tidal wave, boiling the sea, tossing ships, breaking anchor chains, carrying off masts and rigging, hurling ships like toys, careening into each other.

In a few moments which seemed to last forever, the monster wave was gone. But the night had wreaked havoc. The Geneva, part of the Houghton fleet, had been loaded with 2300 tons of cargo, ready to sail in the morning. She was totally wrecked, though Capt. Charles H. MacLoon and his crew were rescued. The Uncle Toby, almost fully loaded, was so badly smashed, she was sold. Eight more Maine ships were so severely damaged they had to spend months in the repair yards.

Cargo manifests considered as reading matter can be dull as a laundry list or as exciting as a mystery novel. I've spent hours looking over cargo manifests which came alive when I had in my mind's eye a picture of the ship and her holds where the cargo was stored, the men who sailed that ship and the people in the distant port who finally bought and used that cargo. I enjoyed poring over lists of general cargo bound from New England to San Francisco during the gold rush days, and the boom of the West. Cargoes contained linoleum (what new settlers would lay it in what new home?); printer's ink (picture of a job printing shop, running off business letterheads and bill forms for a new store in a new town?) frying pans; whiskey (visions of taverns and roughnecks, brawls and bosomy, bawdy women) and railroad iron (pictures of Chinese coolies laying track across mountain passes).

When I look at manifests of thousands of tons of ice leaving the Kennebec, I think of that Maine ice being used in sundown drinks on a plantation porch in Cuba or melting in the sun on a dock in Calcutta, where the stevedores didn't know what ice was; or a manifest for sheaves — Maine cut lumber that would become barrels for molasses from the West Indies.

But, guano?

Spread on the fields of some far distant farm, the guano helped feed mankind. But all I see are the tortured faces, the rheumy eyes, the wheezing lungs of those godforsaken coolies on those miserable rocky islands below the equator, dying as each one hauled his five tons of guano every day to the edge of the cliffs and dumped it down chutes to the holds of ships below.

At least, Maine never built guano boats.

But Maine did build ships to suit other special needs. The early ships, with their special loading transoms in the stern, for putting aboard king's masts, 120 feet tall, bound for England; the lumber ships that carried a million board feet of Bangor, when Bangor was the biggest lumber port in the world. They sailed so loaded their decks were awash and lumber was lashed knee-deep upon those decks. The ice ships of the Kennebec, the lime ships of Rockland, the wheat ships, the slave ships, the granite ships of the islands in Penobscot Bay — all were designed or remodeled to be efficient carriers of different cargoes.

The story of Maine, indeed of all nations, is written in the cargo manifests.

But, guano?

19.

Crews & Bucko Mates:
Brutality at Sea

Despite the tales, few American boys ran away to sea. When they did, most had sense enough after a few years to quit, to get ashore and stay ashore. A seaman's life was too close to hell on earth for most young Americans. Unless, of course, a youngster was smart enough to climb from the fo'c'sle to officers' quarters quickly. If through skill or good connections a young man could get command of his own vessel while still in his twenties, he stayed. But most Americans didn't. So they got off the sailing vessels, took a wife and an easier job onshore which paid more than going to sea. For the fo'c'sle sailor the money was too little, the risks were too great, brutality too common, food too awful, life too unbearable. But if they got a command in six years, they stayed and became the finest kind of captains.

Seafaring ran in the blood of Maine's coastal towns. Thomaston boasted 100 captains; Searsport claimed 77 masters in 1889. Bath, Wiscasset, Portland claimed scores apiece; they bred skippers in Rockland, Castine, Belfast, Boothbay, Bucksport and on down east to Calais and Machias. These men prospered. They built fine handsome homes ashore, when they left sea; the next step was to run fleets from home offices. Their fine homes rivaled each other in grandeur; their wives competed in wearing silks from China and India, hats from Paris. They filled their homes with inlaid tables from Rangoon and Calcutta, served teas from the Orient.

Searsport, Maine, a small coastal town, boasted 77 captains of ocean vessels in 1889; Searsport men captained 10 percent of the entire American merchant fleet.

Searsport wives often went to sea with their husbands. They conceived, bore and raised their children aboard ship. In the Nichols family alone, 35 members were born at sea or in foreign ports. Out of a list of 77 Searsport children born at sea on their fathers' ships, there is only one childbirth death recorded.

Shipowners and captains sometimes brought home to Maine the young sons of men they did business with in foreign ports. These boys became part of the family and went to local Maine schools and colleges. For example, in Wiscasset and Bath schools more than 100 years ago, there were usually a handful of foreign students, some with dark skins, some speaking only Spanish or French. These were the first "foreign exchange" students in small communities.

For the captain and his wife and family aboard ship in the days of clipper ships and Downeasters, there was gracious and exciting living.

The captain's main cabin was aft, generally a good-sized living room, finely paneled, carpeted, furnished with easy chairs, lamps, even a piano. There was a dining salon, the steward's pantry, the captain's office and chartroom, a storeroom; a sleeping cabin for the master and his wife and at least one other cabin for children. In port, all the finery, the ornate candy dishes, the family pictures were brought out. In rough weather at sea, these breakables were stowed, and the furniture was screwed down.

Pride rather than parsimony, signs of wealth rather than penny-pinching, were hallmarks of the master's quarters. This made business sense to the owners; for one way to keep a good captain at sea was to allow him to bring his wife and family and to make them comfortable and happy. From a business view also, it was important to put on "face" in foreign ports, where the captain had to entertain government officials and shipping agents. So owners frequently vied with each other in the splendor of the woodwork, the gilt inlays, the brass fixtures and elaborate furnishings of their captains' quarters.

Household chores were done by the captain's personal steward; the cooking and table-serving was done by one or two Chinese. The food was as good as possible, with fresh meats and vegetables bought at each port. Oftimes a cow and hens were kept aboard; even small vegetable gardens were grown in a sea-going version of window boxes.

If there were young children aboard, the captain's wife was

their teacher. She left her hometown in Maine with the same school books her children's classmates would be studying for that year. She was sent the same tests and examinations.

Joanna C. Colcord of Searsport has written well about her life as a child aboard her family ships. She was born aboard her father's ship in the South Seas off the coast of New Caledonia, and her brother, Lincoln, was born off Cape Horn, and sailed with his father till after his 21st birthday. Miss Colcord took her final high school exams aboard ship at Hong Kong and received her diploma six months later back in Searsport. Growing up aboard, these sea-born children quickly learned to read the weather, to know the stars, to steer by a compass and became expert in the mathematics of navigation and plotting. They picked up at least smatterings of foreign languages in their ports of call, and often from the crew.

The crews were largely foreigners. Many of them knew little about seamanship. Capt. Felix Riesenburg aboard the A.J. Fuller wrote in his book "Under Sail":

> "Mixed with our few real sailors were the worthless scrapings of the waterfront. They came aboard, shipped here by the boarding masters for the benefit of their three months 'advance' and furnished for the sea with kits of dunnage as unreliable and as unfitted for work as the poor unfortunate dubs who were forced by an unkind fate to wear them."

Riesenburg thundered about the necessity of swift, severe discipline to keep such "scrapings of the waterfront" working together as a crew.

> "Over half the crew of most sailing ships were thick skinned clodhoppers, all thumbs on a dark night and useless as so much living ballast. The kicking and moulding into form of this conglomerate mass of deep-sea flotsam called for superhuman efforts. To work a ship the size of Fuller (230 feet long) with 17 men forward, called for man driving without thought of anything but the work required . . . One who has never been

> there can hardly realize the absolute subjugation under which a crew may be placed by their officers."

This old salt captain warned:

> "Young officers are inclined to be a bit "easy" with the men, thinking it will result in more willingness . . . But men who have sailed as merchant officers many years realize that the maintenance of discipline is only possible under a rule of autocratic severity, demanding instant obedience to orders and quick punishment for the first departure from the iron bonds. This is as necessary as life itself. The least hesitation, the slightest possibility of argument, when ordering men to places of extreme danger or difficulty, would soon result in disaster."

Enter the "bully captains and the bucko mates," the belaying pin, the knuckle dusters, the spread eagle and the lash and vile ways to beat up a man in the name of discipline.

Often the safety of the ship may have required it. Sometimes, however, there were captains and mates who relished their positions of absolute power in absolute isolation and abused it to slake a desire to inflict bloody punishment without risk or retaliation. When they went too far too often the word spread, and it became harder and harder for such ships to recruit any crew. The only crew such ships could get were the scrapings from the waterfront. When almost the whole crew was made up of men like that, even the toughest bucko mate was sometimes scared for his life. If the mate or captain was scared, the ship began to look unkept and dirty; the cargo rotted; the voyages took too long; profits dropped; and the home office knew they would have to do some firing.

Sometimes, but rarely, were there mutinies. Crewmen knew that if they fought with an officer, let alone killed him, in front of witnesses, they would get no mercy when the ship finally got to port. In every port the police, judges, juries were stacked against mutiny under any circumstances. Even if a case of outright brutality got into court it was hard to prove brutal abuse months after it had occurred.

Once a law, passed in 1817, required that the crew on any

American ship had to be two-thirds American men. But soon that law had to be ignored. By the 1850s and throughout the heydays of the clipper ships and Downeasters, it was impossible to get enough Americans to work as seamen. So owners and captains gave bribes to boarding house keepers, saloon keepers, madames in whorehouses and jailers to supply the deck hands. When the bodies were delivered dockside, the ship's mate paid in cash for them. Often that cash payment was later docked from the seaman's wages, even though he'd been dragged aboard unconscious or resisting. It was a form of slavery, winked at by authorities in every port, including the United States.

The reports of shipmasters sent to their home offices accurately document how few Americans went to sea. On the Bath-built A.G. Ropes with 34 people aboard, only Capt. Rivers and his family, the mate and the sailmaker were Americans. The second mate was Swedish, the third mate Scottish, the boatswain Irish, the carpenter Danish, the cook Irish and the steward German. The rest were Haitians, Algerians, Maltese, and Orientals. Out of the 17 who were delivered aboard by agents as able bodied seamen, only four knew how to handle rigging.

When Capt. M.A. Woodside took command of the Charles E. Moody, he had only three Americans on deck; the other 15 were Japanese. When the St. Stephen put out the word to body snatchers in San Francisco in 1877 that they needed three able seamen, they got and paid for three cowboys who had never been on salt water until they woke up underway.

The best of ships sometimes had the worst of crews. The huge and handsome Downeaster, Henry B. Hyde from Bath, the ship which once made fast passage from New York to San Francisco in 88 days, needed almost an entirely new crew in New York. Almost the entire previous crew have jumped ship. So the word went out to the body-snatchers, who delivered a new crew, took the body-snatcher fee and left. Next morning the captain found he had to sail his ship with a gang of Bowery thugs.

Capt. Goodwin of the Sewall ship Dirigo left San Francisco for Honolulu and then sailed across the Pacific with two new incompetent mates on board. He wrote to his home office:

> "Each one of the mates I get is a little worse than the last. After this mate got the rum worked out of him, he was sick the remainder of the voyage from San Francisco to Honolulu. The fellow I'd shipped as second mate decided he wasn't a second mate the first day out and went into the forecastle."

Aboard the famous Sewall ships, there was forever crew trouble. Wrote Capt. Richard Quirk, commanding the Edward Sewall:

> "I left Honolulu with six Puerto Ricans that never saw a ship except laying at a dock and six beachcombers that were born tired." The first night at sea Capt. Quirk found out that in a crew of 20 "only two knew what a wheel was, and they steered very poor."

From Rio de Janiero, Capt. Joe Sewall wrote:

> "I have now got a mate, but he is a drunken son of a gun. I dare not leave this ship to conduct urgent business ashore."

Letter after letter from the captains to their home offices, contained complaints about the crew. Matters got even worse for Capt. Goodwin of the Dirigo, who reported:

> "I've got my troubles piled deeper with drunken mates and sailors. The mate has not been sober for two weeks. I will make every effort to get this ship to Honolulu and then it is back to the Maine woods for me. I am about worn out."

His colleague, Capt. Quirk aboard the Edward Sewall, was having his trouble trying to round the Horn and being blown off by storms for 67 days in succession.

> "A sea carried the second mate overboard to his death; hurt the first mate so badly he was abed four weeks and then went insane. Then one of the seamen went mad; and another died; and several broke their legs."

Capt. Joe Sewall wrote his home office that:

> "For 27 years the ships of A. Sewall have put to sea with garbage as crews. I advise you to give it all up and sell the whole fleet. Your ships are not safe at sea with the cattle manning them."

A sailor's pay was less than a dollar a day. Most were bad at dangerous jobs which they had never done before and never wanted to do again. Mates brutalized them to make them work, to get the ship safely to port. Beyond enduring all these afflictions, crews often had to make the hated run to fetch a cargo of stinking guano.

Somehow — maybe due to the drive and brutality of bucko mates — those American ships, mostly manned by waterfront dregs, became the pride of the oceans.

Capt. Joseph Sewall (1854-1925), brilliant seaman, dandy and sometimes called "The Monster." He commanded various Sewall ships with such brutality that the Red Record, the newspaper of the National Seaman's Union, stated "Captain Sewall is one of the most notorious brutes in charge of an American ship."

The Saco River

Canoeing on the Saco; sometimes 600 on a summer day.

20.

First Court in Maine: 1636

The Guilty & the Gutsy

Sinners and villains were named in the court news 347 years ago in Saco. We know them and their judges, thanks to court records preserved since the first legally constituted court in Maine met in Saco on March 28, 1636.

At 7 a.m. on that March morning, the early settlers were summoned to meet at the home of Richard Bonython to see justice done. The assembly opened with a roll on the drums to announce the first court was in session and to create the atmosphere of serious business and severe punishments ahead.

That first district court fined four rowdies five shillings each for drunkenness and ordered George Cleeves to pay a fine of five shillings for "rash speeches." The judges ordered one man placed in the stocks for talking back to the bench in unseemly language. Thomas Cloyse was fined for playing cards. Jeremiah Gutteridge got a judicial tongue-lashing for being an "idle person and not providing for his family."

By 1640 Saco had risen so high on the judicial ladder and was so respected as a flourishing and old settlement, that Saco was named the seat of government. William Gorges, nephew of the founding father of Maine, Sir Ferdinando Gorges, was sent out from London to be governor.

On June 25, 1640 the first General Court met in Saco to pass justice on eighteen civil actions and eight complaints. Richard Vines, early settler in Casco Bay, was one of the four men sitting in judgment; Richard Bonython was another judge. His son would soon be hauled before the court in deep trouble. Those cases and sentences put gusto into the dry, brief records of life in Saco almost three and a half centuries ago. John Lander was fined two shillings for swearing two oaths; Ivory Puddington was fined for being drunk at Mrs. Tynn's; John Smith, an indentured servant, was sentenced to be whipped in public for running away from his master, John Alcot; two other men had to pay a whopping fine of 20 shillings "for carrying bords on the Sabbath."

The trial which made the biggest news was that of George Burdet, held at the September session of the Saco court. The deputy governor, Thomas Gorges, was principal judge for this trial, flanked by Vines and three others. A jury was sworn in to hear the case against the well-known Burdet.

Burdet had arrived in the New World in 1634, declaring himself a clergyman and settled first in Salem. He preached there for a year or two, delivering fine and learned sermons. Within two years he moved to New Hampshire, and so impressed the settlers there with his silver tongue, his good manners and his scholarship, that he quickly supplanted Governor Thomas Wiggin, and took the office himself.

But Burdet was a double-dealer. He had secretly sent letters to Archbishop Laud, a member of the Privy Council in England who was later beheaded. In those letters, the Rev. Burdet accused his fellow colonists of disloyalties to the Crown and the Church. A copy of one such letter was found, and Burdet was run out of New Hampshire. He fled to Agamenticus, near Saco. There, Burdet broke into the unoccupied house of the lord proprietor and stole all its contents, leaving nothing "but an old pot, a pair of tongs and two cob-irons."

In court, the silver-tongue Burdet managed to persuade Judge Vines and two other judges that he was innocent; but he cut no ice with Deputy Governor Gorges, the principal judge.

As his trial went along, Burdet was accused of adultery with Ruth, the wife of John Gouch and daughter of Judge Richard Bonython. He was found guilty of "lewdness, drunkenness and slanderous speeches" and of other breaches of the peace.

Adultery was the worst of his crimes. He was fined 30 pounds for this offense, and 5 pounds for the others. All his property was seized; and he soon fled, sputtering mad, to England.

His partner in adultery, the unhappy Ruth, was also sentenced: "Six weeks after her expected confinement, she shall stand in a white sheet, publicly before the congregation at Agamenticus, two several Sabbath days, and likewise one other day in the General Court."

Judge Bonython came to the rescue and bailed his erring daughter out of her white-sheet appearances by payment of thirty-five pounds.

But no sooner was his daughter out of court than Judge Richard Bonython's son John was dragged before the court for stealing a pig and "dandering the minister's wife."

The court also held an inquest into the death of Mary Haile; and the jury agreed that Mary "was an accessory to her own death with much over eating and drinking."

The same court took action against wolves:

> "In regard of the great Damage the inhabitants of this Province do sustain thro' the loss of their cattle by the devouring wolves, this court decrees that from henceforth if anyone shall kill any wolf between Pascattaqua and Kennebunk . . the parties so killing them shall have twelve pence for every wolf so killed from every family within those limits."

The story of the Saco River and the first white men on it goes back to April 10, 1603. On that day, just a few days after the death of Queen Elizabeth, Martin Pring sailed from England with 30 men and boys aboard Speedwell, a vessel of 50 tons, and with 13 men and a boy aboard Discovery, only 26 tons. After exploring Penobscot Bay, Pring sailed into Saco Bay and explored five miles up the Saco River. He wrote that he was not impressed, and quickly left.

Two years later De Monts and his cartographer Samuel de Champlain sailed into the Saco River, drew accurate maps and wrote detailed descriptions; then they, too, left. For the next 10 years nobody left any record of traveling into the Saco.

Then in 1616 came Richard Vines, sent by the persistent Sir Ferdinando Gorges in a last try to establish a colony in Maine. Vines and his crew spent the winter of 1616-17 at the mouth of the Saco. He called the spot Winter Harbor, which today is known as Biddeford Pool.

This was the winter of pestilence. The Indians in Maine were decimated by a plague of smallpox or yellow fever. It was said that whole tribes were wiped out. Hubbard, in his "History of New England," wrote that "the disease was very loathsome . . . and that many of the dead were left unburied with a multitude of carcasses found up and down the country." Years later their bones, bleaching white, were found by the English near former Indian villages.

Yet Vines and his men miraculously escaped this plague. They returned home to England, the first on record to report that white men could survive, even enjoy, living through a winter in Maine. It was this report from Vines, based on his winter at Biddeford Pool, which encouraged more English expeditions to sail to New England.

Christopher Levett, who became the first island settler in Casco Bay, sailed into the Saco River in 1623. He wrote a lengthy and favorable description, although he was rained out of his wigwam on his first night ashore.

> "In this place Sawco, there is a world of good fowl, much good timber and a great quantity of clear ground and good, if it be not too sandy. There have been more fish taken within two leagues of this place this year than any other in the land."

By 1623, Richard Vines was back, living at the mouth of the Saco again. About the same time John Oldham joined him. Together with their households and followers they established a permanent settlement near Biddeford Pool. By 1630, Vines and Oldham received title from the Plymouth Council to a big tract of land on the south side of the Saco River, four miles wide along the shore and eight miles deep inland; Thomas Lewis and Richard Bonython received title to an equal area on the opposite side of the river.

These grants are in the archives of the Maine Historical Society in Portland. The deeds required that the new owners transport 50 persons to their respective tracts within seven years to "plant and inhabit there to the advancement of the general strength and safety." These deeds show that the kings of England were still cherishing hope that gold and silver mines might be discovered in Maine, for they "reserved one fifth of the gold and silver ore ever discovered to our Sovereign Lord, the King."

Apparently an effort was made to bring in those 50 persons. For the "booke of rates for the minister" in 1636 listed 37 men as heads of families. Each of the families seems to have been given 100 acres of land.

According to a contemporary writer, John Jocelyn, these early settlers on the Saco lived and ate well. "They had a custom of sitting long at meals, sometimes four times a day. They feed generally upon as good flesh of beef, pork, mutton, fowl and fish as any in the world," wrote Jocelyn.

Richard Vines, the true father of the Saco River settlements, sold his lands to Robert Childs in October 1645 and soon thereafter Vines left Maine in a huff and returned to England. He did not stay in England long, but sailed off to start yet another new life in Barbados. Vines had first come to Maine on a voyage for Sir Ferdinando Gorges in 1609; returned in 1616 with 32 men and wintered over at the mouth of the Saco at what is now Biddeford Pool; returned to establish a colony in 1623.

For 30 years Vines had lived and prospered beside the Saco, and held offices from judge to deputy governor. But when the governor general and the commissioners of the American Plantations ruled in March 1646 that Col. Alexander Rigby, of Gray's Inn, London, and not Sir Ferdinando Gorges was the true proprietor and president of the province, Vines decided it was time to leave. Gorges, his friend and patron for over 40 years, had fallen from favor in London, after being accused of profiteering and mismanagement by the House of Commons. When the title dispute between Gorges and Rigby was heard in court at Saco in 1645, no communication was received from Gorges. Title was granted to Rigby. And Rigby's agent in Maine was George Cleaves, a man Vines distrusted and disliked. Then Vines got the news that his patron, Gorges, had died in England. So Vines felt that his star was falling. Vines sold his estates to Childs and left Maine. With his departure, the thread of continuity was broken. Gorges, the father of Maine, and Vines, his trusted man in Maine for 30 years, were out of the picture. Gorges' old rival, Cleaves, exulting that he had the field to himself, ruled the roost. He became deputy president and chief magistrate of the province until his patron in England, Col. Alexander Rigby, died in 1650.

Here in Saco was a microcosm of the way changing political fortunes in faraway England disrupted life and property rights in the American colonies. With Gorges dead and with his family's claim to Maine weakened because the king who had granted it was no longer on the throne, the Puritans in Massachusetts decided the time was ripe for them to extend their control over Maine. Cleaves became their man in Maine politics and used his influence to sway local opinion to favor closer ties to Massachusetts and the protection that it might bring.

When the Massachusetts men had all their ducks in a row, a

court was convened at Wells on July 5, 1653, and the leading citizens of Saco were summoned to attend. There it was proposed to the assembly that Saco inhabitants acknowledge themselves in open court to be subject to the government of Massachusetts. When the vote was taken, the majority was in favor. Then and there they took a freeman's oath of loyalty to Massachusetts. But there was an opposition group from Saco led by the firebrand and oddball, John Bonython. He was so caustic and vitriolic in his denunciations that he was declared "a rebel or common enemy" and a reward of twenty pounds was offered for his capture, dead or alive. Cowed by that threat, Bonython swallowed his pride and took the oath of allegiance; he was then recognized as a citizen in good standing.

Most Saco citizens, like others in Maine, wanted only to be left in peace, to make a living and enjoy their lives and families. Most did not give a hoot who was in control in London or Boston, so long as they were not bothered. Economics came before politics and religion. So to keep on the right side of Oliver Cromwell, who had deposed the king in England's civil war, 71 influential citizens in Saco, Wells, York and Kittery signed a petition dated 1656 to Cromwell asking that their towns continue under the protection of Massachusetts.

All went well between these Maine towns and Massachusetts while Oliver Cromwell was lord protector in England. But when King Charles II overthrew Cromwell's regime and regained the throne, young Ferdinando Gorges, a stout loyalist like his dead father, Sir Ferdinando, petitioned King Charles to reestablish the Gorges claim to much of Maine. The king did. He believed it was in the throne's self-interest to keep the American colonies at loggerheads with each other and to discourage them from unity among themselves. But young Gorges turned out to be far more interested in money than in Maine. In 1678 he sold Maine to Massachusetts for 1250 pounds.

Through similar plots, counterplots and political manipulation, Kittery had become the first Maine town to take an oath of allegiance to Massachusetts. All Kittery inhabitants had been summoned to a court held in Kittery November 15, 1652 at the home of William Everett. After four days of debate, often vituperative, 41 Kittery inhabitants signed papers acknowledging they were subjects of Massachusetts jurisdiction.

The court moved on to Agamenticus and again after some vigorous protest, this town submitted to Massachusetts. Under the name of York, it became the second town in Maine. And then it was the turn of Wells and Cape Porpoise; they became the third and fifth towns in Maine to accept Massachusetts rule.

The boundaries of Massachusetts now reached to Casco Bay. When the General Court met in Boston in 1653 Maine was represented on the court for the first time. John Wincoln of Kittery and Edward Rishworth of York were Maine's representatives.

Saco, which had been the preeminent center and the first town to hold a legal court in Maine, dropped down the ladder of prestige.

Over 160 years later, voters of Saco would get their revenge upon Massachusetts. They voted overwhelmingly for separation of Maine from Massachusetts. Saco became a leader in the drive for separation. In early January, 1816, Saco citizens, including three Cleaves, signed a petition to the Saco selectmen asking that a special town meeting be held "to see if the town will petition the legislature of Massachusetts to . . . make Maine a separate state."

The special meeting was held May 20, 1816, and the vote was 220 for separation and 7 against.

Subsequently, Massachusetts agreed that a vote on the question of separation should be put to all towns on the first Monday of September 1816. If the majority favored separation by a margin of five to four, then a state convention should meet and draw up a state constitution for an independent Maine.

At the September town meeting, Saco voted 215 in favor of separation and 16 against, and named William Moody, William P. Preble and Benjamin Pike as delegates to the state convention.

The convention met in Brunswick, with 188 delegates present. By no means all favored independence. Some shenanigans were played with the ballots.

For example, Eliot, a town near Saco, was dead set against separation. At its town meeting only 20 had voted for separation and 122 had voted against it. But Eliot did not send its own delegate to the Brunswick convention, entrusting its ballots instead "to the care of a gentleman from a neighboring town," with the request they be counted with the rest.

When the ballots were being opened and counted at Brunswick, and the issue seemed in doubt, that "prominent gentleman" decided to throw the Eliot ballots out the window. The Eliot votes were never found and never counted.

Had they been counted, the day might well have been lost for the separationists. For when the ballots were counted, the popular vote was 11,927 for separation and 10,539 against. There were 554 votes less than the 12,481 needed for the required five-to-four majority.

A committee was formed to decide what to do; and on that committee sat Judge William Preble, one of the Saco delegates. They cooked up the scheme whereby the decision would be based on a convoluted formula which gave the narrow edge to separation. The committee of the convention reported 103 delegates in favor and 84 against separation.

More votes were still to be held. At a town meeting in July 1819, Saco citizens voted an overwhelming 325 to 16 in favor of separation. At the constitutional convention in Portland in December of 1819, Saco voted unanimously in favor of accepting the proposed constitution; and Maine was admitted to the Union by Congress on March 4, 1820. Saco's revenge on Massachusetts was fulfilled.

21.

First Lottery in Maine: 1758
Money for Saco Bridge

In 1973, Maine politicians, editorial writers and citizens jumped on their soap boxes to argue whether or not the state should run a gambling game — the Maine State Lottery. From the uproar, you'd think this was the first time legalized gambling had been broached in Maine. Not so.

Saco pioneered legal gambling in 1758, and such prominent citizens as Sir William Pepperrell were involved in it. And, of course, it was all in a worthy cause.

On January 11, 1758, an act was passed in General Court: "An Act for raising the sum of one thousand two hundred pounds for the building and maintaining of a bridge over Saco and Presumpscot rivers." The preamble stated:

> "Whereas the eastern part of said county of York has been formerly broke up by the enemy, and the getting of troops to their relief is extremely difficult, if not impracticable, in some seasons of the year there being no passing in boats or any other way over the rivers of Saco and Presumpscot, and the building of such a bridge will be in the public interest . . .
>
> "Be it therefore enacted by the Governor, Council and House of Representatives . . . that Sir William Pepperrell, Baronet, and Daniel Moulton, Edward Milliken, Joseph Sayer and Rushworth Jordan, Esqrs., Messrs. Benjamin Chadborn and Stephen Longfellow . . . are empowered to set up and carry on a lottery or lotteries,

> which shall amount to such a sum as, by deducting ten percent out of each prize, will raise the sum of one thousand, two hundred pounds, to be applied . . . towards building and maintaining a good and sufficient bridge over each of said Saco and Presumpscot rivers . . ."

The lottery was promoted through advertisements which announced the first grand drawing would occur at York in May, 1759.

Price of lottery tickets was set at $2, and the grand prize was $1,000.

The lottery went on over three years, one drawing following another, until the 1200 pounds needed to build the bridge had been raised. The bridge over the Saco was built in 1760, the first bridge over any part of the river.

For 106 years before the bridge, people crossed the Saco by licensed ferry. The first ferrymen licensed by town vote in 1654 were Thomas Haile, on the west bank, and Henry Warwick, on the east bank. The record of the time reads:

> "Thomas Haile is allowed to take of every one he setts over ye river 2 pence. Henry Warwick is appointed to keep a public house and receive of every one he setts across ye river 2 pence."

Henry Warwick had come to Saco as one of the first settlers. He is listed as one of the 22 residents of Saco in the "booke of rates for the minister," dated September, 1636. He died still in harness as ferryman and innkeeper in 1673.

That was the year Thomas Haile, his partner, was ordered "for the more secure transportation of travellers, to provide a good sufficient boat for carrying persons and their horses, large enough to carry over three horses at one time."

If people had been nervous about Haile's boat until he was ordered to get a bigger and better one, they stayed nervous about crossing over with his son years later.

In 1717, local citizens presented a petition to the General Court, stating that the water was too rough for comfort, and that the ferryman was too negligent for safety. They asked that a new ferry be put into operation higher up the river "where H. Scammon then dwelt, whose father for many years had kept the ferry till, in the late war, he had been driven away by Indians." The request was granted.

The Sir William Pepperrell who had a baronet's finger in the Saco Lottery pie, is the only native baronet York county can claim. He was also the first equivalent to a millionaire.

He was the son of William Pepperrell Sr., a trader at nearby Kittery. He began buying land at Saco in 1717, when the devastated town was recovering from the second Indian War. First property he bought was the ruined sawmill, burned down by Indians. From that beginning young Pepperrell went on to buy more and more prime land along what was to be Saco's main street. He was only 20 years old at the time. He afterward achieved fame, glory and his baronetcy by being commander of the army which captured Louisburg, Nova Scotia, from the French in 1745. By the time Sir William died, July 6, 1759, his Saco estates alone amounted to over 5,000 acres and, with his other vast holdings, he died probably the wealthiest man in New England. But he died without a son to carry on his name. So he left his huge estate to his grandson, William Pepperrell Sparhawk, on condition that when the boy came of age he would drop his last name and be known as William Pepperrell.

Sir William was by no means universally liked in Saco. Records show he sometimes came to town dressed in a bright red broadcloth coat trimmed with lace, and in church would throw a gold coin into the collection — if enough people could see his generosity. Yet he was admired by most, particularly for the money and jobs he brought to Saco.

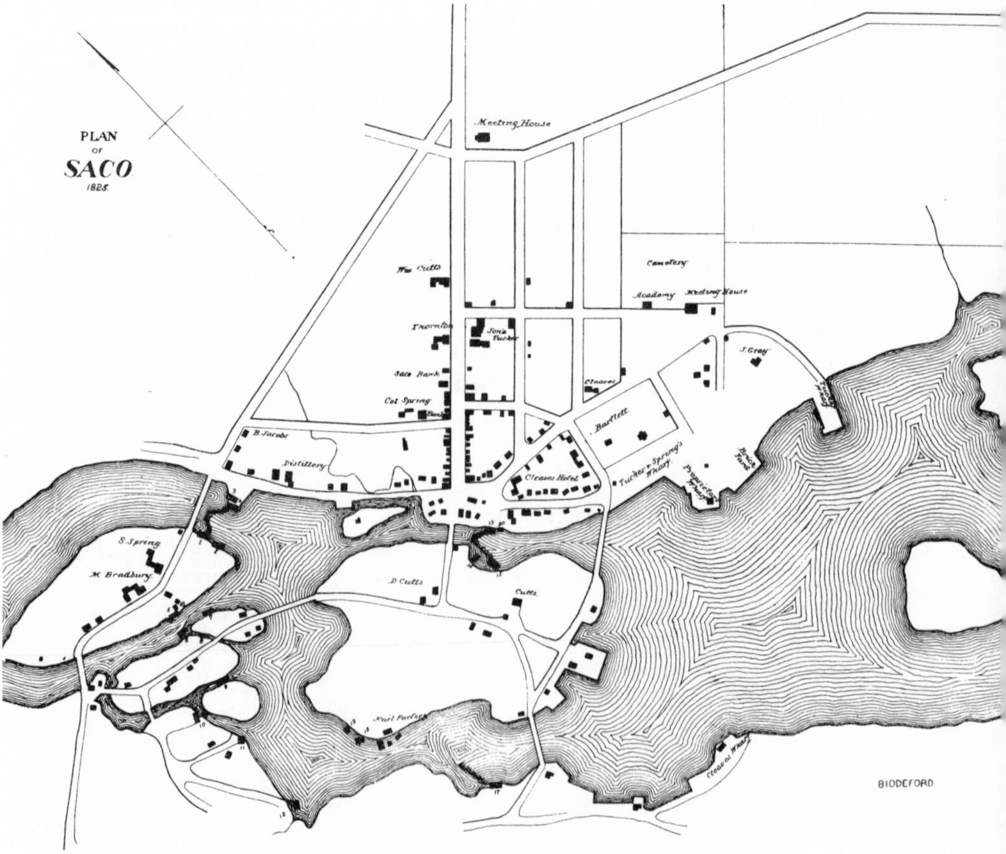

Plan of Saco 1825 (York Institute Museum)

22.

Saco Changes its Name: 1718-1805

Biddeford & Pepperrellboro

For 42 years Saco lost its name and was called Pepperrellboro. This was an ungainly name no one liked, but it clung from 1762 until an act by the Legislature in 1805 gave back the town its rightful name of Saco.

There were several name changes and they happened this way.

After the devastation to Saco by Indians, the townspeople met in 1718, coming from the settlements on both sides of the river; and they voted to change the name from Saco to Biddeford. So Saco became Biddeford from 1718 to 1762. That was the first name change.

During those years, both towns grew on their opposite sides of the river. As the towns grew, town affairs grew complex. It took too much time for selectmen, town clerk, tithingmen, sheep-markers, lumber surveyors, fenceviewers, field drivers, hog reeves and other officials to get back and forth. Two sets of officers were needed, placing an extra cost on taxpayers. But the worst crunch came over church.

In the town meeting of March 1752, the majority voted to build a new meeting house on the Biddeford side of the Saco River. Residents on the opposite or Saco bank dissented and lost. So the next year they had themselves set off as a separate parish. That was fine, but they were then a parish without a meeting house. The building of their own meeting house became the goal and magnet of Saco residents. They went to the rich Sir William Pepperrell, hoping he might give a parcel of land out of the 5500 acres he owned. He agreed to sell but not to give two acres, and accepted the purchase money. Then, when he signed that deed, Sir William generously donated four acres, which became designated on early plans as "Parsonage Land."

The new Saco meeting house was completed about 1754, a plain wooden building without a spire. Yet by 1826 it stood in dilapidated condition, a source of terror to small boys who peered in through its weatherbeaten sides to see the curious pulpit, 10 feet above the floor which was reached by winding stairs painted white. As the church fell to pieces, it became firewood for the poor.

Biddeford, on the other shore, boasted a church big enough to seat almost 1,000 people; two stories high, with galleries and a sounding board. It was torn down in the 1840s, and a house was built from its timbers. But the Biddeford church never got the chandelier sent to it from the town of Biddeford, England. That chandelier somehow got detained in Boston, when it was taken off the ship. It is said that it hung in the Old South Church in Boston.

This split of the single parish into two, one parish on the Biddeford bank and another on the Saco bank, led to the split between the two towns. On June 8, 1762, the General Court passed an act establishing the town of Pepperrellboro. Só again Saco lost its name, in the second name change.

The name Pepperrellboro, beside being clumsy, became politically obnoxious when the spirit of revolution and independence flamed. Sir William Pepperrell had received his baronetcy from the English crown; and his grandson and inheritor was beholden to England's king and openly a loyalist. At a convention in November 1774, the delegates from Pepperrellboro passed the following resolve:

> "Whereas William Pepperrell, Baronet, in his lifetime honestly acquired a large estate . . . and whereas his inheritor William hath with purpose to carry into effect acts of the British Parliament made with design to enslave the free and loyal people of this continent, accepted and now holds a seat at the pretended Board of Councillors in this Province, and therefore forfeited confidence, it is recommended to the people and his lessees to withdraw all connexion, commerce and dealings with him, and to take no leases from his farms or mills; and if anybody does deal with him, we recom-

mend the people have no dealings or intercourse with such an one."

Saco (or Pepperrellboro) sent more than its share of men to fight in the Revolutionary War. The townspeople did their part, drilling in militias and raising money. At a Town Meeting July 12, 1781, it was "Voted to Raise by a Tax 130 pounds in hard money or Equivalent in Paper to Purchase the Town's quota of beef for ye Continental Army."

But the only recorded encounter with the English enemy in the Saco River was a David-and-Goliath skirmish at Cape Porpoise. On August 8, 1782, in sailed an English brig of 18 guns and an English schooner of 10 guns. They captured an unarmed schooner and sloop belonging to a man named Newbury.

This so enraged native Samuel Wildes, who was partially deranged, that he jumped singlehanded into a canoe, paddled out to the enemy vessels, and ordered them to surrender to him. The British mocked their solitary foe and, stung by his insults, ordered him aboard the brig. Wildes refused to obey. They opened fire on the defenseless man, wounding him.

His fellow townsmen had seen the brutality and went to the rescue. They crossed to Goat Island, close by the brig, with their muskets at the ready. The brig sent a boatload of armed sailors to capture them. As the English came close, the Saco River boys let loose with their well-aimed muskets and killed 17 English in the boat, with the loss of one American. The English brig fled.

On the dock at Cape Porpoise almost 200 years later, I talked with a Wildes who is a direct descendant of the Samuel Wildes who singlehandedly took on the 28 guns of two English ships in the same harbor.

Col. Thomas Cutts (1736-1821)

Elizabeth Scammon Cutts, his wife (1766-1854)

These portraits were painted by John Brewster (1766-1854), a Maine itinerant painter who was a deaf mute. About a dozen Brewster portraits are now in the York Museum at Saco. Brewster primitives are in high demand today, at prices exceeding $50,000. (Courtesy York Institute Museum and Dyer Library, Saco)

23.

The Money-Maker: 1756-1829

Thomas Cutts

Thomas Cutts and William Pepperrell, Jr. were the first men in Saco to make very big money and die millionaires by today's standards. But neither was a self-made man. Their fathers and grandfathers had done the donkey-work.

The Cutts' fortune began in a very small way 338 years ago when three Cutts brothers, Robert, John and Richard, decided to get out of Wales and go to the New World. In 1645 they landed on the Isles of Shoals on the Maine-New Hampshire border. But soon Robert sailed off again, first to Barbados, then to Great Island in New Hampshire and lastly to Kittery Point, where he started his very successful shipyard. His two brothers, John and Richard, apparently just as ambitious, soon moved from the Isles of Shoals to the mainland at Portsmouth, where both became wealthy and powerful.

By the time Robert Cutts died in 1672, he had prospered and served as a king's commissioner. He left a big estate to his son, Richard. Richard's son, named Robert after his grandfather, represented Kittery at the General Court for seven years and thereafter was elected a member of the General Council for eight years. It was his son, Thomas, born with a silver spoon in his mouth and a well-respected name on his head, who struck it rich in Saco.

Thomas Cutts arrived in Saco — or Biddeford as it was called then — in 1758, with $100, loaned him by his father, Richard Cutts of Cutts' Island, Kittery.

The town he came to was small, fewer than 500 people on the

Saco side and about 600 people living across the river in Biddeford. It was a frontier town which offered a bounty of 30 shillings on wolves and 15 shillings on whelps killed inside the town boundaries. Salmon filled the river. Indian Island, in midstream, was an unused oak forest where Indians gathered in fishing season.

Cutts bought Indian Island for its central location, paying $2000 for its 40 acres. He linked it to the mainland. Soon he was into shipbuilding (learned from his family yards at Kittery) and was buying and selling cargoes. He made his first financial killing on a big shipment of molasses which arrived just as the Revolutionary War began; he is said to have made $100,000 on that one cargo.

Inflation skyrocketed prices during the war. Wood sold for $300 a cord (and Cutts had lumber); tea sold for $19 a pound (and Cutts' ships brought in tea) and laborers who had earned $1 a day before the war were paid $30 a day. Cutts found himself in a boom town. Population jumped from under 500 when he arrived to almost 1850 people within 20 years. After the war, lumber boomed; 17 sawmills were operating by 1800.

But Thomas Cutts (by now he had the rank of colonel) was already rich. In 1782 he moved his wife and eight children to the huge three-story house which he had been building for five years atop the highest ground on his Indian Island. He had built it to outshine the mansions the Pepperrells and Sparhawks had built at Kittery to show their wealth to the world. His Indian Island was transformed into an array of wharves and factories. From his home he could keep one eye on them, while his other eye watched the harbor, where two dozen of his ships waited to load or unload cargo. He sent his girls off to finishing schools and his sons away to college. Son Richard graduated from Harvard, was elected congressman from Saco, then stayed on in Washington in the executive branch of government, serving under Presidents Madison, Monroe and Adams. The colonel had matters so much under his personal control that Indian Island became known as Cutts' Island, and the post office was moved to it from Biddeford in 1802. Cutts by 1803 was the biggest shareholder in the local bank. By 1811 he was into still another business, an iron works on Cutts' Island which was turning out 3,500 nails a day by 1830, and making noise enough to deafen the dead.

Cutts' wife impressed the local citizens by riding in a spanking carriage, behind coachman and footman. She wore a black silk coat lined with white silk, straight from Paris. Cutts' son-in-law, a prominent doctor, merchant, Republican and scholar, was such a close friend of the Jefferson administration that he was named marshal of Maine in 1813. When President Monroe toured New England in 1817, Cutts arranged for the president to come to town, and greeted him. When the new church was built, with a spire 126 feet high, Cutts was the man who presented a bell for its belfry, made by Paul Revere.

In 1821 Colonel Thomas Cutts died. The island he had bought for $2000 and which had been only a campground for Indians out fishing, now included two sawmills, a huge iron works, a grist mill, the Cutts' mansion. He owned vast land holdings in Biddeford, Hollis and Buxton. He owned a fleet of ships, most of the York bank, timberlands upriver and ten shares in the Saco Boom, which managed the log drives.

A few years later his son, Dominicus Cutts, was to offer the entire empire for sale.

Dams at Biddeford-Saco. Here's the gentle dam from long ago.

And here is the modern dam of today.

24.

The Textile Mills: 1830-1930

Big Business & Water Power

On April 18, 1825, Cutts' Island was sold at auction to Boston businessmen. When the hammer banged, control of this industrial hub left Maine and went to Massachusetts. In came textiles.

The Boston-owned Saco Manufacturing Co. soon built a vast factory and Cutts' Island became Factory Island. The first big building to go up was a cotton mill seven stories high, 210 feet long, big enough to contain 12,000 spindles and 300 looms, and employ 500 people.

No sooner was it operating well, than it went up in smoke. Fire broke out on a Sunday in February 1829 and burned the new plant to the ground, though everyone came to put out the blaze. Even women rushed from churches in mid-service to lift the skirts of their Sunday best and pass the buckets. Burned with the mill were the iron works and other buildings. Gone were the jobs, and 700 people left town.

The new owners of Cutts' Island sold out the ashes; and the buyer was a group of 18 Boston men who issued $300,000 worth of stock to form the York Manufacturing Co. This time the cotton mill was made of fire-resistant brick. The first mill, 210 feet by 46 feet, began turning out products by July 1832, and doing it at such a handsome profit that the directors declared a 20 percent stock dividend within a year and voted to build a second mill.

By 1840, 200 men and 1000 girls and women had jobs. There were three mills, machine shops, dye houses and counting houses, Mountains of textiles were piled on the wharves.

Boss of the operation was Samuel Batchelder, a textile man from Lowell, Mass., who would dominate the textiles industry in Maine for 50 years to come. He would also change the social structure; for he believed in hiring farm girls from upriver to work 12 hours or more a day at his spindles and looms.

The farm girls swarmed by the hundreds into town. But it was Batchelder's policy to be a father to them all. He demanded that they live in approved company boarding houses and live and sleep by the company clock and adhere strictly to the company rules, day and night. He kept them under a strict "moral check," but paid them only 50 cents a day. They had to eat meals supplied by the company, the price of which was deducted from their wages. They might end the week with only $1.50 or $2.00 in cash; but cash was something new, something they never earned doing farm chores at home. So the farm girls came to fill every job offered.

Yet the girls were not chattels. When Batchelder, their paternalistic boss, posted a particular notice they disliked, the girls shocked the world of 1841 by going on strike.

The notice that blew their fuses read:

> "Every person in the employ of the York Company, male or female, except those boarding with their parents, will be expected to board in one of the regular Boarding Houses of the Company, and those who do not comply will be discharged."

The angry women hired the town band and more than 330 of them marched behind it through town to a mass protest meeting at the Baptist church. They carried banners reading: "We scorn to be slaves."

In their protest meeting, the women passed seven resolutions including one which told Batchelder they would cooperate "in preserving purity or morals," but would do it their own way, without being compelled to live, eat and sleep in company boarding houses.

The town and the company were shocked. No strike like this one had been seen before. And it was not approved. "No grievance could justify proceedings so incompatible with the retiring delicacy of the female character," wrote one observer.

But when the marching was over, the women went back to work on company terms. Wages for women stayed about 50 cents a day, for days which lasted 13 hours. Even children under 13 years old worked 10 hours a day in the mills until the 1850s.

Saco and Biddeford fast became boom towns. Because of the new cotton mills, Saco's population doubled and Biddeford's quadrupled between 1830 and 1860. The mill owners used all their political muscle to keep down their property valuations, but even so, valuation in Saco jumped from less than $1 million in 1840 to $3 million by 1860. Across the river, Biddeford's rose faster still, from $323,000 to $4.6 million in just 20 years, as the Laconia and Pepperell mills came to dominate the town. Town governments could not cope; streets were quagmires of mud from the incessant horse and wagon traffic; the sewage overflowed and stank; fires destroyed the Thornton House Tavern, then the Tufts Hotel and flattened half of Pepperell Square and destroyed most of the stores on Factory Island. But not till 1862 did the town vote to buy its first steam fire engine.

Street crime terrorized women workers as they walked home from the mills after dark. The covered bridge from Factory Island was a hangout for muggers and prostitutes, and they used it as their toilet until the stench was so strong that local newspapers called it an Augean stable. To defend themselves while crossing it, girls from Factory Island went in groups, armed with hatpins and cayenne pepper. Newspaper advertisements run by the operator of a public bath called Hygia, urged young ladies to stay healthy by washing more often. Hygia offered hot baths for 25 cents and cold baths for 12 cents. Garbage filled the streets, yet no epidemic of smallpox broke out as feared, largely because Batchelder insisted that every worker in his mills be vaccinated.

After 50 years of expanding the mills, Batchelder retired in 1880 to be replaced by Franklin Nourse, a hard-nosed, cost-cutting boss. Working conditions in the mills were ghastly, partly because of the noise from 35,000 spindles shuttling at high speed, but mostly because of the lint which permeated the air and stuck in eyes, nose, throats of the women. New girls tried chewing gum to keep their throats moist. But soon they switched to "rush kits" for self-protection. They smeared their gums with snuff, which at first made them deathly sick, but eventually worked to keep them from swallowing and near choking on the lint. The men chewed tobacco; the women chewed snuff.

Pay was still low, only 75 cents to $1.50 a day by the 1870s, and the mills were still filled with hundreds of child laborers. Labor unions tried to organize the workers, but the specter of losing their jobs was worse than low pay. When the Maine farm girls showed signs of unrest, Scotch girls, experienced at millwork in Britain, were brought across the Atlantic. By the 1890s, French girls from Quebec were pouring into town, willing to work under any conditions at any wage. When the cotton market boomed, production in Saco and Biddeford soared. When the market softened, workers were laid off without notice. Sometimes entire mills were shut to keep down overhead and keep up profits.

Nourse, the mill boss, left Maine to take a bigger job as mill superintendent in Lowell, and in 1895 a 34-year-old cost-cutting whirlwind named Elmer Page from Norwich, Connecticut, was sent to the mills on the Saco river. He promptly cut wages 10 to 40 percent and increased working hours. Page preached that $1 a day was wage enough for any man and that 70 cents a day was more than enough for any woman.

This was ripe ground for union growth. Hundreds joined the Textile Union, and Page immediately fired the union leaders. Workers walked out. The walkout was answered by the mill owners with a lockout. Page was hung in effigy. In the winter of 1897, Biddeford and Saco mills went on strike. First the weavers, then the beamers, finally the spinners walked off, protesting deeper wage cuts. Thousands from the Laconia and Pepperell mills on the Biddeford side joined 1500 workers from the Saco side, and for three months the strikers took to the streets. After they wrung agreement that wages on the Saco would stay in step with mill wages in the rest of New England, the workers went back and production and jobs boomed again briefly.

By this time, the mill owners had the local governments of Biddeford and Saco by the throat. They demanded that their property taxes be lowered, threatening to move their plants to southern states if they did not get tax cuts, a threat they were to use time and again in the years ahead. Biddeford granted tax cuts to Pepperell and Laconia, and soon Saco followed by giving abatements to York Manufacturing. Mill boss Page, whose original salary of $9,000 had been increasing handsomely year after year, was now earning $14,000, a very big sum then. He bought shares in the company whenever its stock dropped and by the 1900s he was a large stockholder.

During World War I, the mills boomed, turning out cloth for gas masks, and wages rose to undreamed heights. Even after Page died in the early 1920s, the boom went on.

Then came the depression. The demand for cotton slid. The plants switched to making rubberized raincoats. But in 1929, the mills ground to a halt. The number of jobs at York Manufacturing fell from 2000 to 200. The ax of liquidation seemed about to topple Factory Island forever. More than 100 mills in Massachusetts alone had shut. Mrs. Page, a widow and big stockholder, asked what had happened to the $3 million surplus earned in 1920. She charged mogul Samuel Insull with juggling the finances of York

Manufacturing. In desperation, Walter S. Wyman, of CMP fame, purchased (dirt cheap) York Manufacturing along with four other plants to keep them off the auction block. He believed they could again become big customers for his electric utility company. Wyman and his associates poured in millions for new equipment, and jobs rose again to the 1000 mark through most of the depression.

Even so, there was a major and bitter strike in 1934, which was considered so threatening that the National Guard was called out. By 1941, York Manufacturing workers joined with Pepperell and Saco-Lowell workers and voted in the CIO as the bargaining agent for all.

What built Saco and Biddeford into centers for jobs and industry, was not men and their factories. It was the river. As it flows past Saco and Biddeford, the river drops 42 feet in 500 yards. The water power generated by this torrent was the attraction which brought the great mills here.

The Saco Water Power Co., begun in 1839, dominated the 19th and first half of the 20th Century. Upon the Saco Water Power Co. depended the profits of the machine shops and giant cotton mills along the river banks. Those owners made certain they or their agents had control of the lifeblood of their business. And when their cotton business failed and the mills shut in 1929, it was the power interests in the person of Walter S. Wyman and his associates at Central Maine Power who came to their financial rescue. Not because of any love of the milltowns; but for the need of customers, of big users of power. Just as Wyman had helped "Pete" Newall to bring a bankrupt BIW in Bath to new life, not for love of Newall, but for the need of a potential big customer for power on the Kennebec, so Wyman came to the rescue of the closed mills. He needed them and the big machine shops as customers for his power company.

It was the power of the flow of the Penobscot River which made Bangor into the biggest lumber port in the world. The sawmills, powered by the river, gave raw lumber the value-added as cut lumber which was the wealth of booming Bangor.

So it went, in larger and smaller degrees, along the banks of most Maine rivers. The river, fine as it might be for fish or boats, was most of all the source of power; first water power, then steam power, then electric power. The rivers had been the arteries of Maine's business for centuries until trucks and highways became the conveyor belts and coal, then oil, fueled the power plants.

Textile mills on the Saco River at Biddeford. (Dyer Library, Saco)

25.

Living in Saco:
Two Centuries of Fun and Culture

The small doings of ordinary people over the centuries are what makes Saco, like other Maine river towns, come alive generations later.

The will of an early settler named William Scadlock tells how hard men struggled for, and therefore valued, the small comforts. About 1630 Scadlock wrote his will:

> "I bequeath my Bible to my son William. I bequeath unto my son John 3 yards of broadcloth, he upon that consideration, to buy 3 yds of good kersey for a suit for my son Samuel with silk and buttons thereto . . . unto my daughter Rebecca, my worsted stockings . . . unto son William, my new hat, provided he buy another for 10 shillings for my son Samuel . . . a book titled 'Meat out of the Eater' to my son William . . . and a book 'Justifying Faith' to my son John . . . unto my daughter Susanna, a sucking calf called Trubb . . . and unto my daughter Sarah one yard of Holland. . ."

The town selectmen in the 1650s enforced church attendance. What was more, they demanded that citizens stay awake during the long sermons. John Wadleigh paid a fine of two shillings and sixpence for being a "common sleeper" at worship on the Lord's day.

Sextons prowled church aisles, armed with a stave long enough to reach inside the pews, to wake up "common sleepers." At one end of the stave was a rabbit's tail, ticklish and furry. With this end, the Sextons woke up the "Goodies." At the other end was the hard rabbit's foot, pointed claw intact. This end of the prod they used on sleeping boys and men. "Goodies" was the name for "goodwives"; while "Mistress" was the title for ladies of a higher social station.

The first doctor in town was Dr. Samuel White, who began his care for the sick about 1750. His successor didn't like the wild country life of Saco at the time of the American Revolution. He wrote to a friend that too often he had to ride alone to patients in the back country, complaining:

> "riding on stormy nights on bad roads, bye paths, pole bridges, or no bridge at all. Add to these hazards, deer skipping, foxes yelling, wolves howling; music not the most agreeable alone on a trail in a dark winter's night."

The Saco Social Fire Society was founded in 1792. Each of its 30 members had to furnish himself with two leather buckets, suitably initialed, and vow to run to a fire after receiving a special password. The members in the Social Fire Society paid 12 cents for a pint of rum, 3 cents an ounce for tobacco, and meals at the tavern cost them 25 to 50 cents.

In 1834, citizens organized the Saco Mutual Fire Club, a social drinking club whose members passed the leather buckets, and manned the pumpers named "Torrent" and "Plumper." Two years later another friendly organization named the Saco & Biddeford Village Corporation for the Extinguishment of Fires built two reservoirs and formed two branch companies gallantly named Hercules and Tiger. Each group had an eye cocked for its own fame and glory and would sometimes cut the leather hoses of a rival organization at a fire in order to claim credit for fighting and beating the blaze single-handed.

The towns bought two hand operated fire tubs and boastfully christened them Niagara and Deluge. But they could not cope with the blazes which burned the Thornton House Tavern in 1851 and the Tufts Hotel and half of Pepperell Square in 1852 and all the stores on Factory Island in 1854. In 1862 the city fathers finally bought their first steam fire engine, the Saco, and ten years later bought the second, the Governor Fairfield. Then came an arson scare and a $1000 reward was offered for the capture of the firebug. In 1869 more than 50 fires broke out and there was talk in the newspaper of setting up a vigilante committee to fine the culprit and hang him from a lamp post. In 1895 huge fires gutted the interior of Saco City Hall and also Biddeford's public building. Old Orchard Beach went up in flames in 1881 and again 1907.

Saco had its share of pioneers opening new businesses.

Foxwell Bryant, a gnarled old river driver, was the first iceman in town. In winter he harvested ice cakes, then stored them in a sawdust-lined shanty. In summer he hauled them on a wagon, drawn by a white-faced ox, to sell to the mansions of the Cutts and other rich folk. Foxwell Bryant made only $4 during his first summer in the ice business in 1840. But this was the start. Bryant began to do well over the next 25 years, building up a loyal local trade. Then in 1867 entrepreneur James Black from Baltimore plunged into the ice trade on a huge scale. He soon had four huge icehouses filled on Factory Island, a fleet of schooners and 150 men working for him at $1 an hour.

Jovial Joe Weymouth weighed 300 pounds, though he claimed he'd been born a tiny two pounds. He became Saco's top soapmaker. Sweet as the business sounds, it in fact stank. For Soapmaker Weymouth operated a high-class slaughter house, killing herds of cattle and sheep, boiling them down, or rendering them, for tallow. When this first nasty stage was over, Jovial Joe turned the tallow into eight varieties of soap, ranging from strong, plain, laundry soap to delicate, sweet-smelling soap for ladies' toilettes.

Harness-making, carriage-making, barrel-making, brick-making — all flourished in Saco. But the most forgotten Saco business was its cigar-making. Saco was a center of fine cigars. In 1871 half a dozen cigar makers formed a co-op, installed enough machinery to keep 100 people busy turning out 125,000 cigars a week. By 1881, Biddeford and Saco cigar makers were producing 1,500,000 cigars a year. William J. Bradford was the most successful for the longest time. For 20 years his plant turned out Henry Clays, Black Diamonds and tasty Bouquets.

The City Council in the mid 1880s put on a spurt to bring more new business ventures to town. William Abbott began his Hoop Skirt Manufactory, went broke and went on to make a small fortune in cigars.

Silas Gurney, a Boston hotel man, built his Seal Rock Spring Water plant in 1885, the start of a business which prospered close to 100 years, selling ginger ale and sodas to New England by tens of thousands of cases yearly.

National brands found a welcome, too. Once famous remedies such as Sawyer Crystal Blue, Union Twist Drill, and Lydia Pinkham all organized in Saco, under Maine's special incorporation laws, which were more attractive then than Delaware's are today. All the remedies were well laced with alcohol.

Cornelius Sweetsir's name lives on today, with the aura of Saco's best-known benefactor. The reputation is due in about equal parts to the goodness of his heart and the intricacies of his will. He was perhaps the original "matching funds" man. While he left half his fortune in 1881 to local schools, societies and charities, each bequest required so many specific actions on the part of the recipient that the funds stretched out and multiplied. Even today the Sweetsir bequests are evident in Saco life.

Sweetsir arrived in Saco young and in debt in 1845. He went into the shoe business and kept a weather eye on all Saco property being sold for taxes. By 1860, he was worth $60,000; ten years later $100,000 and by the time he died $250,000. He did well in the shoe business, but it was real estate — a knack for buying cheap, selling high, be it slum property or prime business lots — that was the basis of the Sweetsir fortune. He left about $125,000 to a dozen local institutions, from Thornton Academy (for books), to the city (for parks). His bequest to start an orphanage was so complex that the funds lay, accumulating nicely, for 20 years before the orphanage was built; and by then the money had multiplied to $100,000. His Sweetsir public lecture, an annual affair, still is operating.

But my heart warms more to his contemporary and business rival, Luther Bryant. Bryant, a whiz at slum and low-rent real estate, was a Biddeford man of money. He dressed in the cheapest suits and was described as "tall, skinny and moth-eaten."

Bryant owned 15 buildings in Saco by 1868, all bought for unpaid taxes. By 1880 he owned 45, and by 1890 he owned 77 buildings. He owned "half of Biddeford," mostly the slum half, by the time he died. He left $1 million, a fortune four times bigger than Sweetsir's. And there was complications in Luther Bryant's will, too; not because Bryant's will was convoluted with charitable bequests, but because of lawsuits filed by his mistress and live-in housekeeper and his 42 cousins to get their hands on the Bryant fortune.

People in those times had fun; sometimes in ways we have forgotten. Ice skating was the rage. In the winters of the 1890s up to

5,000 skaters were on the frozen river on a Sunday afternoon; 500 were out there by moonlight. When ice went out, roller skating became the summer sport. Crowds watched and cheered the 50-mile endurance races inside City Hall. Then walking marathons became the fad, as jogging is today. Hundreds turned out to walk against the clock to Old Orchard Beach. After that bicycling was the front-runner, with hundreds enrolled in local clubs, until frightened pedestrians joined to pass a town ordinance to keep cyclists off the sidewalks. The Saco-Portland bicycle race drove everything else off the roads. And daring women cyclists revolutionized fashion and scandalized church-goers by wearing "cycle-bloomers" on the Sabbath.

Saco Academy (now Thornton Academy) opened for classes in 1813, with 49 boys and girls paying $3 a quarter. School was in session all year round, six hours a day in winter and eight hours daily in summertime. The boys fed wood to the stoves and rang the school bell; the girls dusted and swept the classrooms. The school got much of its income from a half township of land it owned near Moosehead Lake, but still could not make ends meet. In 1821 Marshall Thornton came to the rescue, donating $1000. The school has been called Thornton Academy for over 160 years since, a fair return for Thornton's thousand dollars. The school burned in 1848 and Saco operated its own high school till 1889, when Thornton Academy was rebuilt where it stands today.

Saco had 5755 people and Biddeford 6074 in 1850. But Saco in 1850 was probably more active culturally and intellectually than it is today. Flourishing in Saco were the Saco and Biddeford Lyceum, the Young Men's Debating Society, the Mechanic's Institute, the Pepperell Club, the Saco Atheneum and the Village Union. In the 1850s these clubs were offering six lectures for $1 a person or $2 for the whole family; and lecturers included such national figures such as Ralph Waldo Emerson, Horace Greeley and Oliver Wendell Holmes.

There were 13 lending libraries in Saco. The Mechanics' Institute alone had almost 5,000 books and lent them out for 50 cents a quarter-year, thereby becoming one of Maine's first public libraries. The York Manufacturing Co. ran its own library where employees could borrow any of its 600 books for 12 cents a quarter-year. By the 1860s the various libraries in Saco had 12,000 volumes on medicine, theology, history, law, agriculture, business.

One Saco-booster wrote a letter to the editor, saying:

> "Now, sir, have the goodness to point out another town in the State with a population like Saco, that has done more for its advancement, morals, religion, and intellect! Show me a town with like population that can point to its eight churches. . ."

Temperance societies gained a stronghold early. Consumption of "ardent spirits" was 24,155 gallons in 1823, when population was just over 2,500. Saco people were two-fisted drinkers, consuming almost 12 gallons per capita, compared to only two gallons per capita in Maine in 1980. After two years of crusading by the temperance societies, consumption of rum and gin dropped to 10,097 gallons, though population increased. When prohibitionist Neal Dow came to town, 2,500 people turned out to hear him. By 1850 the Saco Temperance Society had more than 1,700 members, active enough to exert control on town politics. But it never managed to stamp out all the grog shops and waterfront taverns.

Two final examples of the quirks which enlivened life in the Saco River Valley.

First involved a delightfully scandalous religious sect of the early 19th century called the Cochranites. Jacob Cochran, the leader, was born in 1782 in Enfield, N.H., and he grew up to become a dramatically handsome man and a spellbinding orator. His prime commandment was that the marriage vow of fidelity inhibited full development of the human spirit. He advised wife-swapping. He preached the gospel of wife-swapping to his congregation as the best way to achieve greater holiness of the spirit. And he practiced what he preached.

Cochran's spell mesmerized Sister Mercy, beauteous daughter of a prominent Saco family; and she was the convert who led to Cochran being chased out of Saco, along with his band of faithful wife-swappers. He set up new operations in Limington, Limerick and Parsonfield, but he returned briefly to Saco to abscond with the life savings of a prosperous farmer. For this he was sentenced to prison, but he escaped to his native New Hampshire. The story goes that after his death, admirers smuggled his body back to Saco, where it now lies secretly buried in a cellar.

The second, sadder story concerns John Randolph Watson, born upriver in Standish in 1836. Adventure ran in his blood and he became the first young man from here to seek his fortune in the booming mining town of Helena, Montana. After that he went prospecting in Dawson, capital of Canada's Yukon Territory. While still in his 20s, a mining explosion burned or blew off the lids of both his eyes. For 50 years Watson lived without eyelids. In his waning years, he had artificial ones sewn on, which must have been one of the pace-setting operations in 19th century surgery. That's a Saco man for you.

Early car races on Old Orchard Beach.

Mill workers about 1890 in Biddeford Mill. (Dyer Library, Saco)

The Cutts mansion, built by Thomas Cutts on Factory island. (courtesy Arthur Nadeau)

Saco & Pettee Machine shops at Biddeford. (courtesy Arthur Nadeau)

Saco River Mouth, Camp Ellis. Near here, the first white men settled in the early 1600s.

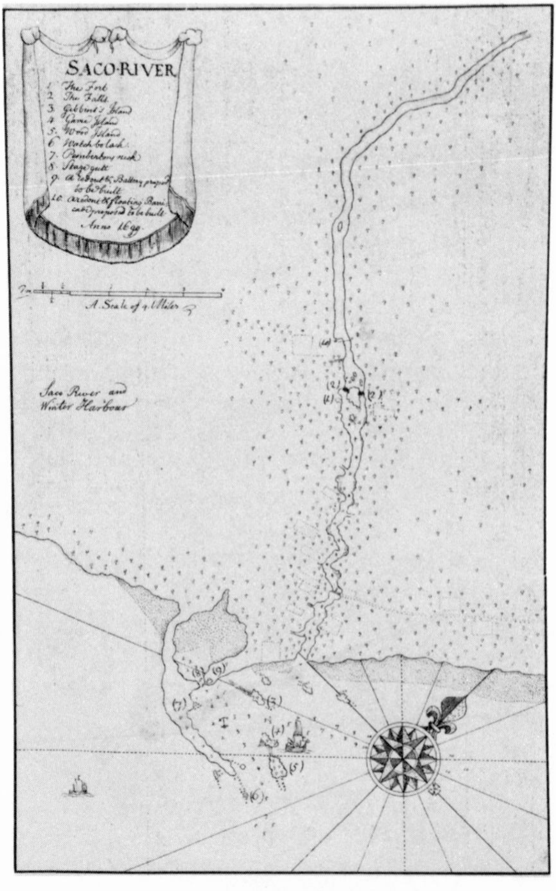

Map of Saco River, drawn 1699. (Maine State Archives, Baxter Rare Map collection)

Old coal sheds at foot of York Hill, looking from Saco to Biddeford. (courtesy Arthur Nadeau)

A River of the Quiet Kind

Town of Damariscotta as seen from the Newcastle shore. (Sturges photo)

26.

Life on the Damariscotta: 1635-1983

Ancient Oysters to Luxury Yachts

Every window in our house looks down the Damariscotta River. We designed it that way. No curtains are ever drawn across those windows unless a bitter gale and driving rain attack us from the south. So we watch our river winter and summer, day and night, in all its moods, all its range of color.

The most glorious oranges and reds and purples are reflected in the mudflats at low tide at sunset. The purest, eeriest color is on those nights when the reflection of a hunter's moon shines out of the wet mud.

We never knew mud could be so beautiful until we began living beside the tidal river, almost 20 years ago.

"I want to be right on the ocean. I want to hear and watch the sea. I want deep water in front of my house, where I can anchor my boat."

That was my heart's desire when we came to live in Maine 19 years ago. It's a common disease, this itch to live with the ocean at your door. Almost everyone who moves to the coast of Maine is afflicted by it at first; which is why ocean-front land is sold at $100 a front foot.

But my wife knew better. "You're the victim of summertime dreams and of living too long in Manhattan. Forget all that. The ocean is wrong for happy year-round living. It is rough and angry half the year. It is grey and lowery and forbidding half the year. And when for the hundredth time you can't see out the windows at your beloved ocean because every window is caked with salt spray, you'll rue the day you built a year-round house on the edge of the North Atlantic."

So we built upriver. Upriver is where sensible settlers in Maine have been building for hundreds of years. Mostly it is summer people who build smack on the ocean.

"Watching the ocean is grand on a summer day," said Barbara. "But watching the ocean 365 days a year, year after year, would make me restless and tense. Only a granite ledge is happy being pounded by seas and wind year-in, year-out."

Time has proved her 100 percent right.

The Indians knew it first. Their settlements were upriver. In summer they'd load canoes and go downriver to summer camps on the ocean or out on the nearby islands. But in fall, winter and springtime they lived by the bountiful, kindly rivers of Maine.

Now we do. And like the Indians long ago, we launch our boat Steer Clear upriver on the first of May. Then we take the boat downriver to the ocean and put her on her mooring in New Harbor. By the first of November we take her back upriver where she spends six months in winter storage. But from May to late October we live as much as possible aboard her, cruising the Maine coast and making trips to home and office as the needs of holding a job or taking a bath or sleeping in a big, soft bed require. We live upriver, but in 15 minutes we can walk out of the house, board the boat and be on the ocean.

Even so, we often poke up rivers on dirty days. It took us years to learn this simple recipe for avoiding days of fog or rough weather at sea. When either came, we used to lie on anchor in an island cove, sometimes for days on end, and moan about the cold, the rain, the fog. But in the last 10 years, we have learned to head up Maine's rivers and find sunshine when there was fog at sea, find flat calm instead of angry, chopping seas.

Mostly these are the quiet rivers, where no fortunes were made, rivers which have stayed out of most history books. Bless them, for they are the meek and lovely rivers. Behind the trees along their banks lie cellar holes of old farm houses overgrown with wild raspberry bushes; old orchards; overgrown pastures for cows and sheep; headstones of graves where generations of the same family buried their loved ones, dead from sickness, drowning, old age and sometimes from being scalped by Indians.

Before there were paved highways, trucks, cars and railroads, these little rivers bustled with far more life than they have today. People, food, cows, sheep, hay, firewood — all the necessities came and went on the rivers.

On the Damariscotta, there used to be boat landings at every village along the 12-mile stretch to the sea. Men would catch the boat (sail, then steam or naphtha, then gasoline) to Damariscotta to do business and bring their wives and children to do the shopping. The mail came and went by boat. Visitors would take the boat from Portland, New York or Boston, get off at the main dock and catch the local boat to their friends downriver. Going by river was cheaper, faster, more reliable and pleasurable than going by horse and wagon or by stage.

There was much business then on the riverbanks of the Damariscotta. Mud, more politely named blue clay, from the mudflats and the low-lying fields made good bricks. So there were dozens of busy brickyards. When a man found the blue clay or mud he wanted, he'd knock off the trees and grass to expose it, then bring in his horse. He'd hitch it up so the horse would turn a long stirrer paddle in circles. He'd blindfold the horse so it wouldn't get dizzy; then all day long the horse would walk in a circle, moving the stirrer paddle through the clay until it was the right consistency. Masses of the clay would be hauled out onto trestle tables, where men would shosh the wet clay into forms the shape of bricks. These were left to stand in the air and sun for a few days to dry, and then were baked in the kilns.

These kilns were fired by wood. Each kiln used at least 200 cords of wood. Sloops loaded with firewood constantly sailed into the brickyard's dock. In 1890, 100 vessels delivered 5,000 cords of wood to the kilns along the Damariscotta. At night the sky was aglow with firelight from the kilns. Each brickyard employed scores of men from May to October. Many were boarders, who were fed 5 meals daily and paid $40 a month.

When the bricks were ready for market, sloops and barges would come in to be loaded, and sail off down the river and along the Maine coast. They'd hug the shore and in poor weather they would put into a handy harbor for the night. Sometimes in the local tavern, the owner would drink with a stranger who might say he was building a new town hall or school or church. And over drinks that night, the Maine man might sell his bricks then and there, ducking the need for a long journey to a buyer waiting in New York. So all along the coastlines of Nova Scotia, Maine, New Hampshire, Rhode Island and Massachusetts there are substantial buildings standing today, made from Damariscotta brick. In 1890, more than 11 million bricks were sold. I often look at my own meadow and cove and see in my mind's eye the kilns burning, the sloops loading, the blindfolded horses walking forever in circles.

Alvin Piper and his father made brick on the cove where we built our house. We went there and dug out of the mud enough of those small rose-red bricks to build a fireplace in our living room. This link between the past and present is meaningful when on a winter night we gaze into the fire and think about the men and horses making the bricks by our river. I'm glad their bricks are in our fireplace; and I hope they are, too.

The boom years for the dozens of brickyards were in the late 1830s. So many buildings were being built from Damariscotta brick that a group of Boston money-men put together a syndicate to market the bricks made by all the small independent brickyards along the Damariscotta River. They found one of their biggest markets in Halifax, Nova Scotia, which was a city being rebuilt in the 1840s. Tens of thousands of Damariscotta bricks were shipped to Halifax in compliance with orders from the Boston money merchants who now controlled most brick production along the river. Damariscotta yards sent the bricks, but never got paid for them. The Boston financiers and the money vanished. Every brickyard along the river went bankrupt. Only a few ever came back to production. Last one in operation belonged to Nathaniel Bryant, ancestor of Paul Bryant who in the 1980s is operating the Bryant shipyard on the river close to the Newcastle-Damariscotta Bridge.

That bridge linking the twin villages was first built in 1797. It was an expensive toll bridge then; it cost 3 cents to walk across and 8 cents on horseback. The tolltaker was Mr. Trumbull, who had first claim to the job since he had rowed the ferry before the bridge was built.

Living beside a Maine river brings a strong feeling of continuity, of kinship to the people who lived on this same river hundreds, even thousands of years ago. The river has not changed very much since their journeys on it. The same sweeping bends, the same narrows, the same rapids, the same ebb and flow of the same tides. The same hidden hazards of shallows and ledges kept those men in their boats on the lookout as they do today. But today we have charts and buoys to help us navigate safely.

This sense of being an inheritor of the river is strongest when we are on the river. In our boat we feel linked to the past.

It begins in the first week of every May when Paul Bryant launches our boat Steer Clear from his Riverside Boat Co. I think of his ancestor Nathaniel Bryant launching boats into this river more than 200 years ago.

Nathaniel Bryant came to Newcastle in 1770 and started his shipyard. Nathaniel died young and soon, at age 33. But his son Nathaniel kept the business alive, moving it to Great Salt Bay, at the head of the river. When this Nathaniel died his son, Cushing Bryant, kept on building ships. And his brother, Nathaniel, III, ran his own shipyard downriver, and built his house nearby in what is now (much enlarged) the handsome Lincoln Home for the Aged. The son of Nathaniel III chose not to stay in boat building; but that did not break the Bryant tradition for long, because Creston Bryant, his son, went right back to building boats on the same site. And now Creston's son, Paul Bryant, launches my boat into the Damariscotta River where his great-great-great-grandfather had launched boats in 1770. He was soon followed by other boat builders.

In the heydays of Maine shipping, scores of fine schooners, clipper ships and big Downeasters were launched from the 24 shipyards along the Damariscotta. Stetson, Hitchcock, Kavanaugh, Cottrell, Cotter, Jonah Morse and 20 others built big vessels in coves which today are mudflats without water enough for a flat-bottom skiff at low tide.

Andrew Carnegie, who gave all the Carnegie libraries, sailed to America aboard a three-masted schooner named Wiscasset and built on the Damariscotta River in 1833 by Abner Stetson.

In 1853 Cyrus Cotter built and sailed the biggest vessel ever built here, the Ocean Herald, a 2,135-ton, square-rigged three-master. A picture of her hangs today over the fireplace in the Damariscotta public library.

Another touch of rivertown continuity is that Capt. Cyrus Cotter's granddaughter sold Sunday newspapers for 70 years, up into the 1970s, from a little shed overhanging the river, by the bridge. She was Mrs. Mabelle Cotter Sherman, a witty, white-haired lady with sparkling blue eyes and an endless knowledge of her town. She bragged that she had been the first woman meat cutter in a butcher shop in the state of Maine.

This linkage, this continuity, is too strong along the river to bypass the story behind the Kavanaugh and Cottrell shipyards.

In 1793, James Kavanaugh, 24, and Mathew Cottrell, 18, made the big trip from a famishing farm in Ireland to the Damariscotta River. Soon they were into every business; alewives and sawmills, bricks and boat building. Between them, they built 25 ships. But as Roman Catholics, they were suspect to the hard line Baptists. Yet there was greater religious tolerance here than, for example, in Bath where they burned out the Catholic church in the 1830s, or in Bangor, where they fought to drive out the first wave of Catholic Irish immigrants. In the magnificent house at Damariscotta Mills called Kavanaugh, the Kavanaugh family sheltered Father Cheverus in 1798 on his way back to Boston from his mission to the Penobscot Indians in Orono. Father Cheverus said Mass in a tiny chapel disguised as a closet. Later that same year of 1798, Mathew Cottrell built a small wooden chapel, St. Mary of the Mills, to serve the 12 Catholic families in the region. Then came the building of St. Patrick's Catholic Church, in 1807, the oldest surviving Catholic church in New England. Kavanaugh and Cottrell brought architect Nicholas Codd from Ireland to design this lovely brick church, and to design the handsome Cottrell House on Damariscotta's Main Street, close to the river; and the Kavanaugh mansion, in Damariscotta Mills.

Today, Damariscotta dominates the river whose name it took. But its twin village, Newcastle, named for the Duke of Newcastle, is by far the senior and larger. Settled in 1630, Newcastle, with its 18,733 acres, was incorporated as the 12th town in Maine in 1773. According to custom, Newcastle received a law book at public expense; and according to Williamson's History of Maine "in regard to the number, reputation and enterprise of its inhabitants, Newcastle has always holden an elevated rank among the towns." Damariscotta, a mere 8,000 acres, became the 347th town in Maine when it was incorporated in 1847.

The Damariscotta oyster shell heaps are the oldest link in the river's history. They tell a story of ancient feasting and gatherings of Indian tribes 5,000 years ago.

These shell heaps measure 45 million cubic feet. In places they are 31 feet deep. They are reputed to be the biggest in the world.

The heaps are upriver, near where the Damariscotta River and Great Salt Bay meet. Today the Route 1 highway runs close by these shell heaps. But very few people inside those fast-traveling cars realize that they are whizzing past the place where tribes of Indians met to celebrate and feast on oysters.

It is not difficult to park the car and walk the river bank to where the mounds, grass covered now, stand high beside the river. You can walk there, too, on a rough path along the Newcastle side of the river. The heaps are on private property which now belongs to the Hart family, who live in the big house through the gates at the end of Glidden Street.

The best way, the most enjoyable way, to get to the shell heaps is by river. You need a shallow draft outboard, a very wary eye and an alert pilot on the bow. For here the river is shallow and strewn with boulders and your boat must go through the white water and swift current of Johnny Orr's rapids.

Don't expect to be thrilled by the sight. The shell heaps are, when all is said, an ancient garbage heap. Indians threw empty oyster shells, millions of them, onto this spot. That may indicate they were, generation after generation, a neat people, who took pains to keep tidy the place where they enjoyed their reunions.

There are three distinct layers of oyster shells, separated by thick layers of mold. Experts say this indicates 300 years or more passed between the ending of one layer of shells and the beginning of the next layer, because it takes 100 years for one inch of vegetable mold to accumulate.

The top layer of mold over these heaps is three and a half inches thick. This indicates that the last oyster shells were thrown in 350 years ago, about the early 1600s, when the Wawenock Indians began to leave the Damariscotta region, and the first white settlers arrived.

In the second layer of shells, traces of iron oxide have been discovered, indicating that the Red Paint people, who used this red paint, or clay, feasted here. Their feasts on this riverbank would therefore have taken place 4,000 years ago.

Below is yet another layer of mold, and then a third stratum of shells, going far back into the caverns of time.

Why are these oyster shell heaps, said to be the greatest assembly of their kind on the entire earth, found here?

The most believable explanation is that the best oysters grew here in enormous plentitude, and that Indians from many different settlements rendezvoused here because of that. In the springtime, after they had done their planting of corn at their permanent settlements inland, Indians headed in their canoes and afoot for the coast for the summer fishing.

They would catch and dry huge quantities of cod and herring to carry home and eat in the winter. They'd hunt seals basking on ledges in the bays, feast off the meat, preserve some of it and dry the hides, which in winter they would make into clothing or into moccasins or snowshoes.

On their spring migration to the coast, these social people would meet, gather massive quantities of oysters, feast on them and dance, wrestle, fall in love and swap news for a few days. In the fall, when they headed back upriver, they'd have another reunion here, eat more oysters and swap more news of the

Brig. Jonathan Chase, built at Damariscotta in 1866 by J. Day Co.

Ship Virginia Dare launched 1916 at Newcastle. (Flye collection)

The Massassoit Engine Co., 1905. Fire fighters of Damariscotta then had little equipment, but very fine uniforms. The firehouse shown here is now a store called The Firehouse. (Gannett file photo)

Schooners at Cottrell's wharf, Damariscotta in 1900s.
At one time, there were more than 20 shipyards on the Damariscotta River.

Alewives netted from the stream, Damariscotta Mills, early 1900s. (Flye collection)

Ancient oyster heaps on Damariscotta. Begun thousands years ago by feasting Indian trib these are the biggest and oldest their kind in the world. (F collection)

Damariscotta ladies take their hats for an outing on the river steamer. (Flye collection)

Boarding the river steamer Newcastle at South Bristol. (Flye collection)

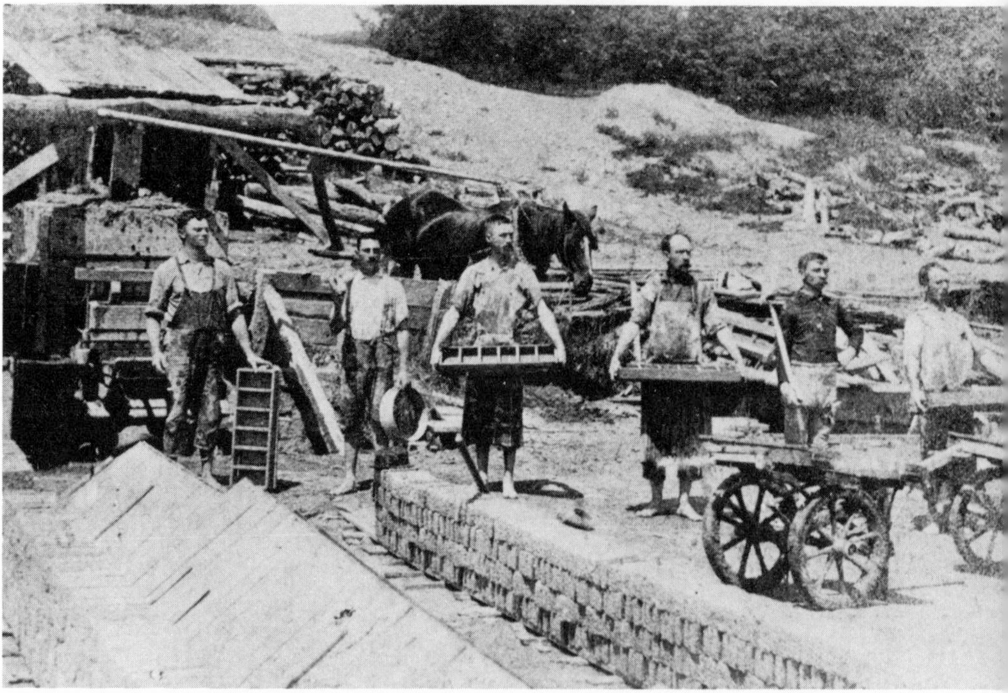

Bryant's brickyard, Newcastle, 1899. More than 11 million bricks were made in one year along the banks of the Damariscotta. (Flye collection)

Knox-Lincoln railroad construction in 1870s. (Flye collection)

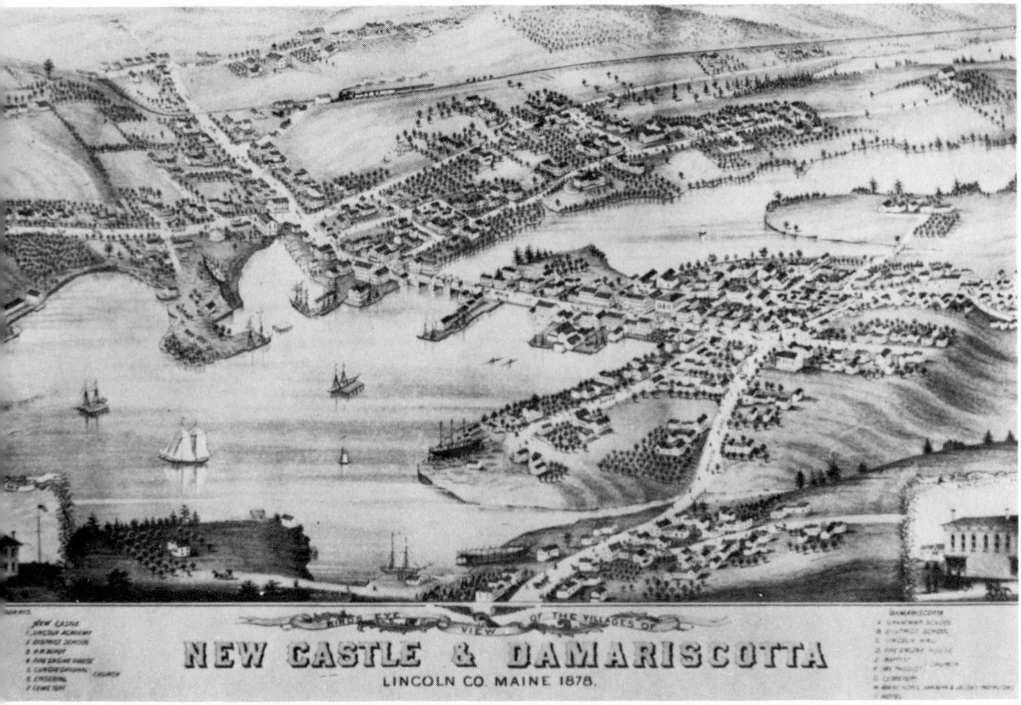

View of Newcastle and Damariscotta, 1875.

Harvey Gamage long headed the yard at South Bristol, across the Damariscotta River from Goudy & Stevens. His yard too produced many of the staunchest Maine fishing vessels as well as large classic yachts.

James Stevens and his brother "Tunk" Stevens run the Goudy & Stevens shipyard in East Boothbay. From here they have launched scores of fishing vessels and world-famous yachts.

summer's happenings, and then go their different ways until the next spring reunion. The reunions and feasts went on over thousands of years; and the only monument to these monumental picnics are the vast oyster shell heaps beside the Damariscotta.

Knowing the scalpings, kidnappings, murders and arson and disease which lay ahead for Indians and white men along this river, I rejoice when I go by the oyster shell heaps to picture the games, flirtations, dancing, gossip and feasting that date back thousands of years. The first shells were probably thrown on this heap about 2900 BC.

When we head downriver in the spring in Steer Clear and come back upriver in late October, we meander. The run down to the mouth of the river is about 12 miles; but it is so lovely, and offers so many coves where families of seals play, that we stretch it from an hour's run to eight hours and sometimes two days. There are no landmarks in the sight-seeing sense, and very few houses to be seen. The river for the most part looks to us as it must have looked to the Indians before the white men found it.

Of course, the white men found it early and easily, for the river mouth opens out hospitably to all vessels. The earliest fishing vessels and the early explorers sailed at least into the mouth of the river, and some sent small boats to scout far upriver. Fishermen on Monhegan and Damariscove Island sailed up here as early as the 1580's. By 1602 Bartholomew Gosnold in his ship Concord sailed in these Maine waters; Capt. John Weymouth in Archangel anchored off Monhegan, 15 miles away, in 1605; and by 1607 the Popham colony was established at the nearby mouth of the Kennebec. Many of them probably explored the Damariscotta River.

Pemaquid, long an Indian summer camp, was settled by 1625, a few miles to the east. John Brown was the first white settler hereabouts. In 1625 he bought land from Samoset, the Wawenock Indian chief, which stretched from the Damariscotta River east to Pemaquid and inland to Waldoboro. He paid 50 beaver skins for it, in what has to be called the first title deed transaction. The deeds are in the county court house at Wiscasset today. John Brown and his family lived here for 50 years. They fled to Boston in the Indian War of 1675, but his widow and son returned to live close to the Damariscotta River again.

There are sometimes nuggets of fun in these old deeds. I like the sale made on January 20, 1652 by three Indians with three unforgettable names. "Be it known to all men," says the deed, "that we,

Robinhood, Dick Swash and Jack Pudding, do hereby make free sale to John Mason one neck of land. . ."

Another named that will ring a bell to all admirers of Boston is Shem Drowne. He is the tinsmith (called America's first sculptor in the Encyclopaedia Britannica) who made the famous Grasshopper, the golden weathervane on Faneuil Hall. Shem Drowne married a Maine girl named Catherine Davidson, daughter of Nicholas Davidson, a mariner, who had a sound claim to the Pemaquid Patent of some 12,000 acres. Through his wife, sculptor Shem Drowne claimed the Pemaquid lands for himself and in 1736 came here to survey them. The Drowne Claim was in and out of law courts over 70 years before it was resolved in 1813. Drowne's heirs got almost 12,000 acres of public lands, mostly elsewhere in Maine.

The first settlers along the river on the Newcastle side were James Smith, Walter Phillips and John Taylor. Taylor came from the Plymouth colony in 1635 and built his cabin in 1638 where Weeks-Waltz Motors sells Fords today. Phillips left for Salem, Massachusetts, where he was last heard from in 1702.

Across the river on the Damariscotta side, three other settlers built their cabins about 1638. John Drowne, son of the Boston grasshopper man, built his on what is now called Belknap Point; Robert Scott was upriver by the old oyster beds; Thomas Kimball overlooked Great Salt Bay.

Downriver they are still building fine ships. The Harvey Gamage yard on the Damariscotta side, near the mouth of the river, and the Goudy & Stevens yard on the Newcastle side have national reputations for building the staunchest of fishing boats and the most luxurious of pleasure yachts.

We knew Harvey Gamage and his wife Jennie and his police dog, Lady, when we summered in South Bristol 20 years ago. By then, in the early 1960s, Harvey Gamage was probably the most respected shipbuilder in Maine.

Gamages have built more than 450 vessels since the first Gamage yard began on the Gut at South Bristol in 1854. Then Harvey's granduncles, Albion O. and Menzus R. Gamage, opened the A&M Gamage yard. They built 87 vessels, mostly schooners, in 48 years between 1854 and 1902. The last was the steamer Newcastle, which carried mail and freight on the river for the Damariscotta Steamship Co. Another steamer was named the Bristol, built for the same company to carry passengers. When the Damariscotta

Steamship Co. went out of business in 1917, the Bristol was sold. But she kept right on carrying passengers — this time prisoners up the Hudson River, headed for Sing Sing Prison.

One oddball craft the Gamage Brothers built was the little 8-ton steamer Anodyne, launched in 1890, and perhaps Maine's first floating billboard. She was plastered with advertising for Anodyne Liniment, whose slogan was "Every Mother Should Have It in the Home"; and thousands did, for it contained 18 percent alcohol. This cure-all was hawked from the deck at every town where Anodyne could dock.

After building scores of staunch fishing vessels for others, the brothers built one for themselves and christened their 222-foot schooner the A&M Gamage. She sailed out of South Bristol on her maiden voyage in 1872 and has never been heard from since.

When A&M Gamage closed in 1902, not another Gamage boat was built on The Gut until 1924, when young Harvey Gamage opened his yard.

Harvey Gamage had been trained as a house carpenter by his father, Warren L. Gamage. He hated the work. When he was 19, he got the job he wanted — as a ship's carpenter, working across the Damariscotta River at Hodgdon Bros., yacht builders in East Boothbay. There he was paid $3 a day until he had learned to work mahogany, when he was raised to $4.50 a day.

Harvey Gamage was 27 years old and the youngest boatbuilder in Maine when he opened his own yard in South Bristol in 1924, starting ambitiously with a shed 35 feet wide and 100 feet long but with no orders. Then he got a telegram from a man who had promised that one day Harvey Gamage would build boats for him. The telegram was from John Alden of Boston, one of the most famous designers, and the order was for a 29-foot Alden sloop called Actala. Gamage launched this sailboat in 1925 and she was still sailing in Maine waters more than half a century later. Gamage built more handsome, small yachts until the Great Depression brought a halt to that business.

The war forced Harvey Gamage into fast production of bigger boats for the Navy. His yard built 128 powerboats, minesweepers and PT boats, some over 100 feet in length.

When the war was over, Gamage hit his true stride and began building the vessels which became the Gamage hallmark — fishing schooners in the 90 foot range, strong enough to weather the most savage seas over Georges and Grand Banks. Strength without frills was the Gamage code. He cut his own oak from his own woodlots in Alna and Jefferson, from trees never less than 12 inches at the butt and often as thick as 42 inches. Gamage vessels skimped on comforts such as hot running water and sinks. But they were filled with thick oak and plenty of it. His first 77-foot dragger cost $23,000 ready to go to sea, in 1945. By 1970, its equivalent cost half a million; and the price he had to charge fishermen horrified Harvey Gamage.

Gamage built some of the finest replicas of old and great American sailing ships. He built the Mary Day, a handsome windjammer working as cruise ship out of Camden; the Shenandoah, a 108-foot topsail schooner; the Clearwater, a replica of a Hudson River sloop. He built the heroic Hero so tough and sturdy she could shoulder her way through Antarctic ice as a research vessel for the National Science Foundation. And when time and economics demanded it Gamage built steel-hulled vessels.

In his lifetime, Harvey Gamage built some 400 vessels. He wore his engineer's cap, his faded denim jacket and work pants and every minute of every day he knew precisely the job every man in his yard was doing.

Harvey had a shirt-sleeve office, up rickety steps from the boat shed, and shared it with Bob Woodward, the smiling man who handled procurement and paper work. Some days Harvey was in his office only 10 minutes in the morning and 15 minutes in the afternoon. The rest of the time he was down in the boatshed. He was a master boatbuilder who spent his working time building boats; and he launched more boats than the mammoth Bath Iron Works. Oddly, the name Gamage was not painted anywhere in his yard.

Right across the Damariscotta River stood the Hodgdon Brothers yard, to which Harvey Gamage used to row to work each morning as a young man, learning the trade. Caleb and Tyler Hodgdon began building boats here in 1818. They launched their first vessel — a pinky called Union — about 30 years before A&M Gamage Brothers began. The Hodgdons ran a sawmill and East Boothbay was long called Hodgdon's Mills. Hodgdon's built schooners for the famed Noonan fishing fleet out of Cape Porpoise; they built the world-renowned Bowdoin in 1921, in which MacMillan explored the Arctic. In all the Hodgdon yards have launched more than 300 vessels. And a Hodgdon is still building fine boats in East Boothbay, not far from where the first Hodgdon yard stood. He is "Sonny" Hodgdon, running G.I. Hodgdon Co. As a hobby Sonny has built half models and his collection now numbers 91, one of the finest in America. Hodgdon's is reputed to be the oldest yard on the Atlantic coast continuously in the same family.

Goudy & Stevens is the biggest yard in East Boothbay nowadays. The firm began in 1921 and its taproot was the Hodgdon yard. Wallace W. Goudy had been a ship's carpenter with Hodgdon's. Their first boat was a 25-footer, built in Goudy's barn. During the years of World War II, and thereafter, Hodgdon's and Goundy & Stevens teamed for joint production, since the yards were cheek-by-jowl.

An extraordinary range of fine shipbuilding is the hallmark of Goudy & Stevens. They have built the most luxurious yachts and the toughest fishing boats. For example, they built the handsome replica of the America — which won the Cowes Regatta in Queen Victoria's time and for whom the America's Cup is named; and hugely successful steel-hulled draggers (at over $1 million a copy now) for the O'Hara fleet. In the summer of 1983 they'll launch the super-luxury sport fisherman for John S. Payson, a boat capable of 40 knots, yet equipped with so much in the way of electronics, video and stereo, and live-aboard luxury that there is close to four miles of wiring aboard this 60-foot Warrior.

However the real story of these yards on both sides of the Damariscotta River is not in the numbers or value of the boats built, but in their continuity; and in the rare skills among the artisans, passed from generation to generation, in these small river towns.

The little harbor at South Bristol Gut boasts the busiest and the smallest swing bridge in Maine. Go through it and hold your breath, and sail on to John's Bay, past Gene Tunney's island, where President Kennedy stayed, and cruise to the Fort at Pemaquid. Three times destroyed and rebuilt, Pemaquid had seen British, French and American flags flying over the fort. Here was the Duke of York's custom house. Current excavations prove it was a flourishing village when the Pilgrims were just settling in at Plymouth.

The links of past to present are everywhere. In the snug harbor at Christmas Cove, for instance, where Captain John Smith, of Pocahontas fame, is supposed to have celebrated Christmas in 1614. Today there is a hospitable inn, restaurant and marina there. In a cove on the Newcastle side is where police made the first big drug bust in 20th century Maine from a steel-hulled luxury power yacht, with London as her hailing port. The smugglers stood out like a sore thumb, arriving in the Damariscotta River in

April in a luxury yacht. They should have asked a local man. Mainers have for centuries been successful smugglers because they always used local boats which blend.

The Indians gave the river its name. Damariscotta means river of many fishes. This is where they trapped alewives as they swam upriver to spawn in Damariscotta Lake. Kavanaugh and Cottrell followed the Indian lead, when these Irishmen set up their alewives fishery almost 200 years ago. On the same fishway today in May there is a big and lively alewives fishery. For generation after generation, part of the proceeds from catching this annual multitude of fishes has been used to benefit the poor in nearby towns.

Oysters which Indians feasted upon thousands of years ago are back again. The Indians might be amazed to see aquaculture farms where millions of seed oysters and mussels are today being raised on the Damariscotta River by methods learned by Japan. The past and the present, the continuity of mankind and the river flow like the tide, forever intermingling.

View of Damariscotta across the river from the Newcastle shore, 1982.

The Penobscot River

Bangor about 1835, from an old painting.

27.

Up the Bangor River:

City of Vigor

In Bangor today, you can't find a place to tie a boat. Thereby hangs a horrid tale.

We came in February by a Coast Guard icebreaker boat up the 24 miles of the Bangor River (now called the Penobscot) and the only half-safe place to tie a boat to was a decrepit piling beside a garbage-strewn, abandoned coal yard. To get a meal ashore we had to walk the railroad tracks into the Queen City. It was a hell of a way to arrive in Bangor.

But that's what has happened to the head tide of the river. A sad, sleazy, deserted slum is what is left of the port of Bangor, which once boasted that here was the busiest lumber port in all the world.

Ephraim Lansil was captain of the Bangor port and busiest man in the city that year of 1860, when his record book showed 3,376 vessels arriving. The Bangor Whig and Courier newspaper of July 14, 1860, said 60 vessels under sail had arrived within the space of two hours. In a single day of summer 250 vessels so choked the water between Brewer and Bangor that a man could walk across the river, deck to deck, without wetting his boots.

Yet in 1980 there was not a mooring, not a dock for a little visiting boat. Not a welcoming tavern, grog shop or eating place asking for the trade of sailors off a boat.

But what a welcome a sailor got in 1860! The Devil's Half Acre, the tenderloin district, behind Pickering Square — all were bursting with bars, girls, music, lights, dancing, whorehouses and fights.

Here were the dives where seamen, pent-up, thirsty and horny from long voyages, clashed with lumberjacks in town after five months in the boozeless, womanless camps of the north woods. To throw pepper on that hot mixture came the loggers, the rivermen, the Bangor Tigers, out for a night on Bangor to ease the tension and salve the wounds from driving the logs downstream.

With pints at their lips or on their hips, these men, fresh from the most dangerous jobs in the world, lined up to get to the girls at Fan Jones' Skyblue House of Pleasure, while others couldn't wait and headed out to Barney Kelly's Saloon and Aunt Hat's place in Veazie.

Money moved fast. Fortunes flowed. Bangor boomed. Bangor bragged. This was the year, 1860, when Bangor shipped out 250 million board feet of long lumber, cut in the 410 sawmills at the river's edge. There was no port in the world to match Bangor, when the Devil's Half Acre was jammed with fast spenders from every rough waterfront in Europe and Asia, with skins from Indian red to Yankee white to yellow and brown to black and speaking a dozen tongues. Bangor brawled. And Bangor boomed.

When spring came to Bangor in those days, there were few cities in America to match it. When the ice went out of the river, the ships sailed in, over 200 a day, to load with lumber. When the snows and ice melted up the Penobscot, the lumberjacks struck camp, tree-cutting over; and the huge log drives began, with the torrents carrying tens of thousands of trees downstream, with rivermen breaking log jams, and finally guiding trees with the right marks of their owners into the right sawmills. With pay in their pockets, thirst in their throats, and a great throbbing in their loins, these thousands of men from the woods and men from the sea swarmed into Bangor in the springtime.

The streets of Bangor turned to quagmires as the frost went out of the ground. The dirt roads were pocked with deep potholes, stuffed with pine branches; and cedar logs were laid to form footbridges over the worst low spots. Planks were laid to provide walkways through the mud. By summer, the roads and sidewalks would turn to choking dust. But from March to November, when the lumberjacks returned to the woods for winter, and the ice kept ships from sailing up river, the taverns and bawdy houses along the waterfront never shut longer than it took to sweep them out.

The madames of some bawdy houses kept order far better than Bangor's night-watch constables. At Ma Hogan's, she made sailors, lumberjacks and rivermen alike play by her rules:

> "Them as orders my vittles, eats them. And them as drinks my rum, likes it. And them as takes a fancy to one of my girls, treats her like a lady or I'll know the reason why. I'll give any man anything he wants, or I'll lend any man money, once. But my rules are: no fighting, no nastiness in my place, and no offensive language either, not counting swearing. Because a man can call a girl a 'goddamn little bitch' and mean nothing but that she's the sweetheart he's always been looking for."

Ma Hogan boasted "a man can spend a winter's pay in my place in 24 hours and get his money's worth, if he's man enough."

Lena Tempest's Palace catered to a wealthier type of customer, the merchants, ship captains and lumber barons. They demanded discretion as much as elegance. No man could simply walk in to Lena Tempest's. The front door was manned by a huge, strong man devoted to the principles of his employer. He admitted only a select few with fine clothes, fat wallets and reputations to protect. Here the harlots were young, pretty, and wore elaborate gowns with very little underneath. Their talents included also an ability to converse, play cards, pour champagne and dance. Their fees were high and their bedchambers as tastefully furnished as the guest rooms in the homes of Bangor's rich. A night at Lena's was so beautifully wrapped, it hardly seemed like sin.

Most famous of the sporting house madames was Fan Jones. Her real name was Parker. She died in Bangor in the 1930s, and lies buried in Mt. Hope Cemetery. Around her grave plot are buried about twelve females — no relation to the famous Fan. Could these have been some of her girls?

Her famous establishment was on Harlow Street, about where the Federal building stands now. There are stories that Fan Jones' Skyblue House of Pleasure got its name from the color of its chimney. She is said to have had it freshly painted every six months, so it would be a visible landmark to sailors coming upriver or lumberjacks coming downriver. This good story may be only legend; but, if true, her chimney was a welcoming beacon to the customers she loved to see. Only one elderly man in Bangor back in the 1960s could be found who would admit being inside Fan Jones's. He could not recall any skyblue chimney; but he did remember pretty girls in revealing slips and Fan Jones, laughing and bossing everyone, with a great wad of bills tucked into the top of her stocking.

Across town, the boisterous boom of Bangor looked different: it was high-hat and highbrow.

Look in on that seat of culture, Norumbega Hall, which opened with a gala white-tie ball on October 19, 1855, and could hold 2,000 people. When Bangor thirsted for culture, the upper-crust could slake that kind of thirst with lectures by Oliver Wendell Holmes and Ralph Waldo Emerson. They could see Edwin Booth play Hamlet or hear the political orations of Hannibal Hamlin, native son and vice-president later to Lincoln, James G. Blaine, presidential candidate and Maine's senator, who was secretary of state under three presidents. James A. Garfield, William McKinley, Cassius Clay, Henry Wilson and Ben Butler all thrilled one part of Bangor, while another part raised hell on the Devil's Half Acre.

Bangor's civic pride and all of Bangor's red, white and blue bunting decorated Norumbega Hall when President Ulysses S. Grant himself arrived to celebrate the opening in 1871 of Bangor's newest, ambitious claim to world fame — the opening of the European and North American Railroad.

Norumbega Hall was not enough. Bangor opened its opera house in 1882 and then its civic auditorium 1897 with a mammoth gala. On stage were 800 singers in the chorus; 60 musicians in the orchestra. For the next 20 years, Bangor's great cultural event of the year was its Maine Music Festival, where the greatest voices of the age such as Schumann-Heink, Melba, Mary Garden and Galli-Curci sang. When the opera season was over, the impressario Charles Frohman brought his Broadway stars to Bangor — Oscar Wilde, Lily Langtry, John Drew, Maude Adams, Ethel Barrymore. Never since has so much talent, so much culture come to Bangor year after year.

To house and entertain the resident rich and visiting VIPs, Bangor built its hotels; the Penobscot Exchange Coffee House with 70 rooms, a big place when it opened in 1827; the Franklin House and Windsor Hotel which by 1865 boasted 140 rooms; and the most famous, longest lasting, Bangor House. The Bangor House opened with a grand gala on Christmas Eve, 1834. The clergyman who gave the blessing, the Rev. Enoch Pond, is the most remembered guest. His invocation ran a little too long, and one of the guests hurled a piece of tripe in protest. The tripe landed precisely in the minister's open mouth.

The Bangor House became a mecca, hosting ever more elaborate and sumptuous balls, banquets and business meetings of big landowners, sellers and Boston financiers.

As the big money flowed along the Penobscot and into Bangor, the new wealthy class began as early as the 1840s to import architects to build them showplace mansions.

Boisterous boom town though Bangor was, there was also an elegance and culture. For example, here is a description of the study or office in a lumber baron's home in 1834:

> "A huge ceilinged room, with tall windows and a vast fireplace of black marble. On the mantel stood two whale oil lamps with crystal prisms, ornamented with gold leaf. The room was lavishly furnished; a marble topped table with a Duncan Phyfe base, half a dozen Chippendale chairs, a Queen Anne wing chair and a Hepplewhite wall cabinet in which fine china and glass ware were kept. The owner sat behind his Hepplewhite desk, with his papers illuminated by light from a candelabra of Waterford glass."

Yet only 64 years had passed since Jacob Buswell, the first ragged settler, had thrown together the first crude shanty on ground that was to become Bangor, busiest lumber port in the world.

"Jacob Buswell is an old damned grey-haired bugger from Hell."

That was how the first settler in Bangor was described by a contemporary. Probably it takes a man like that to become the first settler anywhere in a wild land. He was also a drunk and a wife-beater.

When Jacob Buswell, his wife and nine children arrived in what is now Bangor in 1769, he was a cooper by trade; but in truth he was a poor soldier who'd fought in Canada, had enough of the army and so became the first citizen of Bangor, or Kenduskeag Plantation.

The reports he sent out must have been good, because the next year his son Stephen and his daughter-in-law Lucy came from Castine to join Buswell. Then in 1770 Caleb Goodwin, his wife and eight children arrived from Bowdoinham, followed a year later by Thomas, John and Hugh Smart and their families, who came by sloop from Woolwich, and Thomas Howard, Simon Crosby and Jacob Dennet and their families also arrived. By 1772, there were

12 families; by 1790, the population was up to 169; and the census of 1800 showed 279 people in 45 families, many from Cape Cod. This was fast growth for so remote and hard an outpost.

The minister, the Rev. Seth Noble, enlivened life in Kenduskeag, as it was then called. Noble was 43 when he, his wife, and three children arrived from Nova Scotia in 1786. His salary was $400 a year (rum was three cents a glass). Noble is one of the few early Bangor men whose foibles we know. He was fond of hymn singing and his favorite was one called Bangor; he was even fonder of drinking a dram of rum and swapping stories with his flock as he made his parish rounds on horseback.

The records at Mr. Treat's Kenduskeag store show that between September and mid-November, a 66-day span, the Reverend Noble had been to the well, buying pints, quarts and even gallons of rum with regularity. In those 66 days the Rev. Noble was down on Treat's ledger for 16 gallons of rum. He explained to parishioners that he always carried a supply on his parish rounds "for the benefit of Rhemumatic and Colicky parishioners, whose outlook on life and bodily aches were much improved by a little of my medicine."

This apparently was the kind of preacher the early Bangor settlers liked. For after Noble had been with them only one year, they voted at town meeting to build him a house and give him an acre of land to surround it.

But, alas for poor Noble, no one followed through. The records show he began to lose the respect of his most upright parishioners.

> "He had acquired army habits . . . He could not sustain the gravity becoming to a minister . . . he would drink a dram with almost anyone who invited him . . . his conversation was light."

So Noble continued living in a small log house. He could not collect his pay and wrote complaining letters to the town committee, demanding they pay his salary. To make ends meet, Noble did teaching on the side, but here too he had a hard time collecting his fees. He wrote to Col. Jonathan Eddy in June 1793 saying:

> "I have a small account against Jacob Buswell Jr., which I wish you to collect as soon as possible. Try easy means first . . . To one quarter year's schooling in 1792,

> 1,000 of the best shingles. Ditto in 1793, six shillings and one day's labor. If he will labor for me for four days next week, I will accept it; if not, sue him for six shillings."

Noble holds a special niche in history because he is responsible for Bangor being named Bangor and not Sunbury, a weak name for a lumber port. The story goes that in 1791, Parson Noble was sent to Boston to file papers with the General Court for the incorporation of the settlement on Kenduskeag Plantation into a town to be known as Sunbury. While Parson Noble was waiting for the clerk to fill out the necessary forms, fortified with a few drams of rum, he fell to singing his favorite hymn called Bangor. The file clerk looked up, and asked "What's the name?" Noble, thinking the clerk meant the name of the hymn and not the town, replied "Bangor." The clerk wrote the name "Bangor" into the incorporation papers; and Bangor it has been ever since, the 73rd town in Maine.

Noble's life as a minister was less than stable. After the death of his first wife, who had come to Bangor with him, Noble remarried, this time to Mrs. Ruhama Emery. They moved away in 1797 to Newmarket, New Hampshire, where he had been hired to preach for six months. After that they moved back to his hometown of Westfield, Massachusetts, and from there to Montgomery, Massachusetts, until 1806. His second wife died there. He married again, to Mary Riddle, and became a preacher in Franklinton, Ohio. There he died in September 1807, aged 64, the wandering parson with a taste for rum and wives, the man who saved Bangor from being called Sunbury.

But incorporation in 1791 did not bring quick prosperity to Bangor, its 20,000 acres and its inhabitants. By 1800 the population had dwindled to 277; rose to 750 by 1810 and when Maine became a State in 1820 with a population of 297,839 only 1,222 of them lived in Bangor.

One reason why Bangor failed to grow in the early days was because life on the Penobscot was not safe. The Pilgrims had opened a small trading post at the mouth of the river in about 1630, to trade with the Indians and obtain beaver skins, the best cash crop the Pilgrims found to help pay their debts in London. Their agent, Edward Ashley, did a huge volume of beaver skin business, amounting to a thousand pounds (about $50,000); but he did too much drinking, love-making and trading in gunpowder with the Indians. So the Pilgrims at Plymouth sent Ashley back to England, a prisoner. Thomas Willett took charge of the trading post, but in his absence one day in 1632, the French from Canada sailed in, robbed the post of 500 pounds worth of precious beaver skins and hauled away all the muskets, blankets and trading goods. The French attacked again in 1635 and made Willett and his men sail home to Plymouth. For years thereafter, the mouth of the Penobscot was a perilous place to live: too close to Canada and French fortifications built at Castine, too vulnerable to attack by Indians allied with the French, too far to the east to get protection from Pemaquid, Plymouth or Boston.

Nevertheless in the 10 years since first settler Buswell set foot in Bangor, the population was close to 400. Then in 1779, the British came plundering up the Penobscot.

28.

Penobscot Expedition: 1779

Cowardice and Fiasco

The Penobscot fiasco of 1779 and the day of infamy at Pearl Harbor, 1941, have this in common; they were the biggest and least excusable defeats in American naval history.

As Short and Kimmel were blamed for the disgrace of Pearl Harbor, Col. Paul Revere and Commodore of the Fleet Dudley Salstonstall were the scapegoats for the defeat of Penobscot Bay. Revere was no hero this time; he and Saltonstall were court-martialed for acts of cowardice; some of his officers said Saltonstall was a traitor who deliberately gave victory to the British.

On a summer day, August 14, 1779, the Americans lost 43 ships and a thousand soldiers fled.

Paul Revere, famed rider in the night and celebrated maker of bells, was commander of the artillery. Dudley Saltonstall, son of General Gurdon Saltonstall, was commander-in-chief of the fleet. Peleg Wadsworth was second in command to the Army. He was captured, escaped and came out with his reputation unsullied. Most history books gloss over this biggest and worst American naval defeat before Pearl Harbor. It happened where the Penobscot River runs into Penobscot Bay, near to Castine.

The British had only 650 troops on land at Castine, and only three sloops-of-war and four transport ships nearby when the American fleet sailed into Penobscot Bay with 19 ships of war and 24 troop transports, with close to 2,000 men in the armada.

The time was the third year of the Revolutionary war against England. The British had decided that a fort at Castine would protect their shipping from being ravaged by American raiders off the coast of Maine; and further that a fort at Castine would protect against an American land attack on Canada. Therefore the British landed on June 17, 1779, after obtaining the quick and easy surrender of the inhabitants at Castine.

With them was John Nutting, from Cambridge, Mass. He was a loyalist to the British crown who owned land along the Bagaduce River and knew the local countryside. He had command of the carpenters who were to build the British fort on Penobscot Bay.

When this news reached Boston, the legislature or General Court was so alarmed, it ordered a massive expeditionary force to attack, destroy and drive out the British. The Revolution was going badly and the Colonial forces, suffering from many defeats, needed a spectacular victory by land and sea.

The Penobscot Expedition, they hoped, would be the glorious turning point of the war for independence. Money, men, ships were poured into the grand design with amazing speed. Within 30 days of the British landing, the Penobscot Expedition was ready to sail from Boston to wipe them out. The fleet had 350 guns, carried 2,000 men. The massive effort was to cost $8.5 million, and scrape bare the treasury of the Commonwealth of Massachusetts.

The fleet sailed from Boston for Boothbay Harbor, where 1200 men from the York and Cumberland (Maine) militia were supposed to join it.

Maine didn't produce. General Solomon Lovell, commander of all troops, reported that only 500 Maine men were at Boothbay Harbor. They were short in quality as well as short in numbers. "At least one-fourth appear to me to be small boys and old men, unfit for service," wrote the Adjutant General Peleg Wadsworth (Longfellow's grandfather).

Another officer looked over the men and wrote; "Some were old men, some boys and some invalids; but they were soldiers and could carry a gun." The situation was so bad that more men were rounded up at gunpoint and forced to join. By the time the expedition sailed out of Boothbay Harbor, they had taken aboard another 973 men, still far short of the 1500 expected. On July 24, the American fleet sailed into Penobscot Bay, with orders to demolish the British at Castine.

The British were waiting for them. Spies had carried news to the English that the American fleet was on its way. The English naval commander, Capt. Henry Mowatt (the same man who had burned Portland in 1775, four years earlier) positioned his three sloops of war; and every man available readied the fort to repel the American assault.

The assault never came. Commodore Saltonstall in an act of

cowardice refused to hurl his massive naval and ground strength against the small enemy force.

On the first day after arriving in Penobscot Bay, July 25, a half-hearted effort was made to land 200 troops. But a little cannonading from the enemy and a strong breeze were excuses enough for Saltonstall to call off the attack. On the next day, there was another minor landing of 200 men on Nautilus Island, at the mouth of the Bagaduce River, opposite Castine. The 200 Americans drove off 20 British, and hauled enough artillery ashore to make Capt. Mowatt remove his British vessels out of range. But Saltonstall still refused to fight. So on the third day, July 27, the ship commanders under him signed and delivered an urgent petition to Saltonstall to get on with the battle. "Speedy exertions should be used to accomplish our mission," they wrote. "We think delays are extremely dangerous. We (should) go immediately into the harbor and attack the enemy's ships." Saltonstall rejected their call for action.

Then General Lovell gave Saltonstall reports from spies he had sent ashore, reports which showed that the spies had taken a good look at the British defenses and said they could be easily wrecked by one strong assault. In reply to this, Saltonstall hove up his long chin and said, "You seem to be damned knowing about the matter! But I am not going to risk my shipping in that damned hole!"

At 3 a.m. in the foggy darkness of July 28, three American ships landed 200 marines and 200 militia men to attack British troops holding high ground just beyond Dyce's Head, where the lighthouse stands today. The fight was bloody, lasted only 20 minutes. American losses numbered 14 killed and 20 wounded. They drove off the British, and asked Saltonstall for a major landing to follow them to drive on into Castine and force surrender. But again Saltonstall refused. And for the next two weeks, Saltonstall and his fleet stood off shore, while his commanders grew increasingly disgusted.

General Lovell kept urging Saltonstall not to delay any longer. "Go in and destroy the British ships now and seize the fort. If we keep waiting, reinforcements will arrive," was the gist of Lovell's argument with the reluctant Saltonstall.

On August 11, General Lovell, on shore at the heights he had taken, again sent a strong letter to Saltonstall, still hovering aboard his flagship. Lovell wrote:

"In this alarming state of affairs, I am once more obliged to request the most speedy service from you. It appears to me that any further delay must be infamous. I have it this moment, by a deserter from one of the British ships, that the moment you enter the harbor, they will destroy themselves. The information that British ships and reinforcements are on the way is not to be despised; not a moment is to be lost . . . I feel the honor of America is at stake . . . I have now only to repeat the absolute necessity of undertaking the destruction of the ships, or quitting this place. I impatiently await your answer."

Even this got no action from Saltonstall. With 40 ships and 2,000 men, he was stood off by Capt. Mowatt's three British sloops of war and 650 men ashore. Lovell and Revere, ashore with a few troops and a few artillery pieces, were losing control of their unsupported troops. Each night their men, many impressed into service at gun point, were deserting.

As Saltonstall stalled, British ships from New York were sailing with reinforcements toward Castine. When the frightened Saltonstall got this information, he panicked, and ordered his land forces and Gen. Lovell to give up his land position, and retreat with all men and weapons back to their ships.

August 14 was a day of infamy in American history. Saltonstall thought only of saving his own neck. When he saw seven British warships coming across the bay, he fled. Even though his fleet outnumbered the British men-of-war, even though he had 350 guns and the British had 204, Saltonstall ran for the Penobscot River with his warships, leaving his own transports behind to fend for themselves against the British men-of-war.

Chased by the British, Saltonstall's fleet was in total disarray. Some ships beached themselves on the banks of the river, and the men aboard ran for safety in the woods. Other ships were destroyed. Still others were set afire by their crews, who took to the boats, rowed to shore and disappeared into the forest.

August 14 was a day of disgrace in American history.

"To attempt to describe this terrible day," wrote General Lovell, "is out of my power. It would be a fit subject for some masterly hand to describe it in its true colors, to see four ships pursuing seventeen armed vessels,

> nine of which were stout ships, transports on fire, men-of-war blowing up every kind of stores on shore and as much confusion as can be conceived."

Dr. John Calef, a British sympathizer who lived at Castine and saw the battle, reported 11 American vessels taken and 26 burned by their crews, 70 British killed and wounded, and 474 Americans killed, captured or wounded. Records on the American side report American casualties at about 150 and British about 85.

John E. Cayford in his book, "The Penobscot Expedition," wrote:

> "Commodore Saltonstall, through lack of courage and disgraceful attitude, can be blamed for the loss of the mightiest fleet ever assembled in the Revolutionary War. There have been but few times in American military history when a battle commander, having strength, position, firepower, ever deserted his post, leaving men and equipment to the mercy of an oncoming enemy. Nevertheless, Saltonstall chose this deserter's route. Could it have been possible that the Commodore was guilty of being as traitorous as General Benedict Arnold?"

Saltonstall was given a court-martial, which cashiered him from the service and pronounced him forever banned from holding any military or governmental position. Revere, after many public accusations of cowardice, finally got a full hearing two and a half years later, which cleared his name of the worst charges against him.

The British remained in control at Castine until December 1783.

The cast of characters in the disastrous Penobscot Expedition is worth pursuing to see what happened to them before and after this American defeat on the Penobscot River and Bay.

Commodore Dudley Saltonstall was perhaps the blackest sheep in the long Saltonstall clan. He was a direct descendant of Sir Richard Saltonstall, a contemporary of John Winthrop, the first Governor of the Massachusetts Bay Colony in 1630. He was a grandson of Gurdon Saltonstall, governor of Connecticut in the early 18th century; the fifth of fourteen children born to General Gurdon Saltonstall, Dudley was born in New London, September 8, 1738.

He went to sea as a boy and during the French and Indian wars did well as a privateer. When the American Revolution broke out, he was commander of the fort at New London. When the American navy was born in 1775, Dudley Saltonstall was made commander of the flagship Alfred, and John Paul Jones was his lieutenant. In 1776, Saltonstall was involved in a battle at sea against the British in the Bahamas, and was hauled home on charges that he had allowed the British frigate Glasgow to escape. He was exonerated. By 1779 he had command of the 32-gun frigate Warren of the Continental navy. When the Penobscot Expedition was launched from Boston that year, Saltonstall was the senior naval officer present in the Continental Navy; thus he was made commodore of the fleet. After defeat, Saltonstall was permanently cashiered and forbidden to hold any military or civil office. He went back to privateering, mostly in the West Indies. There he died at Haiti, age 58, in the year 1796.

Capt. Henry Mowatt, the man who defeated Saltonstall, was born in Scotland in 1734, the son of a British naval officer. He followed in his father's footsteps, joined the Royal Navy and by the time he was 24 he was commissioned lieutenant. He served 44 years in the British Navy, about 30 of them in American waters. When he was 41 he attacked and destroyed Falmouth Neck (or Portland, as it was later named) in the fall of 1775. His next command was the sloop Albany, flagship of the three-vessel squadron protecting the British fort at Castine. Mowatt's three ships held off the huge Saltonstall fleet until British reinforcements arrived to defeat the Americans in August, 1779.

Capt. Mowatt died of apoplexy aboard his ship Assistance while on station off Virginia, on April 14, 1798. He lies buried in St. John's churchyard at Hampton, Virginia.

The man closest to Maine was Peleg Wadsworth, second in command of the Army forces under General Solomon Lovell during the disasterous Penobscot Expedition. After that defeat Wadsworth was named commander of Eastern Maine. But that was a big title commanding non-existent armies. Wadsworth, his wife, a five-year-old son and younger daughter, were holed up in a farmhouse outside Thomaston. The British were still after him. He had a footguard of only six militiamen. On the night of February

18, a British sloop from Castine came ashore near Thomaston with 25 men, sent to capture General Wadsworth.

The British surrounded his house, captured all occupants except Wadsworth, who slept behind bars in a strong room, alone. Woken by gunfire, he grabbed a pair of pistols, a fusee and a blunderbuss and put up a hard fight. But when he was shot in the elbow, he surrendered and was taken to Castine.

Held under tight guard for months, Wadsworth and his fellow prisoner, Major Benjamin Burton, staged an escape worthy of mention. They made friends with their barber and from him they obtained a gimlet. With the gimlet they bored holes into the ceiling. They camouflaged the holes by chewing up their breadcrusts into dough and using it to paste over the holes in the ceiling. When the hole was big enough for a man to crawl through, they waited until a night of thunderstorms on June 18, 1781. Then they climbed out through the hole in the ceiling, made a rope from their blankets, and escaped in the downpour. In a remote cove they stole a small boat. Finally they made their way on foot to Plymouth.

The next year Peleg Wadsworth moved to Maine. He was 35 years old when he bought land on what is now Congress Street, Portland. He paid John Ingersoll 100 pounds for the land and spent two years building Portland's first brick house. It still stands today, close to Monument Square, as the home of the Maine Historical Society. Peleg and his wife and six children (later four more were born in the house) moved into their new home in 1786.

In Maine, Wadsworth quickly made a name. By 1785 he was chairman of a convention in Portland debating separation from Massachusetts. By 1792 he was elected senator from his district in the Senate of Massachusetts. Later in 1792 he was elected as U.S. congressman from the District of Cumberland, an office he held for seven terms. (Letters he wrote to his son John, a student at Harvard, from the Congress, then meeting in Philadelphia, have been published by the Maine Historical Society).

In Maine, Wadsworth also made money, for the first time in his life. After he had graduated from Harvard in 1769, he had done some school teaching and later had briefly become a storekeeper in Kingston. But the Revolution was in the wind. He formed and captained a company of minutemen on September 26, 1774. His rise through the ranks was fast. Within 15 months he was a brigadier major and within two years he became adjutant general of Massachusetts. On July 7, 1779 he became brigadier general, second in command of the Penobscot Expedition, which suffered humiliating defeat.

But once in Maine, his fortunes prospered. Six years after moving to Portland, Wadsworth bought 7500 acres between the Saco and Ossipee Rivers. But because of his absence as U.S. congressman from Cumberland, it was not until 1807 that Peleg Wadsworth and his family moved from Portland to the estate and house near Saco, which eventually became the nucleus of the town of Hiram. He turned the brick house on Congress Street, Portland, over to his daughter Zilpah and her husband, Stephen Longfellow. This son-in-law later also went to Washington as U.S. congressman, taking the seat once occupied by Peleg Wadsworth. And the son of Zilpah and Stephen Longfellow became the famous Portland poet, Henry Wadsworth Longfellow.

Wadsworth, by now 73 years old and squire of Saco, came back to his brick house on Congress Street to welcome a guest from France, General Lafayette.

Wadsworth died November 13, 1829, at the age of 81.

Castine, where the British defeated the American fleet and held Wadsworth prisoner, is now where the Maine Maritime Academy trains officers for the sea. The fortifications which the British built are well preserved, and the cove beside the road into Castine is called Wadsworth Cove, in remembrance of the night Peleg Wadsworth waded ashore there. In the church at Castine a Paul Revere bell rings out, an ironic reminder that its maker, Col. Paul Revere lost his artillery and almost his reputation in this part of Penobscot Bay.

But this military fiasco was only a prelude. Ahead were the years when Penobscot waters would be caught up in England's war against Napoleon. First that war brought prosperity through smuggling, with Maine ships selling cargoes at tremendous profits to both sides by blockade running. This resulted in the French seizing American ships trading with Britain, and in the British shanghaiing Maine crews from the decks of their ships. This led to the Embargo Act of 1807, whereby President Jefferson tried to keep the young American nation neutral by forbidding American ships to sail for any foreign port. This embargo led to economic devastation for Maine's river and coastal towns. All this culminated finally in war between the U.S. and Great Britain; the War of 1812, in which Bangor and all the Penobscot river towns surrendered to the British, who swept through Penobscot Bay, seizing

Castine, Hampden, Bangor, Belfast, Camden. Neither the Commonwealth of Massachusetts, which governed Maine, nor the federal government, gave protection to the Penobscot when the British attacked. The river was again under enemy guns on the first day of September 1812.

The British again bedeviled Bangor and Castine and stormed towns along the Penobscot in the War of 1812 against the United States.

The Young America

29.

Mr. Madison's War: 1812

How Maine Suffered

"Mr. Madison's War" pinched all shipbuilding and sea trading towns of the Maine coast long before war was declared in 1812.

The money pinch began in 1807 when President Thomas Jefferson signed the Embargo Act, which prohibited the export of any goods at all from the United States. Jefferson was trying to keep the young United States neutral and outside the conflict raging between England and France, which was to end with the defeat of Napoleon at the heroic battle of Waterloo. But the British were seizing and imprisoning American crews whom they believed were trading with Napoleon. And Napoleon was capturing American ships supplying England. Fearful lest repeated seizure of United States men and ships would force this nation into the war, Jefferson decided to ban all trade with either side. So he forced his Embargo Act through Congress in 1807.

Maine screamed. Our ships, shipmasters, shipbuilders, as well as traders had been making money hand over fist, selling to both sides. The seacoast towns and their Congressmen flooded the White House with protests.

Mainers, of course, took to smuggling. Suddenly little Eastport became one of the busiest ports on the Atlantic. In a single year, Eastport handled 160,000 barrels of flour. It came in from the south at $3 or $4 a barrel; and a quick trip to British Nova Scotia raised that price by 300 percent. In one week 30,000 barrels of flour came and went from tiny Eastport. Maine skippers could load flour in southern ports at $3 and sell it in Jamaica for $25. They could buy lumber for $8 in Maine and sell it for $60 in the West Indies.

Take the case of Ploughboy which left the Penobscot River in October 1808 with a cargo for nearby Castine. But, said her skipper, she was blown off course and ended in Antigua, West Indies, thousands of miles away. When she arrived finally in Castine the next February, her cargo holds were empty; but the owner's pockets were full of gold.

But by 1807 President Jefferson clamped down hard, enforcing the Embargo Act. Maine, which had amassed fortunes, from ship owners to crews, was suddenly impoverished. William King of Bath, later Maine's first governor, watched in misery as his fleet of nine vessels rocked on their moorings, idle in harbor. He complained the embargo was costing him $5,588 a month. Off Bath on the Kennebec River over 100 vessels stood empty and idle. Wiscasset suffered a knockout blow. In 1806 the Wiscasset Custom House had cleared 67 ships. In 1808 it cleared only two.

Disaster hit the Portland waterfront. Within a month after the Embargo Act, eleven of the biggest mercantile houses in Portland went broke. At least 60 percent of the inhabitants of Maine seacoast towns were out of work. Soup kettles were set up in public squares to feed the hungry. Maine peppered the White House with protests.

After 14 months of embargo, the act was lifted on the day President Jefferson left office. Maine ships refitted swiftly and took to the seas fast to make money hand over fist. The little brig Lee, from Portland, owned by Asa Clapp and his partner, Mathew "King" Cobb, made $80,000 on a single trip.

But the destruction and harassment of U.S. shipping by France and Britain were more than our young, independent nation could tolerate. The British had seized 4,000 American sailors in foreign ports and on the open sea and flung them into Dartmoor Prison in England or forced them to serve on English warships.

For example, Captain Stone of Kennebunk saw a press gang from a British frigate capture his entire crew in Kingston, Jamaica. Captain Smith of Portland had been unable to move his schooner Friendship because a British ship had seized all his crew except one mate. Sylvanus Snow, an American sailor from Orrington, had been shanghaied and made to fight at the battle of Trafalgar under Lord Nelson. John Allen of Topsham suffered the same sort of fate, but he had his leg shot off and was turned out from the British navy a human derelict on a foreign shore. Robert Randall and James Cotterill, of Wiscasset, were seized from their ship and forced to sail for 11 years in the British navy until both were discharged as invalids. Hundreds of American sailors were thrown into Dartmoor Prison.

The French seized not crews but complete U.S. vessels. More than 30 ships from Portland, worth $354,967, were seized by the French. Colonel Thomas Cutts of Saco counted losses of $90,000. Kennebunk lost 23 vessels, Wiscasset 9; and so it went in every port along the Atlantic coast. Years later, when the Louisiana Purchase was negotiated, one of the demands made by France was that the U.S. should assume liability for the claims of American shipowners against France for seizure of U.S. vessels. That claim amounted to $3,750,000.

Thus on June 18, 1812, President Madison declared war. Quickly the British forces in Canada responded by launching attacks on the undefended and vulnerable Penobscot Bay and all the east coast of Maine. Maine got no help from the Commonwealth of Massachusetts, of which it was a part. It got no help from the national government in Washington. The young American navy had only six first-class frigates and a dozen smaller vessels, whereas the British had nearly a thousand ships of war.

So a week after President Madison declared war, Congress issued letters of marque, those documents which allowed American merchant ships to arm themselves and attack and seize enemy ships. This was a blank check for Maine to go full gallop into the risky, profitable business of privateering.

Casco Bay sent out a fleet of 45 armed vessels, ranging from the Hyder All, with 100 men and 16 cannon, down to the boat Lark with 4 men and 4 muskets.

The brig Grand Turk, built in 1812 at Wiscasset, captured 30 ships at sea and made a fortune. The Fox, out of Portland, was soon tagged "the multi-million-dollar privateer." One of her richest prizes, the British brig Belise, fetched $205,927. Her fifth cruise netted her owners almost $330,000, with each seaman aboard getting a $1200 bonus.

Best remembered Maine privateer is the little Dart, of South Portland, which was built in five weeks to go privateering. It was her good fortune to seize a British ship bound for Quebec and laden with rum. Not ordinary rum, but the very finest which had matured in casks for years in the vaults of the London docks. The Dart seized 212 puncheons of this fine rum, equivalent of 17,805 gallons. The Dart hurried back to Portland with this special prize, and for the next two generations any mention of old Dart rum brought a gleam to the eyes of Portland connoisseurs.

Fastest of the Maine privateers was Dash, from Freeport. She was so fast she overtook and captured 15 British ships, which she brought back to Maine and sold, along with their cargoes.

Privateers carried enormous numbers in crew, because they had to be able to man and sail the ships they captured. When the Dash foundered on Georges Bank she went down with 60 men aboard, their deaths memorialized in Whittier's poem "The Dead Ship of Harpswell."

The Niles Register lists 89 captured British vessels sent into Maine ports, many seized en route to Canada. But the only battle between British and American naval vessels to have stuck in Maine minds is the fight between the British brig Boxer and the American Enterprise, in which the American triumphed off Monhegan, but only after both young captains were killed. They lie buried in adjoining graves in the old Eastern Cemetery in Portland.

Britain, after two years of severe losses from Maine privateers, decided to begin stern retaliation. England's first move was to change commanders in Canada. Admiral Cochrane was sent out to replace Sir John Warren, and in April 1814, Cochrane got busy against Maine. He sent the Bulwark, 74 tons, to destroy all shipping and scare all fishermen from their grounds. By April 14, Bulwark was in the mouth of the Saco River, at Biddeford Pool, setting fire to one of Thomas Cutts' boats, which Bulwark had chased in from the sea. The British landed and cut another boat to pieces, and took a third as prize. Thence Bulwark staged raids off Kennebunk, then up the Sheepscot River and then up the George's River.

Meanwhile Cochrane was readying a fleet for a large scale attack on the troublesome towns of Penobscot Bay. On August 14, 1814, he dispatched a fleet of 10 transports, carrying 3,500 soldiers, escorted by 9 warships and 6 supply vessels. On September 1, 1814, this armada of 25 British ships sailed into Penobscot Bay.

The British, who had walloped the Americans here in 1779, were back again. They had beaten Saltonstall and his superior forces then. Now they were the superior force; and most inhabitants of Penobscot Bay surrendered quickly and quietly.

The British displayed their force at Castine; and soon after sunrise, September 1, Castine surrendered. A detachment then sailed across the bay to warn Belfast to surrender as 600 troops were soon to be landed there. Belfast surrendered. On September 2,600 more British troops were landed at Frankfort, up the Penobscot River; on September 3 more troops were landed at Hampden. There 750 of the local militia ran almost without a shot being fired. Within an hour, the British captured Hampden. The toll was one soldier on each side. They swept on to Bangor, and Bangor surrendered, without a shot.

The British troops terrorized the Penobscot towns, beginning with Hampden.

> "Here ensued a scene of abuse, pillage and destruction which were a disgrace to the British name," wrote historian William D. Williamson in 1832. "Sixty or seventy of the principal inhabitants were seized and locked aboard ship under hatches, without fresh air, fresh water or any quiet sleep. The people were treated with abusive language; their houses and stores were rifled, their cattle killed and some of their vessels burned, and a bond of $12,000 was extracted from the town. The losses and damages sustained by the people of Hampden amounted to 44,000 dollars."

The next day, September 3, British vessels sailed upriver to Bangor, while British troops marched by land. At Bangor, British officers demanded immediate surrender and food and lodging for their troops, threatening to plunder the village if there was not immediate compliance.

A letter from J. K. Whitney, describing the scene, was later published in a Bangor newspaper.

> "A flag of truce was sent out and Bangor agreed to unconditional surrender. But within two hours the British commenced a scene of havoc and plunder, which the most savage Goth would have shrunk from. Dwelling houses were ransacked, even women's stockings and infants' apparel stolen. What they could not take away, they destroyed.
>
> "The inhabitants had not only to supply the enemy with provisions, but they were forced to cook for them, dig potatoes and draw water for the soldiery. They enforced their demands by threats to burn the town

> down. Doctor Fiske was horse-whipped. Capt. Hammond had his store ransacked. Mr. Dutton, a lawyer and one of John Bull's staunchest supporters, had to draw water for the soldiers and wait upon them like a Negro; he even had to pull a wagon load of soldiers down to the wharf. The parson, a good, pious soul, had a company of soldiers quartered in his house, who burned his wife's muff and tippet and destroyed many of his books."

Thirteen boats were burned and four others seized and towed to Castine. Then, after 30 hours of terror, the British left Bangor and its 750 inhabitants, and went on to loot Frankfort on September 6, demanding 40 oxen and 100 sheep from the village.

This violence and devastation along the Penobscot alarmed the sea ports of Bath and Wiscasset to the west, lest the British soon descend upon them. In Bath, Major General King ordered out a whole division of militia to muster under arms immediately in Wiscasset. All currency was taken from the vaults in Wiscasset and Bath banks. The United States mails were stopped at Hampden on the west bank of the Penobscot. Castine and Eastport became British fortresses. Penobscot Bay spent a hard and frightened winter, under constant fear of more attacks.

But the British in headquarters at Castine were comfortably and peacefully settled in for winter. Their only enemy was boredom. To fight that in typical British fashion, they turned to amateur theatricals and staged a new play every two weeks until spring.

While the Mainers wintered in fear, and the British in comfort, a peace treaty was signed on Christmas Eve, 1814, in faraway Ghent in Europe.

But the news did not reach Maine until two months later. At midnight, February 14, 1815, the stagecoach pulled into Camden, with the driver blowing his horn as loudly as he could, non-stop. The racket awoke the sleeping citizens of Camden, who leaped from bed expecting the worst, perhaps a new British assault. Instead they got the news that peace had come and the war was over.

By dawn Simeon Tyler and a few other young blades had climbed 800-foot Mount Battie to set off the cannons mounted on the summit. Only one year before, Camden, fearing British attack, had installed three big cannons on the top of the mountain so they could fire upon enemy ships entering the harbor. That was when John Grose, poor man, had contracted to cut a road and haul the cannon to the top for a mere $25. Now the cannons were fired for the first time, to signal the news of peace to the rest of Penobscot Bay. Even after that, the leisurely British did not pull out of their headquarters at Castine until the end of April, 1815, four months after the peace treaty had been signed.

Deacons of the First Parish Church, Bangor. Left to right, sitting, Deacon Thatcher, Rev. Gilman, Deacon Allen, Deacon Titcomb. Standing Dr. Pomery.

Fred W. Ayer, president of Eastern Co., Bangor (1855-1935). He sold his stamp collection to King George V of England.

Sailing Ships in Bangor harbor about 1880. (Vickery collection)

Steamboat Penobscot on the Bangor River. (courtesy James B. Vickery)

Market Square, Bangor, Maine taken in 1900.

Pickering Square, Bangor.

Steamer "Katahdin" (after storm of 1886).

Issac Farrar mansion, Bangor, now Symphony House, at 166 Union St. Built in 1833 for lumberman Farrar, the red brick was brought from England, each brick individually wrapped. Slate for the roof was imported from Bangor, Wales. A circular room is finished throughout with mahogany from Santa Domingo.

Gen. Samuel Veazie, Bangor money-maker (1800-88) painted by Jeremiah Hardy. (Bangor Public Library)

30.

Land, Lumber & Money: 1825-1875

Where the Fortunes were Made

With a dime you could buy an acre of Maine forest in the 1790s. Men with plenty of dimes bought millions of acres. They were the first of the Bangor land speculators.

William Bingham, the U.S. senator from Pennsylvania from 1795-1801, bought more than two million acres in Maine and paid, on average, just over 12 cents an acre, hoping to subdivide and sell to settlers at 50 cents to a dollar an acre. But he had tied up so much of his cash that he became strapped for money and sent his agent, Major Henry Jackson, to England to find a buyer for huge tracts. Jackson found his buyer in the Baring brothers, sons of the banking family of London.

The astute William Bingham knew he had made a good connection. So he brought the two Baring boys on a trip to the United States. Once they were here, Bingham arranged a family cruise down east aboard his yacht in 1794. One result was that the two wealthy Baring brothers married the two daughters of Bingham. Another result was that Alexander Baring, at the age of 22, bought a half interest in the Bingham lands. He paid 45 cents an acre for land that had cost Bingham only 12 cents. Having given the father 400 per cent profit, young Baring then married Anne Bingham. Later, after he had become the first Lord Ashburton and was 65 years old, this same Alexander Baring sat down with Daniel Webster and they negotiated the Webster-Ashburton treaty of 1842, which averted outright war between Maine and New Brunswick over a disputed border.

Between 1785 and 1812, Massachusetts had sold more than four million acres of Maine land at an average price of 20 cents per acre. And, to encourage settlement, offered to give 100 acres to any soldier or settler, provided he would clear 16 of those acres within four years. More lands were given away to pay off Revolutionary soldiers.

By the time Maine became a state in 1820, there were still over 11 million acres in public lands. Maine began selling off these lands and within 15 years had sold over a million acres at about 40 cents an acre.

As the lumber trade prospered, more people wanted to buy into Maine. Land speculation became a fever. Prices shot up. At an auction in September 1828, Col. John Black was selling land at $1.50 an acre. (Black, an accountant, had come to Maine 1802, at age 21, as land agent for the Binghams. He made so much money so fast that within a year he was building the famous Black mansion at Ellsworth, now open to the public as an example of gracious living here 180-odd years ago.)

By 1835 the Maine land boom was in wild full swing, and Bangor was the hub of speculators. Fast-traders thronged the Bangor House and other hotels, coffee houses and taverns, and did business on street corners.

In 1835, the money-making Colonel Black was writing to a business friend in Boston:

> "The spirit of land speculation is quite on tip-toe; there is more excitement on the subject of timberlands than I have ever known before. I have made sale of about 250,000 acres this winter, some at $3 per acre."
>
> Black had bought that land for about 15 cents an acre.

The fast money men from Boston crowded into Bangor. Hardly a seat, let alone a bed, was to be had on the boats from Boston. In Bangor, every hotel was filled and men leased out their beds during the day. One man paid 75 cents just to lean against the sign post the first night. Next night he rented out his space for a dollar an hour and made $10.

A Bangor trader, H. McCulloch, who later became secretary of the Treasury, wrote in 1835:

> "Buyers in the morning were sellers in the afternoon. The same lands were sold over and over again until lands that had been bought originally for a few cents an acre were sold for half as many dollars an acre."

Brothers Edward and Samuel Smith began a new fever by buying options on huge tracts. They would pay one-quarter down, and sign a mortgage for the balance, due over one to four years. Then they went out and sold title to small tracts for four dollars an acre, land which they had bought for a dollar or less. One speculator from Vassalboro, named Brown, made $150,000 in short order; and appropriately gave $10,000 toward a state lunatic asylum.

A newspaper of 1835, the Niles Register, carried a report saying:

"Land which was sold by the state of Maine and Massachusetts ten years ago at 6, 12 and 14 cents an acre, will now readily command $8 to $10 an acre."

A newspaper reporter described some of the land speculators:

> "I have noticed among the speculators at the Bangor House several gentlemen who have failed in Boston in the last two or three years . . . Many speculators are men of small means. But they have a kind of daredevil feeling which is far better than money. A man who is not the owner of a hundred dollars will buy a whole township and sell it again within the hour."

The newspaper carried another story out of Bangor which said:

> "The timberlands are all the go in the market, and even the worthy Catholic bishop, it is understood, is dipping in, having purchased a whole township (36 square miles) which he is selling to the Irish to make a Catholic state somewhere in the Maine woods."

According to the Bangor Whig and Courier a township originally bought for $620 was sold for $185,000, even after $14,000 worth of lumber had been cut.

The land speculators ran a fast courier line between Bangor and Boston, which operated along the same principles as a stock market ticker in a broker's office today. Whole townships were sold and resold overnight, sight unseen. Men bought huge tracts of land off an unreliable map, as they later bought oil and silver rights in the western boom towns. Champagne corks popped from breakfast until past midnight. At one lavish land auction big wash tubs were hustled into service and filled with champagne bottles, cooling to seal the sale.

The tallest story concerns two paupers who escaped from the Bangor poorhouse. Before they were caught the next day each had made $1,800 in selling timberland. The price per acre went from $2 to $5 to $8 and to $10 within a few months.

Then came the crash of 1837, when banks across the nation closed and failed. The bottom dropped out of Bangor's brief, boisterous, glorious land boom.

From now on, the profits were to be made from felling, sawing selling and sailing the timber to foreign markets.

If the land boom was over, the lumber boom was just beginning and would last 50 years.

General Samuel Veazie was one of the first Bangor lumber millionaires, a breed which included Samuel F. Hersey and Henry F. Prentiss and still exists in Bangor today.

There is a clue to his personality in that title "general," which he insisted upon. During the war of 1812 Veazie began in the ranks of the militia at Topsham and worked himself swiftly up the ranks to general. Once he had that title, he clung to it all his life.

Veazie's life began in Portland, April 22, 1787. His grandfather had been a minister, the Rev. Samuel Veazie, who came to Harpswell from Nantasket in 1767. His father, John Veazie, apprenticed young Samuel to a baker in Portland. He liked neither the hours nor the pay; and soon went to sea, as a sailor before the mast at $8 a month, sailing to the West Indies.

Even then Veazie found a way to make an extra dollar. He got rights to a little stowage space aboard, and filled it with goods to trade. He sold in the West Indies the goods he could buy cheaply in Portland; and bought in the West Indies what he could sell profitably back in Portland. Soon he had accumulated money enough to buy 100-ton vessels of his own and kept right on trading and profiting. Then he branched into the cigar business, moved to Topsham and went into general trading. The lumber trade on the Androscoggin attracted him and he added lumber to his other business. He soon was shipping his own lumber in his own ships to the West Indies, selling at a high profit, and bringing home molasses for rum. He meanwhile had bought control of the Androscoggin Boom, so every lumberman on the river was paying a fee to Veazie to move his logs downstream.

From Topsham, Veazie kept his eye on the money being made in land and lumber down east on the Penobscot. He got his fingers into the Bangor pie in 1826, when he was almost 40 years old, by buying sawmills at Old Town. Before long Veazie owned 19 sawmills. Every one on the west side of the river belonged to Veazie. And thereafter he kept adding more; he bought 20 mills at North Bangor (later called Veazie) and another 13 mills at Orono. He wound up owning 52 sawmills, more than any man in Maine. "Land's all right and pine's all right," said Veazie. "But it's the sawmills that make the money."

Where Veazie's treasure was, there was his heart and his body also. In 1832, General Veazie moved lock, stock and barrel into Bangor and built the Veazie homestead at the corner of York and Broadway. When a neighbor began building nearby and the neighbor's house seemed as though it might overlook Veazie, the General promptly added another story to his house. "I will not be looked down upon by anybody," he said.

The General had a burr under his saddle when it came to controlling others, however. And a fine way to control other lumbermen on the Penobscot River, was to control the Boom, which handled everybody's logs. Veazie moved in on the Penobscot Boom, just as he had moved in to control the Androscoggin Boom when he lived in Topsham. First he bought a half-interest, then he bought the other half; and for the rest of his life he gloated over the profits and especially the total control which 100 per cent ownership gave to him.

At the Bangor Courthouse, Veazie's critics and detractors liked to exhibit the corporation records of the Penobscot Boom Company. The records show Veazie holding corporation meetings — required by charter — alone in his own home at night, voting himself into office as president, clerk and director and then transacting all corporate business, which was always concluded by unanimous vote of approval.

Owning the Penobscot Boom and 52 sawmills was not enough to satisfy the general's appetite for business. His next move was to get control of the railroad from Bangor to Old Town, the first railroad in Maine. Started in 1836, it was powered by engines built in England by pioneer George Stephenson, which sped along at six miles per hour. The cars were open-sided, eight feet long and six feet wide. The track, about 12 miles long, was made of wooden rails with iron straps over them.

The local citizens who had begun that railroad made a serious mistake when they extended its track in 1850 and ran it across land which belonged to General Veazie. Veazie sued and won a verdict of $17,000 in damages; but he wanted control more than money. So Veazie kept up a drumfire of lawsuits which tied the railroad and its owners in such knots that they finally sold him the original Bangor & Piscataquis R.R. at such a knockdown price that it became another of Veazie's profit-making investments. Until the day he died, Veazie controlled the railroad. And when his heirs sold out, they sold it to nothing less than the European and North American Railroad, another Bangor dream whose story is told elsewhere in this book.

A man like General Veazie needed ready money and fast loans to seize opportunities before his rivals. This meant having the inside track to a friendly bank. So Veazie bought heavily into the Bank of Bangor, until he became its president and sole manager. When the charter of the Bank of Bangor expired, he had it renewed and reissued under a new name; the Veazie Bank.

The Veazie Bank became one of the most reliable in the country. Even travelers to distant parts of the United States felt secure carrying notes and currency issued by the Veazie Bank. They were readily accepted far beyond Maine.

The power of Veazie and the Veazie Bank was vividly proven when silver currency disappeared from circulation during the Civil War. General Veazie stepped in and issued scrip of his own to the amount of $70,000. He issued it over his signature in 10-, 25- and 50-cent denominations, and it was accepted everywhere. Some of this scrip is in private money collections now. Each bill carries a flattering picture of General Veazie.

Veazie was described by a contemporary in the following words, soon after Veazie moved to Bangor and was 45 years old:

> "He had a huge, blocky head, clean jaw and his clamped lips testified to the drive within, while his eyes,

> the right narrowed and piercing, the left wide open with a questioning and half quizzical lift to the eyelid, showed the shrewd ability which marked his career."

Clearly, Veazie was a hard man to beat in a business deal.

Banker Veazie stubbornly refused to merge his state bank into the national banking system after the Civil War. He claimed the right to keep on issuing Veazie Bank currency, despite the National Act which prohibited state banks from printing their own money. When the federal government demanded that Veazie pay 10 percent tax on the Veazie Bank notes in circulation, he flatly refused. He took his case all the way to the United States Supreme Court and lost. Thereupon the Veazie Bank and all State bank currency in circulation ceased to be legal tender.

Veazie was a tiger for litigation. He fought another banking regulation which required the Veazie Bank, and other banks which issued currency, to keep sufficient cash on hand at all times to redeem all such currency in circulation. He flatly refused to abide by such a rule, called the Suffolk Bank rule.

To get his revenge upon the Suffolk Bank, Veazie regularly sent a messenger to Boston with plenty of transferable securities. The messenger would present the securities and demand checks on the Suffolk Bank in payment. Then he would take the checks to the Suffolk Bank and demand specie. With that specie, Veazie would then force the Suffolk to maintain extra cash on hand to redeem all the Suffolk bills held by Veazie. The general tied that bank's officers and bookkeepers into knots and raised their blood pressure to the danger point.

Veazie spent years of his life and much of his money pursuing lawsuits, often to the United States Supreme Court. He hired the best available legal counsel, and relished these court battles, whether he lost or won.

For example, General Veazie saw there was money to be made in steamboat navigation on the Penobscot above Old Town. The fact that the State of Maine had given W.B.S. Moore and his brother the exclusive navigation rights did not deter the general. He built a boat and put it in the river anyway, in open competition with Moore. He said "the damn law stopping me from doing so is illegal!"

He lost his case in the state courts and again took it all the way to the U.S. Supreme Court, where he lost again. But defeat did not down the obstinate general. He simply took his boat apart and shipped it in pieces to California. There he put the boat back together and ran it on the Sacramento River, making far more money than he could have in Maine and paying all his legal bills in the bargain.

Samuel Veazie, among the first of the Bangor barons, died aged 81 in 1868. He left a huge estate, two sons and a daughter by his first wife (Susanna Walker of Topsham, who died in 1852); and his widow, Mary C. Blanchard.

Born into elegance of this kind in 1855 was Fred W. Ayer, son of Nathan Ayer, Bangor merchant and banker in the first Bangor boom days. Young Fred Ayer was sent away to school at Philips Andover Academy. By the time he was 25, Fred Ayer was becoming a power in his own right in Bangor, operating sawmills and icehouses. Then he formed Eastern Manufacturing Co., using wood pulp to manufacture paper. He was the prosperous president of that successful company until 1916.

Astute businessman though he was, there was a touch of the gambler in Ayer's blood. He was a vigorous mixture of plunger, gambler, financier and collector. He played high stakes poker at the Tarrantine Club and there one night he won the big house and property at 99 Broadway in a poker game.

As a boy, he had started collecting stamps. As he grew rich his collection became renowned among stamp collectors around the world. In 1898 he took his collection to England and sold it to the Duke of York, later King George V. Ayer also collected early American furniture and Currier and Ives prints. After his death in 1935 his widow sold his collection of more than 400 Currier & Ives prints, along with his collection of antique clocks, rugs and furniture. Ayer lived the good life to the hilt and owned a little pleasure craft — the 90-foot yacht Helena.

The Penobscot produced scores of millionaires like the self-made General Veazie. When these men got rich, their wives often loved to dress in finery, deck themselves with jewelry and dance in public. But busy lumber barons had no reason, before they became rich, to dance. They knew nothing of the intricate steps of fancy dances such as the Caledonian Quadrille, the Boston Fancy, the Portland Fancy or the Waltz Redowa.

Enter Bangor's first dancing master and instructor in etiquette, John Martin. Soon Martin had 44 newly wealthy men enrolled as members of John Martin's Dancing Fraternity, formed in 1844. Martin estimated they represented wealth of close to $400,000 between them, the equivalent of many millions today. Dancing to Martin's tunes was Zacheus T. Estes, worth $90,000 and owner of an iron foundry; lumber merchant Gorham Boynton and the mayor of Bangor, A.D. Manson. These new men-of-fashion were taught, in Martin's phrase, to "dance scientifically."

Here in this dancing class lay the seeds for the divisions of class; the separations of rich from the poor, owners from the workers, lumber barons from rivermen, shipowners from sailors, which soon split Bangor. It would lead to street riots less than a dozen years after booming Bangor had become the City of Bangor in 1834.

Meanwhile men by the thousands went into the north woods to work all the hard winter in the logging camps; in the spring runoff, other men would drive the logs to Bangor, where hundreds of sawmills cut the trees into lumber and thousands of ships carried the lumber to market. The work meant jobs the north country had never known before; it meant death in icy rivers and desolate woods for some; and a torrent of dollars in the pockets of a few.

> "There stands the city of Bangor," wrote Thoreau in 1846 in his book, "The Maine Woods," "fifty miles up the Penobscot, at the head of navigation for vessels of the larger class, the principal lumber depot on this continent, with a population of twelve thousand, like a star in the edge of the night, still hewing at the forest of which it is built, already overflowing with the luxuries and refinements of Europe, and sending its vessels to Spain, to England and to the West Indies for its groceries — and yet only a few ax-men have gone 'up river' into the wilderness which feeds it."

Pickering Square, Bangor, 1895, near Devil's Half Acre.

31.

Bangor Boom: 1835

The Irish Tide

Bangor boomed. The river town had 1,200 inhabitants when Maine won statehood in 1820; grew to more than 5,000 — a 400 per cent increase — by 1834, when Bangor incorporated as a city; had 8,643 — more than a 50 per cent increase — by 1840; Thoreau reported there were 12,000 living here in 1846; and they had increased to 16,406 by 1860.

The sudden boom in Penobscot lumber caused the boom in population, money, shipping, sawmills, rum, in the building of elegant homes and the spawning of grog shops. It happened very fast. But it started slowly.

The first settlers, the Buswells, arrived in 1769. There was just one rickety, one-man sawmill in 1771. Thirty years later, by 1800, the population of Bangor was only 277. Even by 1820, the Penobscot had the fewest number of sawmills, 36, of any logging river in Maine. But within the next 20 years Bangor had the most, more than 400. The lumber cut was barely one million board feet in 1820; but ten years later the cut was 35 million; by 1842 it was 100 million; by 1860 it was over 200 million board feet a year. (A board foot is a lumberman's measure for a board one foot long, one foot wide and one inch thick.)

Pine was the making of Bangor. Bangor was at the right place. The huge, valuable pine forests lay to the north; from there, fast-flowing rivers carried the logs down as much as 160 miles to the outskirts of Bangor; there sawmills lined the river banks to cut the huge timbers. And handily, just downstream from the mills, was the "Bangor River," the Penobscot, where ships waited to carry the logs to markets the world around.

Begin by being amazed at the virgin pine. John S. Springer, a

Bangor teacher and later a minister, described the virgin pine in 1850 in his classic book "Forest Life and Forest Trees":

> "This was pumpkin pine; its trunk as straight and handsomely grown as a molded candle, and measured six feet in diameter, four feet from the ground. It was nine rods in length, or 144 feet high, about 65 feet of which was free of limbs, and retained its diameter remarkably well."

Now picture the river drive. In the spring floods the immense pines, which had been felled deep in the distant woods in winter, were driven down the racing, foaming, dangerous river. The river became a tormented sea of swirling trees. In a peak year, 125 rivermen drove 216 million board feet to the sawmills. Some trees traveled 160 miles.

At the mills in Old Town, Milford, Orono, Brewer, Bangor and Hampden, the trees were sawn into logs, staves, shingles and barrels for loading onto waiting ships. At the peak 410 mills stood immense barn-like buildings beside the river. As many as 500 men worked in a single big sawmill, operating 30 to 40 giant saws, all roaring, all dangerous. The output of these mills was stupendous. For example, the manufacture at Orono alone in 1854 amounted to 62 million feet of lumber; 2.2 million clapboards; 2 million shingles; 500,000 pickets; 20,000 barrels; 60,000 oars and 40,000 staves.

John Springer sent a questionnaire in 1850 to the major lumbermen in Maine and based on their answers Springer estimated that 5,000 men and 4,000 oxen and horses were working in the lumbering camps which fed the Penobscot mills; that another 1,500 men and 1,000 oxen worked in the forests feeding logs to the Kennebec; another 928 men and 780 horses and oxen worked in the Machias Basin, with still another 1,200 men and 1,000 oxen working along the St. Croix River. More than 8,600 men and 6,700 animals were working in Maine woods in 1850.

From the mills the cut timber was moved and manhandled into the holds of waiting schooners. On a day in July, 220 schooners might be crowded into the headtide waters of the Penobscot River, ready to be loaded. A man could walk across the river on their decks. During the eight months the river was free of ice more than 3,300 ships would sail up the Penobscot, load and depart from the port of Bangor.

Pine was the reason Bangor boomed and kept booming until it was known as the busiest lumber port in the world. In the peak year of 1872, over 246 million board feet of lumber left Bangor. In the 56 boom years from 1832 to 1888, Bangor shipped to the world over nine billion feet of lumber cut from Maine forests, rafted and boomed down the upwaters of the Penobscot, sawed at Bangor mills. The biggest single shipment on record left Bangor aboard the ship F.E. Smith on July 14, 1862, a load of 1,040,000 board feet, bound for Liverpool.

The grandest old lady of the small lumber schooners was Polly. She was built on the Penobscot in 1804, and was still sailing 101 years later in 1905. No one counted the number of trips Polly made up and down the winding, tricky 25-mile run from Bangor to the sea.

That trip is not easy today, when there are few boats on the Bangor river. But during the lumber boom the man at the helm must have been stark with terror at times. He might be steering round a bend and come suddenly upon a dreaded sight — two tow boats pulling 20 or 30 vessels, three abreast, ten rows deep, taking up the whole river.

The boom in lumber meant a boom in building in Bangor. A hundred new buildings went up in 1831, two hundred in 1832, five hundred in 1833. Among them, of course, were some 'uglies.' But though Bangor was a boom town as rough as the boom towns of the brawling American west were to be later, Bangor had a streak of ambitious good taste from the start.

Even as a frontier town in 1801, when fewer than three hundred lived here, three Bangor merchants — Stetson, Lapish, and French — commissioned the famous Boston architect, Charles Bulfinch, to lay out plans for Bangor's future. Bulfinch drew up plans for the development of the choice area called Condeskeag Point on the Penobscot, dividing it into a grid of nine streets and 213 building lots.

These three merchants must have been men with vision for the distant future, or have commissioned Bulfinch after a few rounds of rum flip. Because Bangor even by 1810 did not look at all promising to their fellow business man Jacob Leavitt. In 1810, Leavitt wrote this description of Bangor in his diary:

"The mercantile interest here consists of about 20

> traders, with small stock and small capital, little or no navigation (shipping) owned. No meeting house, several school houses, several tolerable houses partly finished; yet on the whole the place has the appearance of but little wealth . . . I am of the opinion that these slow improvements are the result of idleness, stupor and drinking . . . The country around is very poor, with but few settlers . . . they never pay bills until sued, then their stock, if any, is taken; otherwise their land goes to auction and they go to jail."

Corn, grain and meat, as well as money, were scarce then in Bangor, but disease was plentiful. Between 1808 and 1810 an epidemic killed many, but it is not reported whether it was diphtheria or spotted fever. (Spotted fever swept the Kennebec area in 1814 and 1815.)

Twenty years after Leavitt's gloomy entries in his diary, he was rich and Bangor was growing fast. Even though Bulfinch's plans were not followed, a few handsome new homes were being built each year by the wealthy.

In the poor parts of town, families suffered in shanties, drowning out the world with rum, and plague was rampant amid the slops and mud.

Then came the cholera scare, and the first big Irish influx, two dangers wrapped in one event deeply resented and feared by most of Bangor.

The Irish came sweeping down from Canada in the summer and fall of 1832. Bangor felt threatened by the penniless refugees, and more threatened by the dreaded cholera that they were supposed to be carrying with them.

The sad tale began with famine in County Mayo. American newspapers carried stories of thousands there dying from hunger, and the living fleeing to the land of opportunity across the Atlantic.

By August 1832, 45,000 Irish had landed in Canada and thousands were heading to the United States, on foot.

Bangor was the magnet for them. Bangor by now was famous as a boom town, where jobs and money were to be had for the asking.

As these Irish headed toward Maine, Bangor was rife with rumors that they were bringing cholera. The Irish ship Carricks, out of Dublin, had arrived reportedly infested with cholera. The ship

Constantia, out of Limerick, had lost 29 passengers from cholera on the way across.

So at the June town meeting in Bangor, citizens filed appeals to the Governor of Maine to prevent foreign immigrants coming to Bangor. To get quicker action than they'd get from the governor, the town rushed two of their selectmen, James Fiske and John Hodgdon, to Eastport by stagecoach, with instructions to turn back any Irish refugees heading toward Bangor. At the same time, Dr. Mason was sent hurriedly off to New York to learn the latest ways of treating cholera, should it break out in Bangor. Maine prepared to repel the Irish by setting up citizen picket lines at border crossings. Portland and Bangor refused to permit any Irish immigrants to board steamships at Eastport which were headed to their cities. This action only resulted in making the Irish try to get to Bangor by foot.

It was a hard journey of 200 miles through the wilderness forest of northeastern Maine from St. John, New Brunswick, where many of the refugees landed, to Bangor. But the desperate families attempted it in hordes, straggling along the Wilderness road. The sight was reported by a stagecoach driver, Abner Lee:

> "They came, men, women and children, footsore and weary, with their babies in their arms and worldly possessions strapped on their backs, many of them depending on charity for their food and shelter. Some days no less than hundreds passed along."

Many made it into Bangor. Citizens rioted in the street in fierce anti-Irish demonstrations. No cholera epidemic broke out, perhaps because winter cold came quickly on their heels and killed the germs.

But Bangor would again be a magnet for the Irish after the next potato famine struck Ireland in 1846. This time, cholera came with them; thousands fell sick; makeshift hospitals were all over town; and more than 140 people died from cholera in Bangor before the terror passed.

The Bangor boom pulled the penniless Irish refugees to Bangor. Some became rich and key figures in Bangor life.

One young Irishman who made his splash on both sides of the tracks was Teddy Fields. He arrived a penniless boy from Ireland, worked as a day laborer in Bangor until he and two fellow Irishmen headed west in the California goldrush on 1849. Fields struck it rich and came back to Bangor loaded with new wealth, which burned a hole in his pocket. He moved into a fashionable mansion and plunged into the high-life of race horses and wines and playboy friends. He cut a fine, fast swath in Bangor and when he died young at age 33, he left more than $100,000 — a fortune in those days. One section of his will bequeathed 600 bottles of fine wine and brandy to a special friend.

The Irish in Bangor, as everywhere else, left their happy mark on many a fine saloon. In the area police called Peppermint Row, were the pubs run by Thomas Kelly and James Aarn, and the famous Paddy McAloon Stand. At City Point were the grog shops of Mary Managan, Hugh Gillogly and other countrymen. James Quinn ran one of the best — the Alhambra. Pat Moran was host to many an Irish Ball at his establishment called Moranbega Hall, in mockery of the Norumbega Hall across town, where Bangor's bluebloods staged their balls.

As the Irish arrived in waves following each potato famine in the old country, they became lumberjacks and rivermen and rafters and seagoing sailors. They multiplied and their cousins from County Mayo and Donegal came to join them and to belly up to the Irish bars.

And here in Bangor, as in Boston and other cities hit by the Irish immigrant wave, the Irish were scorned, mocked, mistreated and feared. The Protestants of Bangor feared not only plague of cholera, but feared that the plague of popery had come to torment them.

But the Irish clung on and by the 1850s, the Irish made up one-quarter of Bangor's population. This numerical power seemed a new threat to many Bangor citizens, who were eager to "put the Irish in their place." So when Bangor went to the polls March 15, close to St. Patrick's Day 1855, the "natives" voted into office by a landslide a slate of Know-Nothing candidates for mayor and the city council. Their platform was a thundering promise to strictly enforce Maine law and end foreign influences on the true-blue American way of life in Bangor.

First target of new Mayor J.T.K. Hayward was the grogshops. If liquor could be taken away from the poor, he preached, that would eliminate poverty. As the chief spearhead of the drive, the mayor appointed Bangor's most vocal temperance leader, the

Rev. Philip Weaver. The city council made this hard-shell Baptist preacher city marshal, superintendent of the school committee, chief constable and tax collector. In addition to all these powers, the Rev. Weaver was given control of Bangor's reform police force of 40 men, a sort of paramilitary outfit which wore special leather hatbands with the word 'police' emblazoned in silver. The Baptist minister, dressed in a black frock coat, wore a silver star police badge under his lapel, and a pair of Colt revolvers in his belt. He led the crusade to wipe out liquor.

Weaver, a graduate of Bangor Theological Seminary in 1849, and minister of the Bangor Free Will Baptist Church, went hell-bent after demon rum. He kicked down doors on his raids without bothering to get a warrant; he jailed Irishmen for possession of the merest amounts of alcohol. Within a few months Preacher Weaver and his police had seized over 10,000 gallons of white-eye rum. They went all out to close the Irish hangouts around the waterfront area. When the Irish celebrated the Fourth of July, the special police drew their revolvers against them, but were then forced to retreat under a barrage of Irish bricks. By September 10 tensions had reached the explosion point, and the Irish marched upon the city marshal's house — only to find he was out. A few days later street fights and near riots broke out at Paddy's Hollow. For a month there was near anarchy in the Irish sections of Bangor as mobs stormed Irish hangouts. There were rumors rife that the Irish Catholics were building a nunnery in the basement of St. John's and that papist debaucheries were being celebrated underground. Threats were voiced about putting the torch to the Catholic Church, as Know-Nothings had done a year before in Bath when they burned the Catholic Church there. Countering this rumor was another that Irishmen were standing guard at night around their church, armed with rifles and ready to shoot.

Then came the bomb that rocked Bangor!

The Rev. Philip Weaver was suddenly and totally unfrocked in public. Newspapers broke the news that the great reformer who had led the crusade against rum and sin had all along been a heavy drinker, a sinner and thief himself.

Much of the 10,000 gallons of rum and gin which Weaver and his special police had seized they had sold back to the rightful owners, and Weaver had pocketed the profit. The alcohol he had not sold back, Weaver and his police had drunk. The men Weaver had arrested had been released if they could line Weaver's pockets with a $20 gold piece. The City Council which had appointed Weaver as its battering-ram, now fired him. But Weaver did not stay for the verdict. He fled in the dark of night before the council met. In the next election, that city council itself was fired by the voters.

The Bangor Irish drank a dram to celebrate. They had survived again.

Larry Conner, famous riverman from Veazie, killed on a logging drive in May 1868. He was a Bangor Tiger. (Vickery collection)

32.

Logging Camps: 1840-1890

Rough and Brutal Life

Lumberjacks and rivermen made Bangor. There never would have been 3,300 vessels a year coming up the Penobscot, and Bangor would never have been the world's busiest lumber port without lumberjacks in the woods cutting trees and rivermen driving the logs downstream. Let's look at how they worked and lived and played.

Life in the lumber camps, like life on clipper ships and Downeasters, has been romanticized over the years. We glow today in a false, romantic picture of legendary men who worked the forests and sailed around the Horn. Truth is their life was harsh and dangerous; their food and living conditions were awful; and their wages were slave's wages.

Pay in the depression days of the 1870s dropped as low as $5 a month in the woods and still men went because life at the soup kitchens in Bangor was worse. A top hand with an ax such as David Libby, who was so good that his name has been famous over 100 years, got $2 a day. But most men working the woods between 1860 and 1890 earned 50 cents to $1 a day.

The crews were a motley crowd; some Indians, some half-breeds; a big proportion came, then as now, from Canada. They were mostly wiry, quick-tempered Frenchmen from big families on poor farms, where there was not food enough in winter to feed 15 mouths at the family table. And there were plenty of Irish who had fled from famines in Donegal. There were Finns, Poles, Russians, a cross-section of European immigrants.

A few men from these varied backgrounds became such experts that their names are known a century later.

"Big Sabattus" Mitchell, who weighed over 260 pounds, was the most famous of the Penobscot Indians who were top river drivers during the 1870's. He was joined by Attean Sock, "Black Jack" Solomon, Lewey Ketchum and John Stanley — all Indians made immortal in Fannie Eckstrom's classic stories in "The Penobscot Man."

Fred Gilbert was a Frenchman who began as an axman and finished as the head of the spruce wood division of Great Northern Paper Co. Fred Noad, born in England, was a cant-dog hand who rose to be deputy minister of lands and forests for Ontario. Tom Cozzie was a Russian who began as a swamper cutting tote roads and finished as woods manager for St. Regis Paper Co.

John Ross, the most famous river man on the Penobscot who ever lived, was born in Orrington, Maine, in 1831. Ross was work boss of the Penobscot Log Driving Co from 1864 to 1867 and set records by moving 2 million feet of lumber down the West Branch. Year after year, John Ross welded together a piebald bunch of French, Irish, Indians, Finns, English, Slavs, and transformed them into the Bangor Tigers, whose skill and daring with pikepole and peavey, spiked boot and bateau, have never been surpassed on any river anywhere. Ross died in Halifax in 1913.

A lumber camp might have 150 men inside and close to 100 horses outside in the hovel. The men lived in the remote camps from November till March or April, felling trees. Winter weather in these north woods was cold; there were weeks on end when the thermometer never got above 30 degrees below zero. Some winters the snow was seven feet deep. In the springtime and summer, when crews built the camps and dams, the men were plagued by flies. From the first of May till the end of July the men were tortured by infestations of black fly, moose fly, mosquitoes and, worst of all, the millions of no-see-ums. But woodsmen had a way to fight back; they shaved their heads, and coated themselves with layers of tar mixed with bear grease.

The work day began at 4:30 a.m., when the cold knifed and the sky was dark; and lasted till 12 hours later, every day except Sunday.

The camp was usually two rooms, the living quarters and the cook shack. In the center was a huge fireplace, big enough to take four- or six-foot logs. The fire burned day and night for six months on end, saturating the room with smoke and smell, but keeping it warm, even hot. At right angles to the fire were deacons' benches and empty barrels, the only places to sit or to dry wet and iced boots and socks. For eating, there was a long sawhorse table, where the cook, who ruled the camp, served breakfast and supper. Lunch was taken out to the work sites by the cookees.

Many cooks demanded silence at mealtime. The meals were mostly salt port, biscuits, molasses and beans.

Beans and brown bread for breakfast, brown bread and beans for dinner, and a mixture of the two for supper; and little else until the 1890s, when lumber companies began to compete for crews by the food their camps provided.

As for sleeping, all men often slept in one huge common bunk. On Sundays, in the cleaner camps, the men changed their bunks by throwing out the hemlock boughs on which they had slept for a week, and replacing them with clean-cut boughs. One huge cover was the one blanket for all. Two lengths of blanket material, each 20 feet by 20 feet were sewn together and six inches of warming straw was stuffed between the top and bottom layers. The men would bunk down under this communal cover. It was so heavy that if water got into it, 20 men could not lift it to carry it out to dry in the winter sun. Over the weeks, lice and vermin would infest the straw. Worse, some men, unable to climb out from the middle, would urinate or defecate into the straw.

Men slept in their underclothes, shedding only boots and outer layers, wearing the same clothing for weeks on end. The body heat from scores of men under the same cover, plus the heat of the fire, kept them warm through nights when the outside temperature was 40 degrees below zero. While packed in like sardines under the lid of the tremendous communal cover, one man would wake and cry out "Flop!" and then — without really waking — all would turn over.

As the years went by, the camps became cleaner and more comfortable. Instead of men sleeping in one huge bed on the floor, they slept in bunks in pairs, head to toe. These pair bunks were stacked tiers high around the walls of the single big room. This lasted until the 1940s. Today the lumber camps are more like motels, but with more and better food.

The sleeping arrangements were described by the uncle of Robert E. Pike in Pike's fine book, "Tall Trees and Tough Men." His uncle was 92 years old in 1966 when he described his camp.

> "Starting in October 1892, I stayed 125 days in camp. It snowed every day. And I never saw the camp by daylight, except on Sunday. The first night I arrived I slept in an upper bunk, but the air up there was so bad that the next day I took the only lower one left, in a corner. It had an icicle thick as my leg and three feet long lying

> between a chink in the logs, right next to my nose. I slept beside the icicle for four months and I never had a trace of cold. I was never sick and I never weighed so much again in my whole life as I did that winter, living on baked beans and salt pork and working from before daylight till after dark six days a week."

Scores of reports confirm there was almost no illness in lumber camps, despite the fact men were cold and wet from ice and snow for 125 days and nights, ate coarse, monotonous food, slept in the same clothes in fetid rooms, sharing bunks. The subzero cold killed most bugs. But subzero temperatures did not kill the smallpox virus. In the late 1830s and again ten years later, smallpox swept through many camps. Of course, there were no doctors. But there were lots of accidents and injuries. If a man was hurt so badly he could not recover in camp, then he'd be lashed to a sled and pulled over rough territory to the nearest doctor. The trip could be agony, and take days; so most injured men chose to stay where they were, in camp.

Why did men by the thousand endure such work? Strangely, some loved the hard life and stayed with it till they died. But they were few out of the thousands. Often, the bosses got their crews to the logging camps the same way bucko mates got their crews aboard schooners. They kidnapped them.

Agents were paid $1 per head for each body they could put on a crew. Consequently scores of men in the camps were stuck there against their will for four months, because they had been dragooned while drunk and senseless, taken from some tavern or whorehouse. This happened as late as 1919. Robert Pike reports that when he was at a camp in 1919, the tote-team arrived "with a Boston man with a respectable and profitable business. He had slept it off most of the way from Boston, and when he woke up he was in the north woods, 20 miles from a railroad, and he had $200 in his pocket. In the same camp there were a New York City tailor, a Florida barber, an English remittance man and two alleged murderers."

Such were the men who each year cut millions of dollars of lumber bound for Bangor, over 100 years ago.

33.

Animals, Men & Inventions:
Getting Out the Timber

Rivermen along the Penobscot and all across America where men drive logs, bless the name of Joseph Peavey. His invention has saved thousands of backs and many lives. He invented the "peavey" and his invention killed off the cantankerous old cant-dog.

Joseph Peavey, a blacksmith from Stillwater, was spending an hour in 1858 watching the rivermen work on the Penobscot. Every man was having trouble catching and holding swirling logs with his cant-dog. Peavey listened to them swearing at the logs and the cant-dogs. That heavy cant-dog was hard to swing, and then lost its hold on a log it had grabbed.

As Peavey peered down at the rivermen and their cant-dogs through the slats in a wooden bridge, he got his idea which soon revolutionized the logging industry.

He turned and went quickly back to his blacksmith shop and hammered out a new version of the cant-dog. He put a pick on the end to grab the log; then made a rigid clasp to encircle and hold the log, with lips on one side. He drilled these lips so they'd take a bolt which would hold the hook, or dog, on the log without hampering its up and down movement when the tool was used to turn logs or break loose jammed logs.

Peavey took his new tool back to the bridge. He talked William Heald of Orono and other rivermen into trying it. They found it worked well and told him he had made a marvelous invention. Blacksmith Peavey and his son worked the clock around to meet the demand for his invention. It was soon called a "peavey" everywhere logs were driven.

Alone Peavey couldn't begin to fill the orders which poured in. The Bangor Edge Tool Co. got the patent from Peavey — some say stole it — and by 1878 was making over 2,000 and still couldn't meet demand, even with enlarged production and new quarters. R.W. Kimball of Orono went into the business of making peaveys too, and by 1885 was making 6,000 a year. The price was only $1.50 each. In 1887 the Connecticut Lumber Co. placed an order for 2,500 peaveys, and a Seattle firm ordered 2,000. By 1891 one firm was making 28,000 handles a year for Bangor peaveys. For many years a peavey factory in Brewer sported a ten-foot sign over its front door. On it were two letters, one at each end — P and V. Today a Peavey gravestone in a Bangor cemetery bears a large P crossed by two carved peaveys.

How did lumbermen move a massive tree, 100 feet or more tall and six feet in diameter at the base, out of the forest?

First they cut a track to the nearest stream. To do this required a crew of men called "swampers," to cut down the brush and trees and make a roadway and build bridges over swamps. Then they iced the roadway with water till it was glassy-slippery.

Then they hitched the ox teams and pulled the massive tree to the water. Later horses were used instead of oxen; still later, tractors, and still later, fleets of lumber trucks.

Begin with the ox. When lumbering started, horses were bred too small to haul heavy loads. Oxen were stronger, could pull better, ate less, got sick less. So teams of oxen were driven from Bangor to lumbering camps far up the Penobscot. But oxen move slower than the wrath of God. The trip often took six days. Imagine driving 100 of these beasts for six days through a forest wilderness.

Between 30 and 60 oxen, yoked in pairs, were needed to haul a huge pine. Drivers, with their goads, kept the oxen pulling. Assistants stationed along the way kept them from falling down on each other, or getting their chains crossed, which would break their backs. On a long, heavy haul, four pairs of oxen might break a leg or a back and have to be destroyed. Spare oxen were kept along the track.

Dumb and strong as an ox may be, the animal has legs which forever caused trouble. Due to their cloven hooves, oxen were always cutting their forelegs below the dew claws. And their oddly delicate legs would freeze up from cold at night. So night after night, the drivers had to pick off the ice and patiently rub the legs of their beasts.

Shoeing an ox was the worst job of all, done by the camp blacksmith. Because of their cloven hooves, each hoof required two shoes. And when an ox needed to be shod, the blacksmith could not pick up and bend the leg, as with a horse. An ox had to be lifted bodily up in the air. This required maneuvering the beast into a sling and then winching it up into the air, by hand. The leather sling had a hole punched in it for the ox to pee through, which it always did when getting new shoes. Then the leg to be shod had to be held in a kind of vise and hauled straight out so the blacksmith could work on it.

Despite the problems, oxen were used to haul lumber for close to 50 years, until horses were bred big enough and strong enough to work in Maine winters. By 1890, the ox was out and horses by the thousands hauled lumber in the woods all winter long. The Great Northern Paper Company alone had as many as 1,500 horses in its lumbering camps.

The logistics of supplying men and beasts in the camps were boggling. Two reporters for the Industrial Journal, covering lumbering operations on the Upper Penobscot River in 1887, filed this account:

> "It is estimated that 350 horses and 4,050 men are lumbering in the vicinity of Patten, and that it requires another 40 men and 100 horses to haul in their supplies. It needs about 500 tons of hay and 40,000 bushels of oats to feed the horses and 110 tons of provisions to feed the men. Altogether some 1,400 tons of camp supplies must be moved through Patten; requiring cash outlays of $125,000 for labor, $90,000 for hay, grain and hauling and $25,000 for food for the men. In all close to $250,000 in these expenses."

The ledger books of Joab Palmer for 1880 show that his camp with 160 men and 80 horses ate up the following provisions: 270 barrels of flour, 135 barrels of pork, 300 bushels of beans, 2,000 gallons of molasses, 300 bushels of potatoes, 3 tons of fresh beef, 110 tons of hay and 5,500 bushels of corn and oats. He complained that these supplies were almost all gone, and he still had a full month more of lumbering operations ahead.

In time it became cheaper to clear the forest and make a farm than to tote in supplies. At Chamberlain Farm, on Chamberlain Lake, they harvested 600 acres of hay and potatoes a year for nearby lumber camps. At the Pittston Farm on Seboomook Lake, where the North Branch and South Branch of the Penobscot River join, they raised 5,000 bushels of potatoes in 1924. Until

Pittston Farm became a supply depot, as many as 60 tote-teams a day plodded up the woods road with fodder and food, according to records from 1916. The care and feeding of horses was expensive, requiring thousands of tons of hay and oats.

Then came the machine — The Lombard Steam Log Hauler, which used a lag tractor tread, and was the granddaddy of all bulldozers of today.

Alvin O. Lombard invented it and then patented it in 1901. He was a farmer's son who grew up to be a mechanical genius.

Lombard's invention looked like a huge, primitive locomotive, except that instead of wheels it had a revolving belt of lags which could travel over snow and rough country. The first models were fired by wood, but later models used coal to make steam. Their speed was about five miles an hour. And they worked day and night, unlike horses.

At its best, the Lombard pulled a train 1650 feet long, made up of 24 huge sleds loaded with long logs. The early models weighed 14 tons, had a 75 horsepower engine and could haul as much lumber as 16 horses. Later models weighed 20 tons, were 32 feet long and could haul a load of 125 tons. But they were expensive, $5,000 each in 1908, F.O.B. at Waterville, Maine.

Lombards required a crew of four men: steersman, engineer, fireman and conductor. The steersman had a job more dangerous and hair-raising than any stunt driver of today. He sat up front, looking like a gargoyle wrapped in blankets to fight off 30-below-zero cold. Above him was the smokestack belching smoke that blinded him and sparks which burned him. He had no brakes, but clung onto his heavy iron steering wheel for dear life, hoping he'd stay on the tracks on fast downhill turns. When he drove at night, a blazing acetylene headlight lit the forest and the track just ahead — if the snow was not too blinding.

The fireman hurled logs, and later coal, onto the boiler to keep up steam pressure. The engineer was in charge of fixing breakdowns, which were frequent. The conductor had a primitive telephone to keep in constant touch along the way, reporting progress.

But Lombard kept improving his locomotives and they performed so well that Lombards were in use until about 1930, a life span of almost 30 years. Great Northern in 1928 hauled more than 900 tons of coal to feed its 20-ton Lombard working on Cooper Brook stream, a tributary of the Penobscot.

Lombard stopped making his Steam Log Hauler in 1917, and developed two gasoline tractors, which were great successes. They hauled 200 tons of wood at a time (about 150 cords) and needed only one man to operate them. The Lombard Big Six held its own from 1917 to 1937, when the cheaper, more powerful Caterpillar cornered the market. One Lombard still sits in the Maine woods, near Churchill Depot on the Allagash.

Lumbering in Maine, from Harper's Weekly, 1858.

Lunch stop on river drive. (Paper Industry photo)

Rivermen using peaveys. (Paper Industry photo)

Breaking up a log jam 1890s. (Bangor Public Library)

Bateaux, like those used by Benedict Arnold expedition to Quebec in the Revolutionary War seen being used on Great Northern Paper Co.'s last river drive on the West Branch of the Penobscot River, 1971. (Paper Industry photo)

Lumber camp, 1890s. Note only oxen were used. (Courtesy James B. Vickery)

Lumber camp, 1912. Note the change from oxen to mostly horses, and that the camp is no longer made of logs. The tools were peaveys. (Courtesy James B. Vickery)

Breaking in a landing, early 1900s. (Bangor Public Library)

Lumber camp crew, 1898. Note that the men are as young as 16. Man in front row holds camp kittens, with a fiddler behind him. (Vickery collection)

Bangor as a shipping port about 1870.
Note European and North American Railroad wharf.

A boom house at Ambejesus boom, Penobscot River around 1880. Man on left is holding a pick pole. (Stereo view by A.L. Hinds, courtesy James B. Vickery.)

When logs first moved by truck. (Paper Industry)

A log drive on the Machias near Canaan Dam on Old Stream - 1967 St. Regis Co. drive. (Maine Department of Conservation)

Bangor, world's largest lumber port about 1880.
Note lumber in river by sawmills.

Bucksport on the Penobscot, St. Regis Paper Co. 1952, when logs were still driven on the river.

Last pulpwood drive on the West Branch Penobscot River. 1971. (Maine Department of Conservation)

East Millinocket Mill — Pollution Abatement.

Ships at McGilvery yard, Brewer, 1870s. (Vickery Collection)

34.

Strange Cargoes:
Shooks, Staves & Spools

Today if you stopped anyone in downtown Bangor and asked what a shook is, you'd probably get a glassy look or a wild guess that a shook is something between a schmuck and a sheik.

But shooks by the millions were shipped out of Bangor in the 1880s, headed for Palermo and Naples and exotic ports in the West Indies.

And birch to make millions of spools for cotton thread went from Bangor to Glasgow.

The man who made millions of dollars by shipping shooks and spool wood was Thomas J. Stewart, a self-made Bangor mogul with loudly-voiced political views, especially on the subject of tariffs.

Stewart had gone to sea as a boy, risen fast to be captain of his ship. But after being shipwrecked in 1850, he stayed close to dry land and came ashore to start a grocery store in Bangor. Quickly he expanded into ship chandlery, then into brokerage, then into the commission business, growing until he became the biggest name in Bangor shipping. Shooks were his specialty.

A shook is a slice of pine, about a half inch thick. This wood was used to make boxes, mostly boxes for fruit such as oranges, tomatoes and onions — what we call orange crates.

By 1881, Stewart was shipping overseas enough shooks to make half a million orange crates, enough staves to make 3,600 barrels. In addition, he shipped to Bermuda 128,500 onion boxes, 19,400 tomato boxes and 15,000 feet of lumber. That lumber was only a splinter compared to the two million feet of long lumber he shipped that year to the West Indies, Granada and Port-of-Spain. In ten years between 1878 and 1888, Thomas J. Stewart chartered 66 vessels to carry his shooks from Bangor to the Mediterranean and 53 vessels to carry his shooks and lumber to the Caribbean. He shipped out his shooks in special convenience packages — each holding enough slices of pine to build an orange crate, each wrapped with string.

Another strange use for Maine's tall trees was the conversion of best birch into spools for cotton thread. Stewart cornered this huge market, too, through his dealings with the family firm of J. and P. Coats in Glasgow, Scotland. They were the biggest makers of cotton thread in the world; and they wound their thread on wooden spools made of Maine white birch, shipped to them by Stewart. It was a huge business.

In 1887 and 1888 seven million board feet of birch left Bangor bound for the Coats plant. One British ship, the SS Crawford, left Bangor with 1.25 million feet of birch aboard to be made into thread spools.

By August 1889, Stewart had shipped 5 million feet of birch for spools and contracted to ship two million more. He had trouble finding enough ships to carry his cargo. In March 1890, Stewart died, and the spool trade with Scotland swiftly declined. But J. and P. Coats kept on using Maine birch for their spools in a smaller way. They finally bought a mill of their own in Dixfield, Maine, and were making spools there until 1963, when plastic spools had replaced wooden ones.

Mudlarking was the name for stevedoring in Bangor. Mudlarkers were the men who loaded 100 to 200 ships a day. And they hung around the waterfront by the hundreds, sometimes the thousands, working long hours in bad conditions for small pay.

The pay averaged only about 25 cents an hour because "buckwheat eaters," men from New Brunswick, worked cheaply. They poured into Bangor after their winter work was finished in the logging camps. They blew their money on the Devil's Half Acre in a week or two. So from April until October or even November, when lumbering upriver started in earnest, these buckwheat eaters crowded the wharves, willing to do tough and mean work for a pittance. They kept wages low.

But the old logbooks of Bangor harbormasters show there was usually work for them. Until the river froze over from December till April, there were usually two foreign-bound ships clearing Bangor each day and 30 more leaving on the domestic trade. When the depression hit in the mid-1870s, the traffic dropped two-thirds, unemployment was rife and Bangor ran soup kitchens.

But 1880 was a good year. The domestic trade loaded 123 million feet of long lumber, 145,000 shooks, 100,000 fish barrels, 109,000 bundles of staves. Foreign exports amounted to two million feet of long lumber, half a million feet of shook and 226 spars. Stevedores on the Bangor waterfront kept busy, making $2.50 to $3.00 a day, while young boys earned $1.50. That was as much as a man made going to sea, where an ordinary sailor's wage was $20 to $25 a month. (If this seems low, remember that in 1941, when the U.S. entered World War II, a GI soldier was paid $21 a month.) As late as 1894, Bangor stevedores were making only $3 a day and $3.50 for night work — and those work days lasted 10 hours. Finally they went on strike, demanding 50 cents an hour on Sundays, pointing out stevedores in New York were getting 60 cents on Sundays. Surprisingly, they got it.

While buckwheat eaters from New Brunswick were undercutting wages at the port of Bangor, lumber shippers in the Canadian Maritimes were trying to undercut the lumber shipping magnates of Bangor. And thereby hangs the tale of some of the strangest, hugest vessels ever launched.

Workers at Joggins, Nova Scotia, launched a raft of logs bigger than the world had ever seen. Working under H.H. Robertson of St. John, they cut 2.5 million feet of long logs, shaped them in the form of a tremendous vessel and linked them together with 54 tons of chains, they then launched it all into the Bay of Fundy. The contraption measured 410 feet long, 50 feet wide and 35 feet high. The scheme was to tow it to New York City, and sell whole logs there. The idea was to beat the tariff. The U.S. Customs levied a tariff of $2.00 a thousand feet on sawed logs, but there was no tariff on unsawed logs of the size in this monster raft.

But the raft was so big and heavy that it broke the ways when it was launched July 31, 1886, and the monster settled, half afloat, half sunk. Maine newspapers had a field day, mocking the attempt. But the Canadians did not give up. Instead they made an even bigger monster.

By November 15 of the next year, 1887, they were ready to try again. The new raft was 585 feet long, 62 feet wide, 37 feet high and drew almost 20 feet of water. The lumber in it amounted to 2.7 million feet and the whole thing weighed 120,000 tons.

The day the monster was launched down 1200 feet of ways, it got up such speed that it traveled the 1200 feet in 34 seconds. The friction was so intense that it set the ways afire.

The immense tow got under way for New York City. But off

Nantucket, Atlantic swells parted the towline and the raft was suddenly adrift in rough seas, 300 miles offshore in the coastal shipping lanes. The huge logs in the raft broke apart. For six months thereafter, vessels reported seeing these logs drifting dangerously in the Atlantic. They finally washed up on the coast of Africa.

Bangor rubbed its hands with glee at the fiasco.

Another big raft, launched in 1890, had to put into Rockland and Rockport for repairs. When it got near Portland, it was in such bad shape that it was beached at Peaks Island for more repairs. Finally it was repaired enough to leave Portland on July 28, heading for New York, consigned to the Astor family who wanted to use the huge logs for pilings on new wharves they were building. It put into Vineyard Haven, Massachusetts, to be repaired again, and eventually arrived in New York on August 5, 1890.

Those Canadians, fighting to beat the $2 tariff and undercut Maine, would not give up trying. The next year they launched the most gigantic raft of all, consisting of 3.5 million feet of lumber in logs, built in 16 sections, banded together with iron chains. Out in front, hauling it, were two tugs, each with nine-inch hawsers 900 feet long. But they were not as strong or powerful as the Atlantic. Off Mount Desert, Maine, rough seas broke 13 rafts loose. The tugs put into Bar Harbor and then chased and caught the 13 rafts which had broken loose. Off they went again, only to hit more bad weather and lose more rafts off Massachusetts.

Robertson gave up and took his talents to the Pacific coast. But for years, Maine residents along the coast had a fine supply of huge logs rolling in free.

The most sentimental cargo ever shipped from Bangor was Christmas trees. Christmas trees were an unlikely cargo to come out of the world's biggest lumber port. But in the 1880s, the city folk in New York and all along the east coast were learning to light and decorate Christmas trees. The Christmas trees went out as deck cargo. But as the demand grew greater, they became too much trouble to load aboard ship. So before long the coastal schooners got out of the Christmas tree business and the Maine Central and other Bangor railroads got into it. By 1883 one contractor had orders for 15 carloads for New York City. Each car carried up to 2,500 trees, and he got up to $5 each for the best and biggest. He took in over $150,000 of New York money that Christmas.

Another odd cargo, proving that somebody, somewhere, will buy anything, was sawdust. In Maine, sawdust was used to bank the foundations of houses in winter, to keep out the cold; and the sawmills gave it away. But Bangor found a market for this waste from its mills and sold it for $1.50 a cord, to keep ice cold.

The cargo sailors hated and feared most was lime, shipped from Rockland, seafaring hub of Penobscot Bay. Lime kilns demanded wood, endless cords of wood, day and night. The wood could be the lowest quality scrap, so long as it burned hot and there was plenty of it.

Hundreds of sawmills along the Penobscot were glad to find this ready market so close by for their scrap lumber. Many a man in an ugly boat made a meager living, scouring the Bangor River for "skoots," the remnant boards tossed off by the sawmills, and sailing down the bay to Rockland to sell his load for cash.

The lime kilns had been started by the money-canny General Henry Knox in 1790 as one of the dozen Maine enterprises he ran from his palatial home, Montpelier, at Thomaston. His schooners, the Quicklime and the Montpelier, hauled lime from Thomaston to New York.

By 1835, the kilns were burning 750,000 casks of lime a year. To keep a single kiln burning took 30 cords of wood. So by the 1850s some 500 sloops, schooners, brigs and little "kiln wooders" were hauling thousands of cords of wood into Rockland harbor. This was safe cargo, even though some of the small schooners were run by a one-legged or one-eyed man, going single-handed with only a mongrel dog for crew.

The dangerous job was taking the lime in casks to market. The slightest amount of water leaking into the lime in the ship's hold would start a fire, a fire that could not be put out. With luck, it might be smothered after it had been burning for days below decks.

So the "Rockland limers" were a special breed of ship. Mostly they were old schooners, whose loss would break nobody's heart and hurt their pocket only a little. These old boats were usually planked over below decks, to keep the lime barrels away from the bilge water.

The skipper's nose was the fire alarm. The smell of lime being slaked by water was a fearsome danger signal that the lime was burning. There was only one way to kill it — by suffocation. Every door, every port, every crack and crevice through which air might flow, had to be plugged and sealed tight, using layers of plaster made from the lime.

When a fire started at sea, the vessel hove to, while the crew sealed all air leaks. Then, slowly, she made her way toward the nearest harbor; not to enter, but to anchor far away from other shipping. Here the limer was stripped of everything that could be taken off. The captain and crew, except for watchmen, went ashore, to board out at a house with a clear view of their ship. She might burst into full, roaring flame at any time. Or, with luck, the fire might be suffocated and die. Sometimes the long wait lasted three months, when fire finally died from lack of oxygen, and the ship was saved. Other times, the fire won and would not be smothered. Then the ship was towed out to sea and scuttled. Or sometimes she was towed to a remote cove, where her sea cocks were opened to allow the ocean to pour in, in the hope it might put out the fire. This seldom happened. More often the water made the lime swell as well as burn; and the expansion of the cargo burst the decks and the hull or broke the back of the vessel; she died an ugly death and was left to rot on a mudbank.

Today lime is towed to market in fireproof barges made entirely of steel.

Across Penobscot Bay from Rockland lies the island of Vinalhaven, 12 miles offshore. The strange cargo from here was granite, hundreds of thousands of tons of granite. The first granite was shipped from Vinalhaven by Richard Tuck in 1829 to build prison walls in New Hampshire. Ironically this cargo moved aboard his vessel named Plymouth Rock.

This Vinalhaven quarry supplied the granite for the great columns of the Cathedral of St. John the Divine in New York. These four columns each weigh 120 tons and cost $20,000 each. Joseph R. Bodwell, who later became governor of Maine, headed the Bodwell Granite Co. during its peak days of production. At the height of the boom more than 3,800 people worked on Vinalhaven, more than double the number who live there today. Maine granite was used to build hundreds of big office buildings, monuments, post offices and street curbs in major cities.

Strangest cargo to be lost in Penobscot Bay was aboard a British steamer called the Royal Tar. In a northwester on an October night in 1836, running between St. John, New Brunswick and Portland, she caught fire in the Fox Island Thorofare, between Vinalhaven and North Haven. She went down only a few yards from shore. The crew and 72 passengers were rescued. But the Royal Tar was transporting a circus; an elephant, two lions, a tiger, a leopard and other wild beasts were lost, drowned at sea.

This river driver is using the famous peavey, a logging tool which was developed in Maine many years ago by Joseph Peavey of Stillwater.

The beautiful City of Bangor steamship. (Vickery photo collection)

35.

Bangor Boats and Railroads:
Wonderful Way to Go

Going to Bangor used to mean taking the Boston boat; or not quite so much fun, the overnight sleeper on the train from New York. Today it means only a plane ride. Gone are the luxury and excitement of the Bangor boats and the Bar Harbor Express. And a big loss, too.

On December 28, 1935, Capt. Alfred E. Rawley stood on the bridge of his beloved white steamer Belfast. This time he listened sadly to her great whistle blow three long departing blasts. They were her farewell to Bangor as she pulled out on her last trip to Boston.

Rawley, born in St. George, Maine, had been working the coastal steamers all his life; 20 years on deck, 22 years as master. His next stop, this day as always, would be Tillson's wharf in Rockland; more farewells there and then the final journey to Boston.

That night of December 28 marked an end to a beloved era of steamboating. Since 1834, 101 years earlier, people had been riding steamboats back and forth from Maine ports on Penobscot Bay to Boston. The boats and their skippers had become a special, sentimental part of life along the coast of Maine.

First steamboat on the Penobscot River was a mongrel with the thoroughbred name of Maine. She was an ungainly sight, made from two schooner hulls, with a wheel suspended between them, and she steamed upriver to Bangor on Sunday, May 23, 1824. On Monday the Maine took 120 curious and daring Bangor citizens for their first steamboat ride. It took all day to get to Bucksport and back. That summer the Maine ran weekly trips between Bangor and Portland. It was better than the stagecoach line which Moses Burley had started in 1821 to Augusta, a rough and bumpy overnight trip. There you transferred for another uncomfortable stagecoach ride to Portland.

The first "Boston Boat" service began in 1834, from Boston, with a 400-ton boat called Bangor. She ran for eight years and then took a jump up the social ladder and became a yacht for the Sultan of Turkey.

But Bangor people didn't enjoy the dominance of a Boston-based company serving their river. So in the 1840s a seafaring Bangor family, headed by Capt. Menemon Sanford, began its own steamship line. This competition on the Penobscot led to the same cut-rate price wars that happened on the Kennebec. The fare from Bangor to Boston, which had been around $7, dropped to $1 in 1848. This was surely the finest bargain in cruising the Maine coast ever offered.

Sanford died in 1852, but a handsome 244-foot vessel named after him was launched in 1854 and became the fastest boat on the run. On July 5, 1856, she left Boston at midnight for Bangor; and two and a half hours later she ran hard aground on Thatcher's Island, off Cape Ann. She survived, which few vessels have done after smacking into Thatcher's Island. Thanks to calm summer weather, she was hauled off, losing 20 feet of her hull.

But the passengers aboard were mad. They said the officers were suffering from too much Independence Day rum on July 4th, and accused them of criminal misconduct.

She was patched up and returned to service. But the Sanford was born an unlucky ship. On another July night, four years later, she hit Dry Salvages Ledge near Cape Ann. She was repaired and in November 1862 she was taken over as a troop carrier in the Civil War, earning $950 a day to carry troops to New Orleans. But within a month a treacherous pilot ran the ship aground with 800 troops aboard, in calm and clear weather. She was abandoned as a total loss.

Fairhaired child among the steamers was the Katahdin, which spent 30 years on the Bangor-Boston run from 1863 to the last turn of her paddles in 1893. In 1895, she was burned for junk at Nut Island, Quincy.

Last and finest of the Sanford boats was the Cambridge, a paddlewheeler 250 feet long, launched in 1867. She and the Katahdin would pass each other going to and from Boston. She survived the whirlwind of September 1869 by a near miracle. The whirlwind and raging seas demolished her rudder and broke her main steam pipe, and she was floundering between Pemaquid Point and Monhegan. She ran out both anchors and their chains held during the worst of the storm, while she pounded just a few yards from the ledges on Franklin Light.

These same waters killed her on a clear moonlight night. She was a mile off course and hit Old Man's Ledge, a few miles inside Monhegan, and broke up under heavy seas. All passengers and crew were rescued.

She was the only boat lost on the Bangor/Boston run in more than 100 years of service.

The best remembered, because they were the last, were the Belfast and Camden, 320 feet long. They began on the Bangor to Boston run in 1909 and 1907 respectively and ran until 1935, when they were sold to serve between New York and Providence. In World War II, the Camden became the Army Transport Comet, and the Belfast became the Army transport ship Arrow. They served in Hawaiian waters. The old Camden achieved new fame as a rescue vessel after the disastrous tidal wave demolished Hilo. In 1948 she was towed to Shanghai to work in China seas. Her propellers, each four feet in diameter, were removed for the trip as their drag would have added four days to the trans-Pacific tow.

Her sister ship, the old Belfast, went aground at Ocean Park, Washington, while in Army service. The government kept watchmen aboard her for a year. But she sank deeper and deeper. Finally her spars were taken off and used as entrance markers to the Park; and her whistle was brought home to Belfast, Maine. There it blew again, to summon sardine packers to work at the Belfast Packing Co. But the old Belfast was abandoned and sank below the waves.

Railroads, and later highways, killed the demand for shipping in Maine's rivers, just as steam power and later the gasoline motor killed the demand for thousands of horses, oxen and axmen in the Maine woods. Bangor and the Penobscot River were at the heart of these changes.

The Bangor and Old Town Railroad was chartered in 1832, second oldest railroad in New England. It traveled a distance of only 12 miles, at about five miles an hour. It carried clapboards, shingles and skoots, lumber that was too small to be rafted, to the loading docks for ships near Exchange Street in downtown Bangor. It ran until 1869, when the little railroad was sold to the grand-sounding European and North American Railroad.

The second lumber railroad was the Whitneyville and Machias. It was chartered in 1836 and ran for 50 years. Its primitive engine, the Lion, can be seen still at the Crosby Laboratory at the University of Maine in Orono. The freight in 1866 amounted to 10 million feet of lumber, a million shingles, 10 million laths.

The quaintest and crudest railway in Maine was the Moosehead Lake Railway at Northeast Carry, chartered in 1847. Just two miles long, its first tracks were made of pine logs, fifty feet long, and its wheels were wooden discs. The locomotive power came from horses. The gauge was three feet, six inches. It was used mostly for transporting lumber camp supplies from the head of Moosehead Lake to the West Branch of the Penobscot. This quaint and crude railroad was destroyed by fire started by blueberry pickers in 1863.

King Ed Lacroix, last of the great oldtime loggers, built another strange railroad 80 years later. Deep in the Maine woods, Lacroix built a 13-mile logging railroad that might defy the imaginations of engineers today. He ran it for 13 years and it carried a million cords of pulpwood from 1927 through 1933, from Eagle Lake to the West Branch of the Penobscot River.

To build it, King Ed hauled in his 90-ton locomotive and sixty flatcars through 50 miles of forest, on iced tote roads and across frozen lakes. At his terminus on Eagle Lake, King Ed built three conveyor belts, each 225 feet long, which raised the pulpwood 25 feet up out of Eagle Lake and carried it to his huge cars. Each of these 60 cars was 32 feet long and carried over 12 cords of wood. His conveyors delivered a cord of wood to the cars every 90 seconds, so it took him only 18 minutes to load a car. He ran three twelve-car trains a day, carrying 450 cords of wood. His track traveled over rivers and streams on long trestles; the trestle crossing the Allagash was 1,500 feet long. His trains negotiated the dangerous bends on the trestles so slowly it took three hours to make the 13-mile trip.

After King Ed Lacroix had operated his railroad for six years, he was finished logging this area. So he left it all behind; 90-ton locomotive, rolling stock, rails and trestles. Today canoeists on the Allagash Wilderness Waterway stare in disbelief when they see an abandoned 90-ton locomotive miles from anywhere, deep in the Maine woods. King Ed Lacroix was the man who brought it there in 1927.

The man with the biggest railroad dream was John A. Poor, a Bangor lawyer, who had once worked as junior counsel to Daniel Webster. His dream was to create the European and North American Railroad. At Bangor's Centennial Dinner on September 30, 1869, Poor mesmerized his audience as he spoke of the railroad which would "form a golden belt around the world; connect the commercial centers of Europe and Asia, spanning the continent of North America between the Atlantic and Pacific seas."

After crossing the United States, the railroad was to run from Bangor through Eastern Maine and New Brunswick to Canso, a port on the eastern tip of Nova Scotia. At one time, Poor had envisioned a railway bridge and trestle spanning the Atlantic. But by 1869 he had tempered that dream. Instead, he envisioned steamers awaiting at Canso to take aboard freight cars and passengers, then sailing to Galway, Ireland, in five days. There trains would carry passengers to Dublin, where they would catch a boat across the Irish Sea to Holyhead and from there take a train again to London. From London, freight and passengers had only a short sail to France, Holland, Belgium, where they would link up again with the European and North American Railroad. Another rail link there would carry them to Asia.

Poor's vision may seem a wild one to us, 135 years later. But he was a practical man, who achieved results. This same Poor had turned Portland into a major rail and shipping center. Thanks to John Poor, Portland became the winter shipping port for millions of tons of Canadian wheat, bound for Europe. Thanks to Poor, the Grand Trunk railway between Portland and Montreal was built.

Poor had been promoting the European and North American Railroad idea since 1850, and with success, too. He had persuaded the State of Maine to donate 700,000 acres for right-of-way for the tracks, and the City of Bangor had pledged a $1 million loan. By 1868 a spur of the railroad had been run from Bangor to Mattawamkeag, and by 1870 it had reached Vanceboro on the Canadian border, 114 miles from Bangor. The great European and North American Railroad had become so solid an undertaking that in 1872 President Ulysses S. Grant came to Bangor to celebrate its opening. Unhappily, Poor had died only six weeks before the president of the United States came to dedicate his European and North American Railroad.

It never grew much further. By 1882, the E. & N. A. went into trusteeship. But even that downward move was made with class, for Hannibal Hamlin, vice president to Abraham Lincoln, was named a trustee.

Best ride for a penny was on the Bon Ton Ferry. For 55 years, Bon Ton ferries carried thousands of people between Bangor and Brewer. When the first Bon Ton started in 1884, the fare was a penny. The last of three almost identical 30-foot Bon Tons caught fire at its dock and was destroyed in 1939. Now all traffic is by highway bridge.

The days of work and glory for the Penobscot as a river of fortune were long over.

So much trade had ruined the river. The pollution was rife and the stench was bad. Sunken logs, tree bark, city and ship wastes, jetsam from hundreds of sawmills had turned the once crystal clear waters of the Penobscot to a sick brown. No one had safely been able to drink or swim in that water. Even salmon could not survive in it. The Penobscot had become a man-made cesspool. It stayed, decaying and disgusting until the late 1960s.

Then massive, multimillion dollar cleanups began and continued for more than a dozen years. Today the water is clean and salmon are back in the Penobscot again. The story of its comeback is told in the last chapter.

The famous Bangor-Brewer ferry Bon Ton III, with S.S. Belfast behind it.

Clean Water

After the clean-up of the Penobscot, the salmon are back in the Bangor salmon pool and the catch runs over 900 fish in 1983.

36.

Maine Cleans its Rivers:
Salmon and Swimming Again

Men made fortunes from Maine rivers; and the fortunes made filth. By the 1960s the Penobscot and the Kennebec had been turned into cesspools and sewers. Their once clear, clean waters had been made vile-looking and vile-smelling. Vapors rising from the Kennebec were so rank they peeled paint from cars and houses. In the polluted Penobscot, fish could barely live. Chemicals, trash, foam, stinking sludge from paper mills so fouled the river that not even the rashest boy would dive into it.

Atlantic salmon had fled from the Penobscot salmon pools where once they flourished. In the 1850s, before the mills and the people desecrated the water, commercial fishermen caught 25,000 Atlantic salmon a year on the Penobscot. So many salmon swam into the Kennebec that in the early days of the 1800s, salmon sold for a penny a fish. But by 1875, the Penobscot catch was down to 15,000; by 1900 down to 12,000; by 1910 down to 2,500. By 1947 the river was so foul that no commercial fishing was allowed on it. Between 1957 and 1970 not a single Atlantic salmon was taken on rod and reel from the Penobscot. It had become a dying river, horrible to see, sickening to smell.

The salmon count is an accurate measure of the decay and death of the river. These splendid fish are reliable detectors of poisons in water, in the same way that canaries are detectors of poisoned air in the mines. Miners kept canaries in cages near them as they worked, to serve as their early warning devices. When the air in the pit killed the canary, the miners fled lest they be the next to die.

Today, the Atlantic salmon are back in the Penobscot. The dead river has come to life again, after a multi-million dollar, 10-year clean-up. Again the Atlantic salmon tell the story more vividly than the chemists.

Bill Walker of Brewer was 76 years old in the spring of 1983 when he told Jerry Harkavy, an Associated Press reporter who works where I work, that he had not been able to catch a single salmon from the fable Bangor salmon pool for 22 years, from 1953 until 1975. Walker's sad account is confirmed by the records kept by the chief biologist for the Atlantic Sea-Run Commission, Alfred Meister. Those records show that only one salmon was caught in 1970, three the next year, four in '72, 14 in '73, 30 in 1974.

From then on, increasing catches of salmon prove the rejuvenation of the Penobscot River. As the cleanup progressed, the catches climbed; to 343 in 1977; to 801 in 1980. Last year, 1982, 937 Atlantic salmon were caught on rod reel; 45 splendid fish being taken in a single day. The salmon run in the Penobscot will be close to 5,000 in 1983 and reach 12,000 by 1990.

The natural return of Atlantic salmon from the ocean to spawn upriver is being increased by a scientific spawning program at the Green Lake National Fish Hatchery near Ellsworth, built at a cost of $7 million in 1979. "This is the largest Atlantic salmon hatchery in the world," says Meister. "We plan to stock half a million salmon a year from it."

Today, the banks of the Penobscot, even in downtown Bangor, a city of 33,000, are lined with salmon fisherman during the season, May 1 to Oct. 15. Lured by stories of high-leaping salmon weighing up to 20 pounds, salmon enthusiasts from across the nation are crowding every available motel room around Bangor at the height of the fishing season. Unlike many rivers, the Penobscot is not an expensive salmon preserve where only the rich enjoy the sport. Because the Penobscot is tidal for 25 miles up to Bangor, Maine residents paid only one dollar to get a salmon stamp on their fishing license. In 1983, the fee was raised to $4. As a result of this low cost, millworkers, garage mechanics, grandmothers, housewives and even children are today casting their salmon flies into the Penobscot.

At the noon hour on a Bangor workday, the rocks in the Penobscot are often crowded with businessmen. Dressed in three-piece suits, they skip lunch to cast for fat silvery salmon. When school is out, kids race their bikes across town, with a nine-foot salmon rod over their shoulders, as they head for an afternoon of fishing inside the city limits.

Once again in 1983 the first Penobscot salmon of the season was sent to the White House to grace the president's dinner table

— a tradition begun in President Teddy Roosevelt's time and revived now Atlantic salmon are back, rising in the Bangor Pool.

The Saco above Biddeford and Saco never suffered from the industrial pollution which blighted the Penobscot and the Kennebec. Today, the Saco is the cleanest and most sparkling of Maine's major rivers. It is a paradise for both white water experts and for families paddling their canoes on a summer afternoon. At least 75,000 people canoe on the Saco each summer. Not only is the river beautiful, but it is amazingly convenient for canoeists too. Because it meanders around so many curves, canoeists can paddle for 20 miles and end up only two miles from where they parked their cars.

The people of the Saco River Valley have long treasured their river. Back in the days when zoning was a fighting word in other parts of Maine, the people here petitioned the state Legislature to impose a super-zoning agency to preserve the beauty of their river. The Saco River Corridor Commission was formed, with two representatives from each of 20 riverfront towns serving on it. This Commission has zoned the river banks to prevent summer cottages from crowding onto handkerchief sized lots, a blight which mars the Saco at its headwaters in the White Mountains in New Hampshire.

The Saco, particularly above Biddeford, is pure and clean enough for trout, bass and pickerel to flourish. Striped bass are plentiful in the tidal estuary at the mouth of the river too. But the Atlantic salmon have not yet returned in force, although the state has recently stocked the river with 40,000 baby salmon.

Reasons why salmon have not returned may be the six dams which harness the hydroelectric power and their inadequate fishways.

On the Kennebec, the same story of a river's near-death and then multi-million dollar rescue was played out in recent years.

When the poisoning of the river began, no man foresaw the havoc which lay ahead. They thought the vast Kennebec was too big and too strong to be ruined. Into the river poured waters from eight major tributaries, 1,000 streams and 300 lakes. The flow of the Kennebec is so enormous that by the time the river swirls past

Popham and Georgetown into the ocean, a torrent of six million gallons a day pours into the Atlantic.

Even so, the Kennebec was almost killed by the men who took fortunes from it. Paper mills dumped sulphurous wastes; sawmills dumped bark and sawdust; and during each springtime river drive tens of thousands of logs sank, to lie mouldering on the bottom. Adding to this foul brew, every village, town and city along its bank emptied its human sewage into the river.

Again, the fish fled from the poison.

Almost nobody stopped to measure the damage being done under their eyes and noses. When the smell got foul, people held their noses and put up with it, saying "that's the smell of money; that stench is my paycheck, which puts food for my family on the table."

The Scott Paper Mill at Winslow put plenty of food on plenty of tables. But every day until 1977, when it was shut down, this one mill dumped as much pollution into the Kennebec as would come from the untreated sewage of a city of two million people. That is twice the population of all Maine, and an indication of the amount of poison just one mill poured into one river every day.

Scott Paper was not alone by any means. All paper mills using the sulphite process were poisoning the rivers where they dumped their wastes. The Kennebec suffered no more than the Penobscot. The pollution poured into the Penobscot was the equivalent of the untreated sewage from five million people, according to a report by the State of Maine Water Improvement Commission in 1964.

Reports like this gave new authority to the lonely voices in Maine which were crying for a clean-up. Until 1964, those voices came mostly from those ardent groups of naturalists, canoeists, wilderness buffs who clung to each other for support because no one else would pay attention. The old Maine excuse "payroll or pickerel" had become ingrown in most minds. People wanted clean rivers only if the cleanliness did not put the paycheck in danger. And that fear of losing jobs influenced voters and legislators. The fear was fanned by the paper companies which at first said that if clean-up costs were imposed upon them by unrealistic environmentalists, the expense would force them to leave Maine. The cities and towns feared the close down of paper mills would bankrupt municipal budgets. Workers feared it might cost them their jobs.

Nevertheless the warnings of the environmentalists began to be listened to across the state; and when scientists backed them up with facts, the voters caught fire. In 1967 the Maine Legislature acted. It passed new laws setting clean water goals and standards for the rivers and made it illegal to discharge any material into a waterway which would lower water quality standards.

In Washington, Maine's Senator Edmund S. Muskie championed the Clean Water Act and guided it through Congress. Muskie became known as Mr. Clean. He had grown up in Rumford, where he had smelled and eye-witnessed the way Oxford Paper had polluted the Androscoggin.

Cleanup became a crusade in Maine. Newspapers which had relegated such stories to a short paragraph buried inside, now bannered pollution and cleanup stories on Page One. As an example of this, only one newspaper reporter covered the legislative hearings in 1963 which set clean water standards for the Kennebec. He was Bob Cummings, a cub reporter for the Bath Times, a weekly with only 3,000 circulation. Cummings latched on hard to the environmental beat as it became the big news story of the 1970s and soon became an award-winning environmental reporter for the Gannett chain of newspapers in Maine.

By the mid-1970s, Maine was leading every state in the nation in the river/cleanup program, despite the fact that Maine was without great financial resources and the even more potent fact that its state Legislature had long been dominated by the lobbyists of the paper and power companies, biggest employers and biggest landowners and biggest money-men of Maine.

The cleanup job was immense. It cost hundreds of millions of public and private dollars. Yet the results have been fast and spectacular. Within the past 10 years, most of the damage caused over 100 years, has been repaired. To do it has taken the force of law, the cooperation of municipalities and industries and the support of taxpayers at state, federal and town levels, whose pockets paid for it all.

The wastes which did the worst damage came from the giant paper mills which used the sulfite chemical process to turn resinous, soft woods into the pulp necessary to make paper. The first pulp and paper mills on the Penobscot began operations 101 years ago, in 1882.

St. Regis Paper stopped sulfite pulping at its Bucksport mill in 1968 and by the mid-1970s had spent $10 million to build primary and secondary treatment plants to purify wastes which used to be dumped untreated in the Penobscot. At Old Town, Diamond International shut down its sulfite pulping operation in 1975 and constructed a $7 million wastewater treatment system, which reduced its pollution of the river by 75 percent. Great Northern Paper at Millinocket and East Millinocket spent $36 million between 1969 and 1976 on pollution abatement. To operate its treatment plants costs more than $6 million a year. Five other mills along the Penobscot have spent $50 million since 1973 on pollution control.

Along the Kennebec other big paper mills were cleaning up. In 1977, after 77 years of operation, Scott Paper shut down its pulp mill at Winslow, the one which caused as much pollution as a city of 2 million people. To replace it, Scott spent $250 million to build a new mill. Scott estimates the operating costs of waste treatment facilities at the new plant at $50 million a year. At Madison, the Madison Paper Industries have spent $7 million on treatment facilities. In Augusta, Statler Tissue spent close to another $7 million.

The Paper Industry Information Office estimates its members have spent over $150 million for new wastewater treatment systems in Maine.

The towns along the Penobscot and Kennebec were as guilty as the industries when it came to dumping untreated wastes into their rivers. Close to $93 million was allocated to improve municipal sewage treatment plants between 1972 and 1981 in 32 towns along the Kennebec. Along the Penobscot another $33 million was allocated for 23 towns to clean up their sewage before dumping it into the river. On the Saco River, Biddeford and Saco were alloted over $4 million.

The total job is still far from done. For example, Maine has $100 million of municipal treatment projects pending and unfunded after 1985, at this writing. But the worst of the pollution has been stopped, but only just in time before the rivers died.

Maine's rivers have recovered more quickly and more completely in 10 years than many knowledgeable people believed possible. The costs have not broken the back of either the paper mills or the taxpayers. In fact, industry has been finding new ways to make profits from wastes they used to throw away into the river. Land values of river towns have increased as the rivers became once again lovely to look at, fine to fish in and sweet to smell.

The length of Maine's 5,000 rivers and streams amounts to 32,000 miles — almost 10 times as long as Maine's fabled coastline. Most of them are small enough not to have been harmed by men and industry. But the big rivers into which they fed were grossly harmed and harnessed, especially during the 100 years between 1870 and 1970.

Men harnessed the power of the rivers to make water power, then steam power, then electric power. Men dammed the rivers, and the lakes which fed them, often without regard for the damaging long-term consequences, provided the short-term profit was clear.

The first big dam on the Kennebec was built in 1837. That was when the Kennebec Dam Co., with the blessing of the state legislature, built a big dam at Augusta. The law stated that a fishway would have to be included, so the salmon and other fish could get upstream to spawn. It wasn't built. And the Legislature did not argue about it.

Over the next 100 years dams galore were built, seemingly whenever and wherever power companies could economically harness lakes, streams, rivers to sell their product.

As oil and coal became cheaper, hydroelectric power was no longer needed so much. Dam construction fell off. Then when oil prices shot skyhigh in the late 1970s and 80s, Maine was swamped with entrepreneurs eager to build new dams or repair broken down and abandoned dams to sell electricity.

To prevent new dams damaging Maine's most scenic rivers, the governor of Maine, Joseph E. Brennan, introduced legislation in the spring of 1983. His proposals basically prohibited new dam construction on 1,100 miles of Maine's best scenic, and fishing rivers. The bill was warmly greeted by most of Maine and the Legislature. Partly to avert opposition from labor unions and the large paper companies, Brennan's bill allows Georgia Pacific to build new dams on the St. Croix river, near the Canadian border, to supply power for mill expansion at Woodland, Maine, where 1200 workers are now employed. The bill would also allow Great Northern Paper Co., which employs more than 4,100 people, to build a major new dam on the West Branch of the Penobscot, to provide electricity to its Millinocket mill. Central Maine Power Co. withdrew its earlier application to build a major new dam which would have flooded the Kennebec River gorge in northern Maine.

However this legislation would encourage development of hydroelectric power generating dams on many of Maine's other rivers, in an effort to offset Maine's extreme dependency on imports of foreign oil. But no future dams would be licensed unless they provided adequate fishways.

To protect the banks of the cleaner rivers from a rash of residential building which might spoil the looks of the rivers, Maine now has laws which generally prohibit new construction or cutting of trees within 250 feet of a river or seashore without a special hard-to-get waiver.

The rivers of Maine are a success story. Over the centuries they have given Maine beauty, sanctuary, food, timber, ice, ships, power and enjoyment. They have supplied the raw materials and the transport on which fortunes have been made. They have supplied the jobs from which tens of thousands of families have earned their livelihoods. The rivers suffered gigantically from severe pollution by the very industries and cities and towns which they nourished along their banks. But while the pollution was happening, few people gave a thought to the damage being done. The handful of men and women who fought first and almost alone to clean up the rivers were looked upon by charitable fellow citizens as being touched in the head. But they were honestly hated by many others who feared these zealots would cost them their jobs.

But as matters turned out, the cleaners of the rivers created new jobs. Their clean-up brought new prosperity. Land values increased. And the dying rivers came alive again.

Thus, these generations of Maine people have made a fine and valuable mark upon the state they love. They are leaving the great rivers of Maine markedly purer and cleaner than the rivers they inherited. That is a monument more worthy and more lasting than most of the fortunes made from the rivers of Maine.

THANKS

Thanks to all who have written about the rivers of Maine before me. Thanks to the ship captains and wives who left log books, diaries and letters of their voyages; to clerks in boatbuilders' offices who kept records of ships; to tavern keepers and merchants who kept records of prices and debtors over the generations. Thanks to town clerks and law clerks who kept tabs on town happenings and court sentences. Thanks to journalists and magazine writers who told the stories of what they saw day by day, centuries ago. Without them much Maine history would have been lost.

Thanks to authors who have spent lonely years writing of the lumber business in the north woods and the log drives. To their labor and scholarship I am indebted for many of the facts and details of what happened along the rivers.

Finally, my thanks to my contemporaries who have lent me their special knowledge. Particularly to James B. Vickery, historian of Bangor, who vetted the chapters of the Penobscot in manuscript; to William F. Mussenden of Bath who vetted the chapters on BIW on the Kennebec; and to Earle R. Warren who vetted the chapters on the Hydes; and to boatbuilder of renown, James Stevens of East Boothbay who vetted the chapters on the Damariscotta River and the chapters on ships and sailing men.

As always, the librarians and researchers helped enormously and patiently. I'm indebted especially to the State Library, the Maine State Archives, the Maine Historical Society, the Maine Maritime Museum, the Bangor Public Library, the Patten Free Library at Bath, the Maine Room of the Portland Public Library and the Special Collections at the Fogler Library, University of Maine.

BIBLIOGRAPHY

The following books were very useful sources and are recommended for those interested in reading further into the topics they cover.

Saco River Section

The Length and Breadth of Maine by Stanley B. Attwood.
Sands, Spindles and Steeples by Roy P. Fairfield.
History of Saco and Biddeford by George Folsom.
Old Times in Saco by Daniel Owen.
Saco Valley Settlements and Families by C.T. Ridlon.
History of York County, Maine, by W.W. Clayton.
Sir William Pepperell by Neil Rolde.

Penobscot River Section

A History of Lumbering in Maine 1820-1861 by Richard G. Wood.
Forest Life and Forest Trees by John S. Springer.
The Penobscot Man by Fannie Hardy Eckstrom.
Penobscot Boom by A.G. Hempstead.
The Maine Woods by Henry David Thoreau.
Yankee Loggers by Stewart W. Holbrook.
The Forests of Maine by Austin H. Wilkins.
The Penobscot Expedition of 1779 by Peter J. Elliott.
Gen. Solomon Lovell and the Penobscot Expedition by C.B. Kevitt.
Tall Trees, Tough Men by Robert E. Pike.
Bangor Bicentennial by James B. Vickery.
Penobscot, Down East Paradise by Gorham Munson.
Sailing Days on the Penobscot by George S. Wasson.
Steamboat Lore of the Penobscot by John M. Richardson.
Sail and Steam Along the Maine Coast by Vincent Short & Edwin Sears.
The Penobscot Expedition by John E. Cayford.
History of Lumbering in Maine 1861-1960 by David C. Smith.

Kennebec River Section

Kennebec Yesterdays by Ernest Marriner.
Kennebec by Robert P. Tristram Coffin.
History of Bath by Henry Wilson Owen.
History of Bath and Kennebec River Region by William Avery Baker.
Sewall Ships of Steel by Mark W. Hennessy.
Cradle of Ships by Garnett Laidlaw Eskew.

Ships & Sailors Section

The Maritime History of Maine by William Hutchinson Rowe.
The Down Easters by Basil Lubbock.
Travelling by Sea in the 19th Century by Greenhall & Gifford.

History of American Sailing Ships by Howard I. Chapelle.
The Clipper Ship Era by Arthur H. Clark.
New England & The Sea by Albion, Bake and Labaree.

General

History of the State of Maine by William D. Williamson.
A History of Maine, A Collection of Readings editor Ronald F. Banks.
History District of Maine by James Sullivan.
Pioneers on Maine Rivers by Wilbur D. Spencer.
Modern Maine by Richard A. Hebert.
Maine: A History by Louis C. Hatch.
Maine: A Literary Chronicle edited by W. Storrs Lee.

INDEX

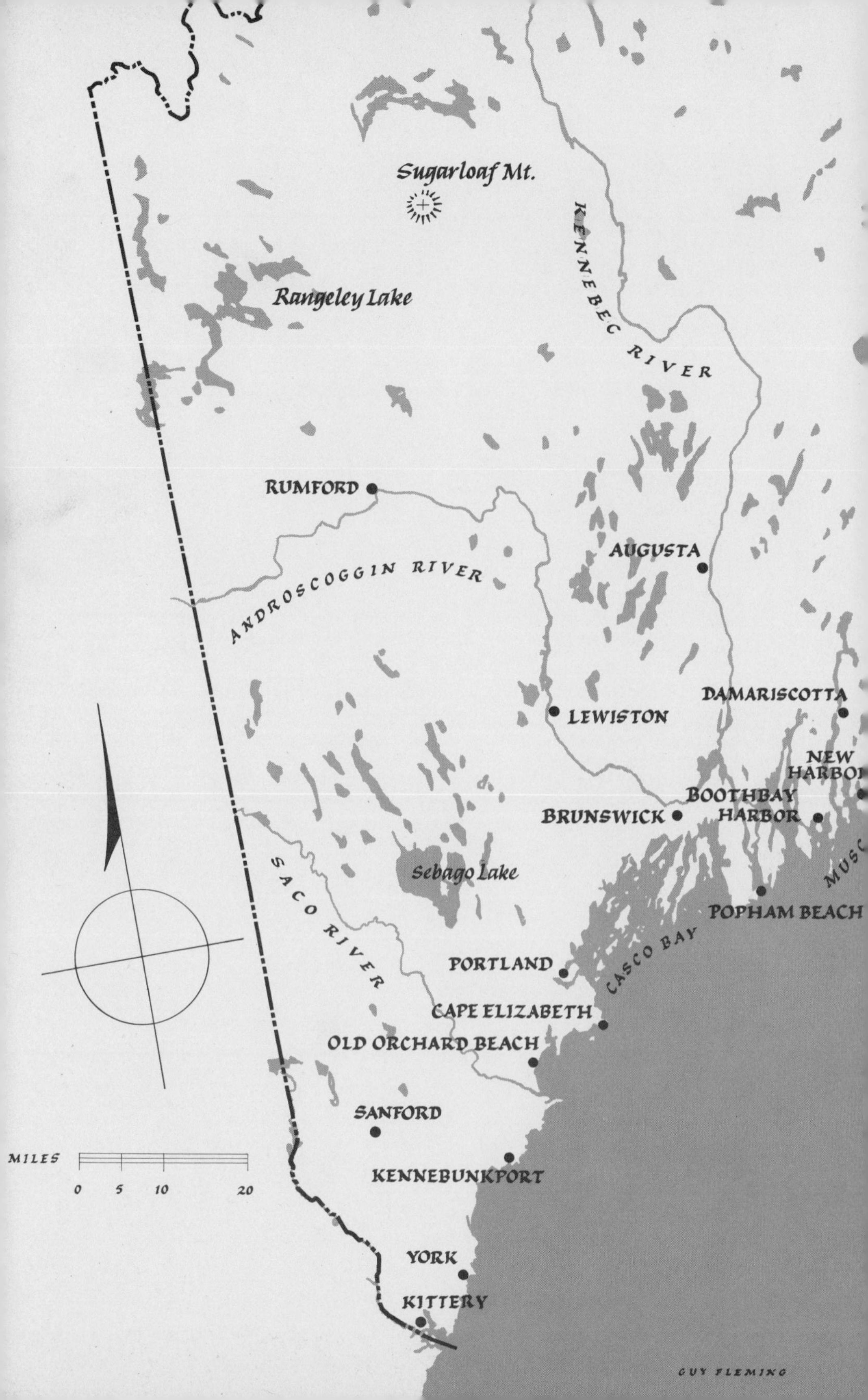

Sugarloaf Mt.
KENNEBEC RIVER
Rangeley Lake
RUMFORD
AUGUSTA
ANDROSCOGGIN RIVER
DAMARISCOTTA
LEWISTON
NEW HARBO
BOOTHBAY HARBOR
BRUNSWICK
SACO RIVER
Sebago Lake
MUSC
POPHAM BEACH
CASCO BAY
PORTLAND
CAPE ELIZABETH
OLD ORCHARD BEACH
SANFORD
MILES
0 5 10 20
KENNEBUNKPORT
YORK
KITTERY
GUY FLEMING